Primitive Coptic portrayal
of the Holy Trinity riding in the
Divine Chariot

Studies in Milton's Theology
Hunter, Patrides, Adamson

Bright Essence

University of Utah Press
Salt Lake City
1971

Contents

Contents

To the Reader

For well over a century following the discovery and publication of his *Christian Doctrine* in 1823, Milton was viewed as a heretic who had denied the divinity of Christ and as a consequence had so fallen into the heresy of Arius that the name of Christian should not be applied to him. But in the mid-1950s the three authors of this book came independently to the conclusion that critics had misunderstood Milton's religious beliefs, that he was not an Arian, and that he should be recognized as a Christian although the tradition upon which he developed his faith has been in great part lost to modern dogma. There is no little irony in the fact that, after long hesitation and reconsideration of the evidence, two of us in the same month submitted substantially the same article with the same conclusions to the *Harvard Theological Review*. Even the titles were similar: "Milton's Arianism Reconsidered" and "Milton's 'Arianism'." The editors of the *Review* printed the first in full and kindly accepted as much of the second as had not appeared in the former. Both are reprinted here.

Having successfully dispensed with a century-old misunderstanding, we each proceeded to explore some of the implications of this reversal of critical tradition. Just how heretical Milton was is indeed of slight moment; but to believe that he was an Arian is inevitably to discount the role of the Son of God in his writing. By emphasizing its centrality, we have discovered a new Milton for whom the Son is of fundamental importance in the act of creation, the revelation of the Godhead within history, and the salvation of man. Some of the results of this change of critical focus appear in the remaining essays which comprise this volume.

The fact that we concur upon the centrality of the Son in Milton's thought does not, however, mean that we are in complete agreement upon every detail. A careful reader will observe slight inconsistencies among the various essays. Perhaps after due consideration we could have come to full harmony with each other, but we have permitted these differences to stand in the belief that the reader may find in them further stimulation of his own thought. In any case, we do not judge that any major issues are involved.

Our provocative interpretation of Milton's beliefs has inevitably led to rejoinders. Two are particularly important: Maurice Kelley's "Milton's Arianism Again Considered," *Harvard Theological Review* 54 (1961): 195–205, and Chapter VI of Barbara K. Lewalski's *Milton's Brief Epic* (Providence, R. I., 1966). In this book, however, we have made no effort to reply directly to these studies, which certainly should be consulted by anyone who takes Milton's thought seriously. On the other hand, we have taken advantage of the opportunity which reprinting has afforded to make a number of minor revisions in all of the essays. Somewhat more extensive modifications appear in Adamson's essay on the War in Heaven and Hunter's studies of Milton's Muse and of the Incarnation, but in no instance have we seriously altered the conclusions of the essays as they first appeared.

Throughout the collection we have relied upon Merritt Y. Hughes's edition of the poetry (New York, 1957) and upon the Columbia edition of the prose (New York, 1931–38) except as we have found it necessary to retranslate parts of the *Christian Doctrine*. For permission to reprint, we wish to express our appreciation to the following publishers and editors:

ELH, A Journal of English Literary History, for "Milton on the Exaltation of the Son: The War in Heaven in *Paradise Lost*," 36 (1969): 215–31.

Harvard Theological Review, for "Milton's Arianism Reconsidered," 52 (1959): 9–35; "Milton's 'Arianism'," 53 (1960): 269–76; "Some Problems in John Milton's Theological Vocabulary," 57 (1964): 353–65.

Journal of English and Germanic Philology, "The War in Heaven: Milton's Version of the *Merkabah*," 57 (1958): 690–703; "Milton and the Creation," 61 (1962): 756–78; "The Godhead in *Paradise Lost*: Dogma or Drama?" 64 (1965): 29–34.

Journal of the History of Ideas, for "Milton and Arianism," 25 (1964): 423–29; "Milton on the Incarnation: Some More Heresies," 21 (1960): 349–69.

Language and Style in Milton, R. D. Emma and J. T. Shawcross, eds. (New York, 1967), for "*Paradise Lost* and the Language of Theology," pp. 102–19.

Modern Language Notes, for "The Meaning of 'Holy Light' in *Paradise Lost* III," 74 (1959) : 589–92, partially reproduced here as "Milton's Muse."

The Clarendon Press, for "Milton on the Trinity," in C. A. Patrides, *Milton and the Christian Tradition* (Oxford, 1966), pp. 15–25.

Studies in English Literature, for "Milton's Urania," 4 (1964) : 35–42, partially reproduced here as "Milton's Muse."

University of Texas *Studies in Literature and Language*, for "*Paradise Lost* and the Theory of Accommodation," 5 (1963) : 58–63.

We also wish to express our appreciation to Trudy M. Evans for her excellent copy-editing of the manuscript.

W.B.H., C.A.P., J.H.A.

1. Problems in Definition

Milton on the Trinity: The Use of Antecedents

C. A. PATRIDES

τὴν ἐξ ἀρχῆς παράδοσιν καὶ διδασκαλίαν καὶ πίστιν τῆς
καθολικῆς Ἐκκλησίας, ἣν ὁ μὲν Κύριος ἔδωκεν, οἱ δὲ
ἀπόστολοι ἐκήρυξαν, καὶ οἱ πατέρες ἐφύλαξαν.

ST. ATHANASIUS, *Epistola ad Serapionem*, I. 28

The doctrine of the Trinity has proved the "Sphynx of Divinitie" to theologians as well as to Milton scholars.[1] Without access to Milton's theological treatise *De Doctrina Christiana*, we should probably have agreed with Bishop Thomas Newton (1749) that *Paradise Lost* is entirely orthodox, and we might have been tempted to accept even Charles Symmons's verdict (1806) that the poem is "orthodox and consistent with the creed of the Church of England."[2] The discovery of *De Doctrina Christiana* in 1823, however, drastically changed opinions which had to be agonizingly reappraised. Henry Todd was not the only one to retract his previous approbation of Milton's orthodoxy and to charge him now with a number of heresies. By 1855 Thomas Keightly summed up the considered view of scholars when he observed that *Paradise Lost* expounds the Arian heresy in a "plain and unequivocal manner."[3] This view led in 1941 to a study minimizing the differences between *Paradise Lost* and *De Doctrina Christiana* and concluding

---

[1] The quoted phrase is borrowed from John Day, *Day's Dyall* (Oxford, 1614), p. 57.

[2] Ant Oras, *Milton's Editors and Commentators . . . 1695–1801* (Dorpat, 1930), p. 227, and Herbert McLachlan, *The Religious Opinions of Milton, Locke and Newton* (Manchester, 1941), p. 17, respectively.

[3] McLachlan (see note 2 above), p. 25.

too readily that the poem is "an Arian document." [4] Certain critics, however, protested against the assumption that "a poem is essentially a decorated and beautified piece of prose," and one argued that the treatise could not have in all respects served as the blueprint for the poem because of the subtle differences between them.[5] In time it became equally clear that even the Arian element so hastily detected in *De Doctrina Christiana* is an extension of the "subordinationism" upheld by the early Christian writers to the Council of Nicaea and revived by the Cambridge Platonists in Milton's own age.[6] I need not repeat here the evidence printed elsewhere in this volume contradicting the relationship assumed to exist between Milton's views and the Arian heresy,[7] but I should at least attempt to explain what is really at issue and to select from the family of traditional ideas current during the Renaissance those which relate to Milton's *De Doctrina Christiana*.

I

Milton's opinions of the Trinity in his theological treatise are, though couched in the intricate terms of theology, clearly understandable. The Trinity as such is not rejected. The Father, the Son, and the Holy Spirit are proclaimed to be "one" in love, communion, spirit, and glory. More important still, each is termed "God" (*deus*), and each is specifically said to share in the divine substance (*substantia*). Thus the Father "imparted to the Son as much as he pleased of the *divina natura*, nay of the *divina substantia*." The Son is made expressly of the Father's *substantia*, and so is the Holy Spirit.[8] Milton does, however, reject their equality in terms of the divine essence (*essentia*). He avoids the term "three persons," and tells us they are not "one in essence." On the contrary, even while they partake of the same *substantia*, each has the *essentia* or *hypostasis* proper to himself ("*essentia* and *hypostasis* mean the same thing").[9]

---

[4] Maurice Kelley, *This Great Argument: A Study of Milton's "De Doctrina Christiana" as a Gloss upon "Paradise Lost"* (Princeton, 1941).

[5] Cleanth Brooks, in *English Institute Essays 1946* (1947), pp. 127–28, and Arthur Sewell, *A Study in Milton's Christian Doctrine* (London, 1939), respectively. See also the review of Kelley's book (*This Great Argument*, note 4 above) by A. S. P. Woodhouse in *Philological Review* 52 (1943): 206–8.

[6] See William B. Hunter, "Milton's Arianism Reconsidered," reprinted in this volume. A useful seventeenth-century compendium of the early "subordinationist" ideas is John Biddle's *The Testimonies of Irenaeus . . .* (1649?).

[7] See C. A. Patrides, "Milton and Arianism," reprinted in this volume.

[8] *Works*, 14: 193, 187, 403.

[9] *Works*, 14: 401, 221, 43; cf. 311.

These conclusions, Milton informs us in the preface to *De Doctrina Christiana*, are grounded solely on a "most careful perusal and meditation of the Holy Scriptures." Their appeal is to the exclusively Protestant doctrine which allows the individual freedom to interpret the Bible guided solely by the *testimonium Spiritus sancti internum*. Were we prepared to accept such a claim at face value, we should perforce have to concede the essential truth of Milton's conclusions, since biblical scholars now assure us that the scriptural evidence for the doctrine of the Trinity is "singularly disconcerting." [10] Yet neither Milton nor "the whole Protestant church" he invokes in his treatise did in fact bypass *humanae traditiones* altogether. The following table presenting the various formulations of the doctrine of the Trinity indicates both the highly flexible terminology sanctioned by tradition and the line of descent of Milton's particular conception.[11] The divine "substratum" constitutes the essence or substance common to the entire Godhead, and the "mode of existence" designates the specific essence or substance peculiar to each Person within the Godhead:

	GODHEAD	
	its divine "substratum"	its "mode of existence" [$\tau\rho\delta\pi\sigma\varsigma$ $\upsilon\pi\alpha\rho\xi\epsilon\omega\varsigma$]
Greek view:	$\mu\iota\alpha$ $\sigma\upsilon\sigma\iota\alpha$ [one *ousia*]	$\tau\rho\epsilon\iota\varsigma$ $\upsilon\pi\sigma\sigma\tau\alpha\sigma\epsilon\iota\varsigma$ [three *hypostaseis*]
	↓←proper Latin translation→↓	
	one *essentia*	three *substantiae*
Augustine's view:[12]	one *essentia* = *substantia*	three *personae*
Usual Catholic view:	one *substantia*	three *personae*
Usual Protestant view:	one *essentia*	three *personae* = *hypostaseis*
Some Protestants affirm:	one *essentia* = *substantia*	three *personae* = *hypostaseis* [sometimes *subsistentiae*]
Milton's view:	one *substantia*	three *essentiae* = *hypostaseis*

---

[10] K. E. Kirk, in *Essays on the Trinity and the Incarnation*, A. E. J. Rawlinson, ed. (London, 1928), p. 199. The "triadic pattern" sought by Arthur W. Wainwright in *The Trinity in the New Testament* (London, 1962) is not quite so readily apparent to biblical scholars.

[11] The crucial terms *substantia, hypostasis*, etc., are explained by J. F. Bethune-Baker, *An Introduction to the Early History of Christian Doctrine*, 2d ed. (London, 1920), pp. 116 f., 231–38, and E. J. Bicknell, *A Theological Introduction to the Thirty-nine Articles*, 2d ed. (London, 1925), pp. 63–65. On the differences between the Greek and Latin views, consult G. L. Prestige, *God in Patristic Thought* (London, 1936), chaps. 8–10, and Vladimir Lossky, *The Mystical Theology of the Eastern Church* (London, 1957), chap. 3. See also the study by William B. Hunter, Jr., "Some Problems in John Milton's Theological Vocabulary," reprinted in this volume as "Further Definitions: Milton's Theological Vocabulary."

[12] Augustine was aware that the correct translation of the Greek formula (one *ousia* and three *hypostaseis*) should be one *essentia* and three *substantiae*, but maintained that "be-

The Catholic Church adopted not Augustine's version but Tertullian's, one *substantia* in three *personae*,[13] which Protestants altered by moving in a number of directions at once. The majority of their commentators adhered to Calvin's lucid exposition: "vnder the name of God, we vnderstande the one onely and single *essentia* in whiche we comprehende thre *personae* or *hypostaseis*."[14] Some, however, offered interpretations resembling Milton's in *De Doctrina Christiana*. But here clarity falters. The term *substantia*, for example, which Milton employed to characterize the divine "substratum" (the Greek *ousia*), corresponds to Catholic usage but walks in Protestant treatises in bewildering guises: as *essentia*, or as *essentia* in the original Latin but as "substance" in translation, or as *substantia* in Latin but as "essence" in translation.[15] Lest the confusion in Milton's age reach into our own, let us ask simply whether Milton's term *substantia* had been traditionally used in the West to mean the divine substratum, whether any biblical scholar during the Renaissance had endorsed such a use, whether any Reformer had conceded that *essentia* could be replaced by *substantia*. The answers to all three questions are decisively in the affirmative. The term *substantia* had indeed been used in Milton's sense by numerous Western theologians such as Tertullian and St. Ambrose. The three divine *hypostaseis* had been described by Erasmus as "of one and the same substaunce or nature or of one essence," while Bullinger and Polanus, two Protestant theologians of major stature, agreed with Luther that the Greek term *ousia* signifies *essentia* or, alternatively, *substantia*.[16]

---

cause with us the usage has already obtained, that by *essentia* we understand the same thing which is understood by *substantia*, we do not dare to say one *essentia*, three *substantiae*, but one *essentia* or *substantia* and three *personae*" (*De Trinitate*, 5. 8. 9, and 10. 10; in *Patrologia latina*, 42: 917–18, and *Nicene and Post-Nicene Fathers*, 3: 92). In fact, however, Augustine's view was based on his failure to grasp the difference between *ousia* and *hypostasis* (*De Trin.*, 5. 8. 10) since he knew Greek only moderately — as he himself states in the Preface to Book 3 of *De Trinitate*.

[13] Tertullian, *Adversus Praxeam*, 11–12 (*Patr. l.*, 2: 166–68, and *Ante-Nicene Fathers*, 3).

[14] *Institutes*, 1. 13. 20; trans. Thomas Norton (1561) [the original Latin in A. Tholuck's edition (Berlin, 1846)]. Thus also Hieronymus Zanchius, *De religione christiana* (Basle, 1585), p. 10; Wolfgang Musculus, *Loci communes* (Basle, 1560), pp. 8 f.; Gulielmus Bucanus, *Institutiones theologicae* (Geneva, 1609), p. 7; Amandus Polanus (see note 16 below), 1: 555; William Ames, *Medulla theologica*, 3d ed. (Amsterdam, 1628), p. 16; Johann Wolleb, *Compendium theologiae christianae* (Cambridge, 1648), p. 9; Johannes van Marck, *Compendium theologiae christianae* (Amsterdam, 1690), p. 93; etc.

[15] Thus Beza's "vnam esse diuinam essentiam quam Deus appellamus" (*Tractationum theologicarum* [Geneva, 1570], 1: 1) was translated "there is one onely dyuyne substaunce whych we call God" (*A briefe . . . Summe of the Christian Faith*, trans. Robert Fyll [1565?], sig. B8). Cf. 39 Art., 1 and 5. Conversely, Daniel Heinsius's *substantia* (*In Theophania . . . homilia* [Leyden, 1612], p. 9) was translated "essence" (*The Mirrour of Humilitie*, trans. John Harmar [1618], p. 5).

[16] Seriatim: Tertullian (see note 13 above), and Ambrose, *De fide orthodoxa*, 3. 14 (*Patr. l.*, 16: 611); Erasmus, *A Playne . . . Declaration of the Cōmune Crede*, trans. Anon.

Milton's *substantia*, like the Greek word *ousia* it is supposed to translate, is not a biblical term, even though Milton himself claims that his *De Doctrina Christiana* rests solely upon the Holy Scriptures (*solo Dei verbo*). Aware of this discrepancy, Milton probably turned with considerable relief to another crucial theological term which does occur in the Bible. According to the Epistle to the Hebrews (1: 3), the Son of God is χαρακτὴρ τῆς ὑποστάσεως αὐτοῦ [τοῦ Πατρός], meaning — if we are to trust the Authorized Version — that he is "the express image of his [the Father's] person." But the translation of ὑπόστασις (*hypostasis*) as "person" (*persona*) finds warrant only in Beza's Latin version of the New Testament (1556) and in its English offspring, the Geneva Bible of 1560. Nearly all other versions agree with the Vulgate's translation of *hypostasis* as *substantia*.[17] Milton appears to have taken an independent line. He rejected both Beza's *persona* and the more common *substantia*, and chose instead the term *essentia*. In his words,

the *essentia* of God, being in itself most simple, can admit no compound quality; so that the term *hypostasis* Heb. i. 3. which is differently translated *substantia*, or *subsistentia* [=*persona*], can be nothing else but that most perfect *essentia* by which God subsists by himself, in himself, and through himself. For neither *substantia* nor *subsistentia* makes any addition to what is already a most perfect *essentia*; and the word *persona* in its later acceptation denotes not the *ens* itself, but the essence of the *ens* in the abstract. *Hypostasis*, therefore, is clearly the same as *essentia*, and thus many of the Latin commentators render it in the passage already quoted.[18]

Did Milton adopt the equation *hypostasis* = *essentia* because he felt that these terms were occasionally flexible enough to admit of interchange?[19] Did he

---

(1533), sig. B8 [the original Latin is quoted below, note 20]; Luther, *Commentariolus in epistolam divi Pauli Apostoli ad Hebreos* (1517), in *Werke* (Weimar, 1939), 57. 3. 100: "usia, quod 'essentiam' seu 'substanciam' significat." Cf. Bullinger, *Compendium christianae religionis* (Zürich, 1559), fol. 21, and Polanus, *Syntagma theologiae christianae* (Geneva, 1612), 1: 370. Later Johann Heinrich Heidegger was to write, "Deus Pater Filium suum ab aeterno ex substantia sua genuit" (*Corpus theologiae christianae* [Zürich, 1700], 1: 125).

[17] Thus Erasmus, *Nouum Testamentum graece & latine* (Paris, 1543), 2: fol. 105ᵛ; Gwalter in his revision of Erasmus, *Novi Testamenti aeditio postrema* (Zürich, 1547), fol. 256; Sebastian Castellio, *Testamentum Novum* (Basle, 1551), sig. R1; Bullinger, Pellikan, Bibliander, et al., *Biblia sacrosancta* (Zürich, 1543), 3: fol. 95ᵛ; as well as most English versions (Wycliffe, Tyndale, Cranmer, and of course Rheims). Brian Walton's monumental edition (*Biblia sacra polyglotta* [1657], 5: 850 f.) translates both the Greek *hypostasis* and its Syriac equivalent as *substantia*, but the Arabic and Ethiopic equivalents as *persona*. Consult also the observations by Cardinal Cajetan, *Epistolae Pauli* . . . (Paris, 1532), fol. 189ᵛ; Jacques Lefèvre d'Étaples, *Epistole diui Pauli . . . cum commentariis* (Paris, 1517), fol. 180; Willem Hessels van Est(ius), Chancellor of the University of Douai (d. 1613), *In omnes d. Pauli epistolas . . . commentarii* (Mainz, 1859), 3: 26 f.; the great biblical scholar Cornelius à Lapide (d. 1637), *Commentaria in omnes divi Pauli epistolas* (Antwerp, 1734), pp. 835 f.; David Dickson, *A Short Explanation of . . . Hebrewes* (Aberdeen, 1635), pp. 7 f.; and John Mayer, *A Commentarie upon all the Epistles of . . . Paul* (1631), pp. 584 ff.

[18] *Works*, 14: 41, 43.

[19] Cf. Zacharias Ursinus: "Filius . . . gignitur a Patre, de essentia Patris: Essentia autem Filii, nõ gignitur . . ." (*Opera theologica* [Heidelberg, 1612], 1: 542). See also Bartholo-

even assume that Erasmus had actually sanctioned this equation?[20] But Milton himself disposes of our need to speculate. He informs us specifically that the translation of *hypostasis* as *essentia* had already appeared in "many of the Latin commentators." Unfortunately he names none, but they must have existed, since Calvin also refers to them as "some expositours" in his militant observations on the meaning of *hypostasis* in Hebrews 1: 3. According to Calvin,

> The apostles namyng the sonne, the engraued forme of the *hypostasis* of his father, he vndoubtedly meaneth, that the Father hath some beeyng, wherin he differeth from the sonne. For to take it for *essentia* (as some expositours haue done, as if Christ like a piece of waxe printed with a seale didde represent the substaunce of the Father) were not onely harde but also an absurditie. For sithe the Essence of God is single or one and vndiuisible, he that in hym selfe conteineth it all and not by pecemeale, or by deriuation, but in whole perfection, should very vnproperly yea fondly bee called the engraued forme of hym. But because ẙ father although he be in his own propretie distinct, hath expressed hymselfe wholly in his sonne, it is for good cause sayde, that he hath geuen his *hypostasis* to be seene in hym. . . . Surely by the Apostles wordes we gather, that there is a certayn propre *hypostasis* in the father, that shineth in the sonne: whereby also agayne is easily perceiued the *hypostasis* of the sonne that distinguisheth him from the Father. Like order is in the holy ghost. . . . Yet this distinction is not of the *essentia*, whiche it is vnlawfull to make manyfolde. Therfore if the Apostles testimonie be credited, it foloweth that there be in God thre *hypostaseis*. This terme seying the Latines haue expressed with the name of *persona*, it were to muche pride and waywardnesse to brawle about so cleere a matter. But if we list worde for worde to translate, we may call it *subsistentia*. Many in the same sense haue called it *substantia*. And the name of *persona* hath not ben in vse among the Latins onely: but also the Grecians, perhaps to declare a consente, haue taught that there are three *prosopa*, that is to say Persons in God. But they, whether they be Grekes or Latins that differ one from an other in the worde, doo very well agree in the summe of the matter.[21]

I have quoted Calvin's statement at some length to show that the orthodox arguments are not necessarily the most persuasive. Milton certainly did not find them so, and his dissatisfaction led him to "many of the Latin commentators," among them, surely, the great Italian Hebraist Emanuele Tremellio (1510–80). Though most often referred to as "that learned Jew,"[22] Immanuel Tremellius had first been converted to the Catholic faith by Cardinal

---

maeus Keckermann's observations on the Son's *essentia*, in *Systema s.s. theologiae* (Hanau, 1602), pp. 62 f.

[20] Cf. "Tres sunt proprietatibus distincti, sed trium eadem est substantia siue natura, aut quod uerbu quidam arbitrantur aptius, *essentia*" (*Dilucida et pia explanatio symboli* [Basle, 1533], p. 19). But Erasmus, in his annotations on the New Testament (Basle, 1535, p. 705), accepted only *hypostasis = substantia*.

[21] *Inst.*, 1. 13. 2 [the original in Tholuck, as before, note 14 above]. See further Calvin's *Commentarie on . . . Hebreuues*, trans. Clement Cotton (1605), pp. 12 f. Estius (note 19 above) also notes that some expositors translate *hypostasis* as *essentia*.

[22] Gilbert Burnet, *The History of the Reformation* (Oxford, 1865), 2: 256.

Pole and later to Protestantism by Peter Martyr (Vermigli). Obliged to leave Italy for Germany, he then went to England at Archbishop Cranmer's invitation. In 1549 he was appointed Regius Professor of Hebrew at Cambridge; but the accession of Queen Mary forced his return to Germany, where in 1561 he obtained the Chair of Old Testament Studies at Heidelberg. After a second visit to England about 1565, Tremellius secured a lasting reputation with his translation of the New Testament from Syriac into Latin, first published in 1569 and dedicated to the *regina potentissima* Elizabeth I. He then collaborated with the celebrated French scholar François du Jon (Junius) to produce a Latin translation of the whole Bible (1575–79) which was "for long the standard Protestant Latin translation." [23] Tremellius, in his version of the New Testament, often reprinted since it was so widely acclaimed by many Catholics and almost all Protestants, translates the word *hypostasis* not as *substantia*, or *persona*, but — as Milton translated it in his theological treatise — *essentia*. [24] Search will undoubtedly reveal other precedents, but in the meantime Milton's reference to so important an authority as Tremellius [25] suffices to establish that in *De Doctrina Christiana* he had not leaned exclusively on the Holy Scriptures but had availed himself of Renaissance biblical scholarship.

The hard core of Milton's thesis remains, nevertheless, the "subordinationism" espoused by the early Fathers whose views Tertullian well summarized: "Pater enim tota substantia est: Filius vero derivatio totus et portio." [26] These, then, are among the antecedents of Milton's *De Doctrina Christiana*.

II

Considered in the light of *De Doctrina Christiana* and the Christian tradition, *Paradise Lost* is far from "an Arian document," and does not even

---

[23] *The Oxford Dictionary of the Christian Church*, F. L. Cross, ed. (1957), p. 1373. See also Basil Hall, "Biblical Scholarship," in *The Cambridge History of the Bible*, S. L. Greenslade, ed. (Cambridge, 1963), pp. 72 f.

[24] I consulted Tremellius's 1569 translation of the New Testament (Geneva, Ἡ Καινὴ Διαθήκη. . . , fol. 617) and the first English edition of the Tremellius–Junius Bible (*Biblia sacra* . . . [1579–80], 5: 161; first published in Frankfurt, 1575–79). Since Junius kept revising Tremellius's labours, I checked also some of the seventeenth-century editions of their Bible (the Hanau ed. of 1602 [2. 381], the Geneva ed. of 1617 [3, fol. 379]), but found that *hypostasis* continued to appear as *essentia*.

[25] Milton never named Tremellius, but his six references to Junius in *De Doctrina* (*Works*, 14: 292; 15: 126, 132, 164; 16: 358; 17: 308) are in fact to the Tremellius–Junius Bible (cf. previous note). Kelley (note 4 above [p. 42]), while convinced that Milton ordinarily followed this Bible, seems not to have realized the importance of his statement.

[26] *Adversus Praxeam*, 9: "the Father is the entire substance but the Son is a derivation and portion of the whole" (*Patr. l.*, 2: 164; *Ante-Nicene Christian Library*, 15: 349).

espouse the "subordinationism" of the treatise. Not that the doctrine of the Trinity in *Paradise Lost* is uttered in "plain and unequivocal" manner, much less in a manner sufficient to confound the ignorant and amaze the very faculties of eyes and ears. The council in Heaven and the differentiation between the Father and the Son clearly evident there (3. 56 ff.) is one of several incidents in *Paradise Lost* which show up so absurdly naïve a conclusion. It will therefore be valuable to examine here some of the differences between *Paradise Lost* and *De Doctrina Christiana*, and in the poem the expression of ideas present immemorially within the circle of the Christian tradition.

Paradise Lost is a poem, *De Doctrina Christiana* a treatise. It sounds too obvious, yet we should hardly be well advised — as has been done — to overlook the difference even for a moment. Each work elicits from us a different response because of obvious differences in form, mode of expression, range of language, metaphor, structure. In *De Doctrina Christiana* we have, for example, the precise theological statement that the Father and the Son are not equal ("non aequalibus").[27] By contrast we have in *Paradise Lost* the Father's assertion that the Son is

> Thron'd in highest bliss
> Equal to God, and equally enjoying
> God-like fruition . . . . [3. 305–7]

Take the phrase "God-like fruition." It has studied generosity, and should be judged according to the sort of metaphorical language that starts off in Book 3: "Hail holy Light, offspring of Heav'n first-born . . . ."[28] What is afterwards stated not only reinforces the structure of the poem by contrasting the fruition within the Godhead to the sterile and perverse relations within the infernal Trinity — Satan, Sin, and Death (2. 648 ff.) — but testifies also to a divine unity that far outstretches the mere unity in love, communion, spirit, and glory that Milton argues in *De Doctrina Christiana*. It is not only that the Son reflects the paternal glory in full resplendence (5. 720; 10. 65) and that in him dwells the fullness of the divine love (3. 225). Of even greater significance, the Son is said to be the image of the Father in all things (6. 736), to shine all the Father forth (3. 139; 7. 196; 10. 66), and to express "all his Father full" (6. 720). The traditional language Milton employs in *Paradise Lost* is partially illuminated for us by John Day in his summary (1614) of

---

[27] *Works*, 14: 50, 190, 210, 310, 328, 342; 15: 4.

[28] See further my discussion in "*Paradise Lost* and the Language of Theology," reprinted in this volume. Cf. William B. Hunter's argument (in "Milton's Muse," appearing elsewhere in this volume) that Milton addresses the Son of God at the beginning of Book 3 as well as in the invocations which begin Books 1, 7, and 9.

the most common metaphors used by patristic writers to set forth the Trinity. Metaphors have been borrowed, we are informed,

as first from the similitude of the *Sunne* and his *Beames*, so *Iustin Martyr, Tertullian, Cyprian,* and *Lactantius*: From the similitude of the *Fountaine, Floud,* and *River,* so *Tertullian* againe, and *Cyprian,* and *Lactantius*; from the similitude of the *Roote,* and *Stem,* and *Bough of a tree,* so *Tertullian & Cyprian*: from the *Vnderstanding, Memory,* and *Will,* so S. *Austen*: from the three faculties of the Soule, *Rational, Irascible, & Concupiscible,* so others.[29]

We may better appreciate the differences between *Paradise Lost* and *De Doctrina Christiana* by reminding ourselves that in his treatise Milton expressly avoided "the drama of the personalities in the Godhead,"[30] yet in his poem that very drama formed the basis of the entire council in heaven. This distinction might well seem to argue that the "subordinationism" of *De Doctrina Christiana* is even more explicit in *Paradise Lost*. But Milton's conception of the heavenly council in *Paradise Lost* makes the poem not less but more orthodox and certainly traditional. We need not doubt that Milton was aware of the immemorial allegory of the debate among the four daughters of God[31] which, once joined to the Protestant theory of the Atonement, yielded emphatic differentiation among the persons of the Godhead in Book 3 and elsewhere.[32] But that differentiation may also stem from the theory of accommodation Milton drew upon,[33] or from a widespread idea touching the council said to have been convened in heaven before the creation of man, resting on Genesis 1: 26 ("Let *us* make man in *our* image . . .") which is claimed to offer the earliest biblical evidence for the doctrine of the Trinity.[34] At the

---

[29] *Day's Dyall* (Oxford, 1614), p. 57. On the analogy of the triune Godhead to the tripartite soul, see Donne, *Sermons,* ed. E. M. Simpson and G. R. Potter (Berkeley, 1953–62), 3: 145, 154, 5: 149, 9: 83 f., etc.; the sources mentioned by Mary P. Ramsey, *Les Doctrines médiévales chez Donne,* 2d ed. (London, 1924), pp. 208 f.; and the writers I cited in *Philological Quarterly* 39 (1960): 120 f. The *locus classicus* is Augustine, *De Trin.,* 10. 17–19.

[30] *Works,* 14: 197.

[31] Cf. Richard Heinzel, "Vier geistliche Gedichte," *Zeitschrift für deutsches Alterthum* 17 (1874): 1–57, and Hope Traver, *The Four Daughters of God* (Bryn Mawr, 1907), and *PMLA* 40 (1925): 44–92.

[32] See my article on "Milton and the Protestant Theory of the Atonement," *PMLA* 74 (1959): 7–13; restated with additional documentation in *Milton and the Christian Tradition* (Oxford, 1966), pp. 131 ff.

[33] Cf. Roland M. Frye, *God, Man and Satan* (Princeton, 1960), *passim,* and the supporting evidence I cite in "The Theory of Accommodation," reprinted in this volume.

[34] For a representative statement see Hilary of Poitiers, *De Trinitate,* 4. 17; consult also Adelheid Heimann, "Trinitas creator mundi," *Journal of the Warburg Institute* 2 (1938–39): 42–52. Judaism interprets Gen. 1: 26 as implying a council between God and the angels (Talmud: Sanhedrin, § 38b; Louis Ginzberg, *The Legends of the Jews* [Philadelphia, 1909–38], 1: 5; and H. Wheeler Robinson, in *Journal of Theological Studies* 45 [1944]: 151–57).

same time, Ephesians 1 : 11 ("[God] worketh all things after the counsel of his own will") was held to argue that God according to the reference in Genesis first "taketh counsel with his wisdome & vertue," and second, before creating man, called "a councell, and [did] consult," "deliberating with himselfe, the Father with the Sonne and the holy Ghost, and they with him." [35] If the same arguments are applicable to the council summoned before the creation of man (*PL*, 7. 505 ff.), they are applicable also to the councils in Book 3 and elsewhere (7. 131 ff.; 10. 21 ff.).

Milton's differentiation of the persons within the Godhead in *Paradise Lost* derives, I suggest, from four traditions: the allegory of the daughters of God, the Protestant view of the Atonement, the theory of accommodation, and the belief in the convocation of a council before the creation. But these are, I insist, peripheral considerations only; as I earlier argued, *Paradise Lost* as a poem must remain our chief concern. Did Milton achieve any balance between manner and matter, between the poetic utterance and the traditional material that constitutes that utterance? The principal evidence is a strange "coincidence": Milton differentiates between the Father and the Son *only* during their verbal exchanges in the various councils that took place in heaven, but as soon as these councils end and the Godhead acts beyond the confines of heaven the distinction between the two persons is abruptly dropped. Thus during the council before the creation of the universe the Father and the Son are clearly differentiated (7. 131 ff.), but once the Creator embarks on his mission outside heaven he is specifically termed "God." During the council after the Fall of Man the Father and the Son are again clearly differentiated (10. 21 ff.), but once the Judge leaves heaven for the Garden of Eden he is once again termed "God," even "the Lord God" (10. 163). The idea underlying all these incidents in *Paradise Lost* may well be "the common known *Maxim*, constantly and uniformly received in the Catholick Church," as Bishop Robert Sanderson called it, which Samuel Hoard restated in 1636 when he wrote that

it hath been a rule of constant credit among all Divines, that *opera Trinitatis ad extra sunt indivisa,* the externall operations of the Trinity are undivided. But yet it hath pleased God to appropriate as it were, and affixe some of these works to the Father, some

---

[35] Seriatim: the Geneva Bible (1560), marginal note to Gen. 1: 26; John Swan, *Speculum mundi* (Cambridge, 1635), p. 496; and Thomas Cartwright, *Christian Religion* (London, 1611), p. 25. For an authoritative statement consult Anselm, *Meditationes*, 1. 1; but consult also Humphrey Sydenham, *Natures Overthrow* (London, 1626), pp. 4 f.; Joseph Hall, *A Plaine . . . Explication* (London, 1633), 1: 4; and Donne, *Sermons*, 1: 289; 2: 337; 5: 157; 6: 154, 266, 296; 9: 60, 69, 137.

to the Sonne, and some to the Holy Ghost, that wee who are of weake capacities in conceiving such deepe mysteries, as that of the Trinity is, might by this meanes be inabled in some measure to apprehend the truth of it.[36]

As I read *Paradise Lost*, Milton achieved the proper balance between matter and manner by preserving the unity of the Godhead even when, for dramatic purposes, he differentiated between the Father and the Son.[37] This does not, however, end the matter. It simply begins it.

    Grammatici certant et adhuc sub iudice lis est.

---

[36] Sanderson, *XXXV Sermons*, 7th ed. (London, 1681), 1: 42, and Hoard, *The Soules Miserie* (London, 1636), pp. 19–20. See also the statements by Christopher Lever, *The Holy Pilgrime* (London, 1618), pp. 3 f., and Henry King, *A Sermon of Deliverance* (London, 1626), p. 17.

[37] See further my article on "The Godhead in *Paradise Lost*: Dogma or Drama?" reprinted in this volume.

Further Definitions:
Milton's Theological Vocabulary

W. B. HUNTER

Throughout the history of western Christianity, a major stumbling block has been agreement upon the definition of certain terms. Milton and his critics have shared in the difficulty of communication which lack of a common terminology has caused. Nowhere is this more evident than in his discussion of the Son of God in the *Christian Doctrine*, where his employment of "substance," "subsistence," "essence," and "hypostasis" has confused students who were attempting to understand the complex meanings which lie back of these words. Milton has often not followed the interpretations of these words usually held in Christianity; rather, he has adopted meanings which were very early associated with them but which lost currency centuries ago, even though they have never been completely forgotten.

Let us begin with the distinction which Milton made in Chapter 5 of the *Christian Doctrine* between substance and essence, one of the most perplexing to be found in the whole area of theological and philosophical thought. In this chapter Milton never confuses the two words or what he means by them. According to him, substance (*substantia*) is the substratum or stuff of God the Father which underlies the Son. It is not common to both but derives only from the Father. "God," he says, "imparted to the Son as much as he pleased of the divine nature, nay of the divine substance itself" (14: 193);[1] "he was properly the Father of the Son produced from his own substance" (14: 186). Likewise, the Holy Spirit "was created or produced of the substance of God" — that is, of the Father (14: 403).

---

[1] All quotations from Milton are taken from the Columbia Edition (New York, 1931–38).

Now essence (*essentia*) has often been used with exactly this meaning of substance. But Milton sharply distinguishes the two words. According to him, essence is a synonym for hypostasis. Unfortunately for clarity, *hypo-stasis* by etymology is the Greek equivalent for Latin *sub-stantia* or *sub-sistentia*, whereas *essentia* is akin to Greek *ousia*. Milton ignores these etymological relationships in identifying essence with hypostasis. Instead, he says that "the term *hypostasis* Heb. i. 3. which is differently translated *substance* [*substantiam*], or *subsistence* [*subsistentiam*], or *person* [*personam*] can be nothing else but that most perfect essence [*essentiam*] by which God subsists [*est*] by himself, in himself, and through himself." He concludes, "*Hypostasis*, therefore, is clearly the same as essence" (14: 41–43). Milton means that both of these words represent individuality or individual being. The persons of Father and Son are two; they receive their individuality from the fact that they are different essences. "Neither *substance*," he says, "nor *subsistence* makes any addition to what is already a most perfect essence" (14: 43). Substance, rather, as we have seen, provides the substratum for these beings, not their separate existence. Substratum is only a part of a complete essence.

Milton is very emphatic on the topic because upon it rests his distinction between Father and Son. From the definition of essence which he is following, if one were to argue for the coessentiality of the Father and Son, their distinction would vanish, and they would be merely two modes of existence of a single God. This is the Sabellian heresy, which deprives the Son of real existence apart from the Father. But in Milton's eyes, the Word must possess its own hypostasis or essence. The Father and Son no more can share their essences than two different men can share their individuality and remain separate individuals. To assert a common essence in Milton's meaning of the term would be to deny their individuality, and again and again Milton underscores the inconsistency of such an assertion: "since a numerical difference originates in difference of essence, those who are two numerically, must be also two essentially" (14: 203); "the Father and the Son are one," but not in essence (14: 211); "the Son now at least differs numerically from the Father; but . . . those who differ numerically must differ also in their proper essences" (14: 309–11); the Son does derive (*habeat*) his essence from the Father, but this by no means indicates that their essences are identical (14: 311–13). Many other passages could be marshaled. The best word to translate *essentia* in Milton's terminology is probably *individuality*. Throughout these and many other passages he is asserting the numerically separate being of the

Son apart from, though dependent upon, the numerically separate being of the Father.

Milton is thoroughly consistent in his use of these terms throughout his discussion of the Son in this chapter of the *Christian Doctrine*. But most unfortunately for the understanding of his meaning, his translator, Bishop Sumner, is not. From the original discussion (14: 41–43) of the synonymity of essence and hypostasis which has been quoted above, Milton repeats his conclusion that the words mean the same thing (14: 221) and then goes on to argue that "there can be no real difference of meaning between the adverbs *essentially* [*essentialiter*] and *hypostatically* [*hypostatice*]." But Sumner translates the latter term as *substantially*, exactly reversing the purport of the whole chapter and destroying Milton's carefully drawn and significant distinctions. The translation then blunders on: "If then the name of God be attributed to the Father alone *essentially*, it must also be attributed to the Father alone *substantially* [*hypostatice*]," instead of *hypostatically*. This is, of course, sheer nonsense in Milton's terminology. But the confusion of words led Arthur Sewell into an erroneous analysis of the relationship between *Paradise Lost* and the *Christian Doctrine*,[2] which Maurice Kelley corrected by giving the accurate translation.[3] Unfortunately, however, Professor Kelley himself did not understand the issues involved, for he went on to assume, "as Milton apparently did, that *substantia* and *hypostasis* are synonyms" — which they most certainly are not. The errors resulting from this misapprehension continue in Professor Kelley's latest statement on the subject,[4] where he argues strongly in favor of Milton as Arian on the basis of the poet's frequently repeated statement that Father and Son differ in essence and hence are not *coessential*. He fails, however, to observe that for Milton they are *consubstantial*, though the poet avoids using this word.

Although Milton employs the term *subsistence* several times in this chapter, he has no real need for it, because for him it is pretty much synonymous with substantial essence (14: 195) or substantial existence (15: 267), which for him means an individual possessed of a substratum in which qualities may inhere. In this identification he is traditional; when, as we shall see, *substantia* developed meanings which forbade its being identified with hypostasis, its

---

[2] *A Study in Milton's Christian Doctrine* (London, 1939), p. 88.

[3] *This Great Argument* (Princeton, 1941), pp. 29–30.

[4] "Milton's Arianism Again Considered," *Harvard Theological Review* 54 (1961): 195–205, in part addressed as an answer to my own study, "Milton's Arianism Reconsidered," reprinted elsewhere in this volume, in which I tried to show that Milton was not an Arian.

etymological doublet, another doublet was adopted: *subsistentia*. Hooker, for instance, writes that each Person of the Trinity "hath his own subsistence, which no other besides hath, although there be others besides that are of the same substance." [5] Accordingly, Milton is at no particular pains to define this term. Where he employs it, it generally means a real being — a substantial essence. For him the important and distinctive words are *hypostasis* and *essence*, which despite differing etymologies he interchanges and which for him mean a real entity or real individual. Another is *substance*, which means the substratum underlying being, derived in the case of the Son from the Father. In Milton's view, then, the Trinity may be defined as either three essences or three hypostases in one substance which is derived from the Father. This is just exactly the reverse of Augustine's definition of the Trinity as "one essence [*essentia*], three substances [*substantiae*]"; Augustine does not, of course, recognize any synonymity between essence and hypostasis. [6]

The distinctions which I have pointed out are not negligible, unimportant though they may seem today. At issue is the understanding of the most important word in the Nicene Creed, *homoousios*, a question which rocked the early church to its foundations. The Creed affirms that the Father and Son are homoousian, that is, coessential, whereas, as we have seen, Milton denies their coessentiality at every opportunity. But this denial must be understood, of course, in the light of what he means by essence and substance. Thus, though he flatly and repeatedly denies the coessentiality of Father and Son, he never hints, as I have observed, that they are not consubstantial; and I have already demonstrated what a vast difference he makes between substance and essence. As Milton wrote, Father and Son are consubstantial: God "was properly the Father of the Son produced from his own substance" (14: 186).

Now it is a fair question to ask where Milton may have found this unusual but not unprecedented distinction between essence and substance and what ecclesiastical authority he had for employing these words in these meanings. To answer it, we must first see what problem he was trying to solve. At issue is the Christian affirmation of the Trinity — a Trinity in which the three persons are clearly distinguished, but not so completely that they become altogether independent entities. One early answer was that of Sabellius, already mentioned, who affirmed that the three "Persons" were actually only

---

[5] *Of the Lawes of Ecclesiastical Politie* (London, 1907), 5: 51.

[6] On the Trinity, 5. 8. 10, in *A Select Library of the Nicene and Post-Nicene Fathers* (first ser.), 3: 92. See also his argument (7. 5. 10) as to why "God is improperly called substance."

appearances or modes of operation of a single God. This modal Trinity was rejected, as was its opposite, which posited a Father who created out of nothing the other two persons, making them indeed distinct from the Father but so distinct that it was impossible to conceive how Son and Spirit were divine. This was the heresy of Arius. A position between these two extremes was finally reached at Nicaea in 325. In its Creed the council asserted belief in Father, Son, and Holy Spirit, thus achieving the desired integrity of each of the three persons; but it achieved unity in the three by declaring that they are all of the same *ousia* as the Father: that the three are homoousian. This conclusion was reaffirmed in the Creed of Constantinople (381), known in Milton's time as the "Nicene" Creed; together with the Apostle's Creed it was the standard statement of Christian belief.

Ultimately back of this definition lies an understanding of what is meant by individual being. According to Milton in the *Art of Logic*, "Single things, or what are commonly called individuals, have form single and proper to themselves; certainly they differ in number among themselves . . . ; number, as Scaliger rightly says, is an affection following an essence. Therefore things which differ in number also differ in essence, and never do they differ in number if not in essence" (11: 59). Milton then adds in italics: *"Here let the theologians awake."* The conception of essence here is identical with that in the *Christian Doctrine*; in both works Milton employs the word to mean individual being. Back of his statement lies Aristotle's discussion of individuality. According to the *Metaphysics* (7. 1. 1), the term *being* (τὸ ὄν) first denotes the individuality of a thing. Its primary sense is the *ousia* to which all other attributes adhere. "That which *is* primarily, not in a qualified sense but absolutely, will be *ousia*" (*Meta.*, 7. 1. 5). *Ousia* most obviously appears in bodies of all sorts (*Meta.*, 7. 2. 1), but it may be used in several different senses. The major distinction appears most clearly in the *Categories* (5), where Aristotle develops the concepts of two aspects of *ousia*. The first, which for Aristotle is the primary sense of the word, is "neither predicable of a subject nor present in a subject." It thus represents particular individual beings, "for instance, the individual man or horse." If, following this definition of individual being as *ousia* in its first and most primary meaning, one should assert (as Milton does time and time again) that Father and Son are not coessential (homoousian), he would mean *ousia* in this sense of first *ousia*: individuality. He would assert, then, the separate reality of each of the persons of the Trinity.

At the same time, quite different traditions of *ousia* entered early Christian thinking in its attempt to show how the three Persons could be one. Available, for instance, was the concept of Aristotelian second *ousia* or specific genus, which was widely adopted. Second *ousiai* are "those things . . . within which, as species, the primary substances are included; also those which, as genera, include the species" (*Cate.*, 5). Milton himself uses this definition in *Paradise Lost* (5. 473), which recognizes "various degrees / Of substance," that is, various species or genera. But he does not employ it in his discussion of the Son. As he recognizes, such a definition of *ousia* does not mean individual, as does first *ousia*; rather, "if one divine essence be common to two persons, that essence or divinity will either be in the relation of a whole to its several parts, or of a genus to its several species, or lastly of a common subject to its accidents" (14: 195). This is the Augustinian conception of *ousia* as substance, that is, as second *ousia*.

Also available was a third conception of *ousia*, that of the Stoics. Originally it meant constituent matter, but in Christian thought it came to denote a substratum for any real being. As Prestige observes of the influence of this tradition, "The being or substance of God, without being considered as material, came to be regarded as something which could, at least by a sort of metaphor, be thought of as in extension." [7] As we shall see, this conception of *ousia* as substratum is especially associated with Tertullian.

To summarize, we can recognize three definitions of *ousia*. It can mean Aristotle's first *ousia* or individual. In this sense Milton translated it as essence and applied it to the three persons of the Trinity to state their individual existence. Augustine (and others) translated it as substance and applied it in exactly the same way. Second, it can mean Aristotle's second *ousia* or specific genus. Milton was entirely aware of this definition and on occasion employed it, but not in relation to the unity of the Trinity. Augustine (and others) translated it as essence and did use it to show the unity. Finally, in the Stoic sense *ousia* can mean substratum. Milton translated this as substance and used this concept to support the unity of the Persons in a common substratum derived from the Father. Augustine and Milton, that is, are saying much the same thing, but such is the ambivalence of these theological terms that they superficially appear to be in flat contradiction to one another. In Chapter 5 of the *Christian Doctrine*, Milton consistently uses substance

---

[7] G. L. Prestige, *God in Patristic Thought* (London, 1956), p. 193. See also Harry Wolfson, *Philosophy of the Church Fathers* (Cambridge, Mass., 1956), 1: 325.

in the sense of substratum and essence in the sense of first *ousia*. His probable reason lies in the development of the concepts of hypostasis.

Like *ousia*, "hypostasis" also has two well established theological meanings. It seems to have developed as an equivalent to the term *hypokeimenon*, widely used in classical philosophy. Etymologically, both words mean almost the same thing: "hypostasis" a "standing under" and "hypokeimenon" an "under-lying." As for applied meanings, *hypokeimenon* originally refers to the raw stuff or matter out of which an object is made — the substratum. In this sense it is equivalent to the Stoic *ousia*. But as we have already seen, an individual may be described as a first *ousia* (*Cate.*, 5), and Aristotle elsewhere holds that the individual may be described as a *hypokeimenon* (*Meta.*, 5. 8. 4). Thus, *hypokeimenon* and first *ousia* may be considered to be synonymous, both meaning an individual. In summary, *hypokeimenon* may mean either substratum or individual, depending upon whether it is being used to translate Stoic *ousia* or Aristotelian first *ousia*.

Origen distinguishes Father and Son according to *ousia* and *hypokeimenon*, both words being used in the sense of individual.[8] He seems also to have been the first to describe the persons of the Trinity as hypostases,[9] the equivalent of *hypokeimena*. From his time, that is, Christian writers could use hypostasis as first *ousia*, just as even earlier usage had accepted the antecedent of hypostasis, *hypokeimenon*, in the same sense. But in their original meaning of "substratum" both words could also mean the Stoic *ousia*. Thus hypostasis and *ousia* developed as synonyms in both senses of both words, meaning either the concrete individual or the substratum. They are treated as synonymous in Athanasius and in Epiphanius,[10] where both are used in the meaning of substratum, Milton's "substance." This must be recognized as the earlier meaning of the words. As Prestige observes, "To the mind of the Fathers, down to the time at which the terminology became fixed and technical, the practical meaning of the two terms was substantially identical. They both indicated . . . the particular slab of material stuff which constitutes a given object." [11] But the other meaning then developed in the vigorous discussion at Nicaea and later, where the two words (still synonyms) came now to mean "positive and concrete and distinct existence, [that is] the particular individual,"[12] mak-

---

[8] *De Oratione*, 15; Wolfson, p. 318.
[9] E.g., *Contra Celsum*, 8. 12; cf. Prestige, p. 179, and Wolfson, p. 319.
[10] Prestige, p. 167.
[11] Prestige, p. 168.
[12] Prestige, p. 174.

ing them equivalent to first *ousia* in Aristotle. Milton follows this sense of the two words when he insists that the three persons of the Godhead are hypostases and not coessential; and he carefully restricts "substance" to the earlier meaning of substratum.

So far the history of these words has been followed in Greek. Tertullian seems to have introduced to theology the use of *substantia* as the Latin translation of *ousia*, and he employs *substantia* in both senses of the Greek word. First, he writes against Praxeas, "you will not allow Him [the Word] to be really a substantive being, by having a substance [*substantiae*] of His own; in such a way that He may be regarded as an objective thing and a person, and so be able . . . to make two, the Father and the Son, God and the Word." [13] Here *substantia* is evidently used as synonymous with *persona* or hypostasis or first *ousia*. Thus, one could follow Tertullian and state that there are three substances in the Trinity. As we have seen, this is the meaning of *substantia* which Augustine later adopted. But for the common unity of the Trinity Tertullian also uses the same word *substantia*, now meaning substratum. Commenting upon the verse "I and my Father are one" (John 10:30), he says that they are one "in respect of unity of substance [*substantiae*], not singularity of number." [14] As Wolfson observes, by *substantia* Tertullian must here mean unity of substratum, which derives from the Father.[15] Several times elsewhere, Tertullian employs this second meaning. For instance, he writes that "the Father is the entire substance but the Son is a derivation and portion of the whole," [16] or the Son derives "from the substance of the Father," [17] or the Trinity are three "not in condition, but in degree; not in substance, but in form; not in power, but in aspect; yet of one substance, and of one condition, and of one power," [18] or finally, the distinction of Father and Son is to be explained "on the ground of Personality, not of Substance — in the way of distinction, not of division." [19] This second use of *substantia* in Tertullian for Stoic *ousia* or substratum is precisely that of Milton, who is thus echoing what appears to be the earliest technical meaning of *substantia* in any Latin theo-

---

[13] *Against Praxeas*, 7, in *The Ante-Nicene Fathers*, 3: 602. See also Prestige, p. 220, and Wolfson, pp. 323 ff.

[14] *Against Praxeas*, 25.

[15] Wolfson, p. 326.

[16] *Against Praxeas*, 9; Wolfson, p. 326.

[17] *Against Praxeas*, 4; Wolfson, p. 326.

[18] *Against Praxeas*, 2; Wolfson, p. 328; Prestige, p. 220.

[19] *Against Praxeas*, 12.

logical writer. Neither man uses the term *consubstantial* in this context, though both could have.[20]

Another point of similarity between Tertullian and Milton (aside from their subordinationism, which I have argued elsewhere) is the fact that both derive the second and third Persons from the substance of the Father. For neither writer is there a common substratum underlying all three members. Tertullian's view continues in the Nicene Creed (325), which anathematizes all "who assert that the Son of God is of a different hypostasis or *ousia*." The two words are used synonymously here — a well-established practice by this time with reference to the substratum in the Son, begotten of the *ousia* of the Father, as an earlier clause of the original Creed states.[21] Milton, thus, is following the earliest tradition of the Latin church. Augustine, on the other hand, later established the view that a common substratum underlies both Father and Son,[22] and this became the accepted interpretation.

Likewise, not long after Nicaea, under the influence of the Arian controversy, the Cappadocian fathers, especially Basil and Gregory of Nyssa, distinguished *ousia* from *hypostasis*. The former was henceforth relegated to "substance" in the sense of Aristotelian second *ousia* or substratum. The latter was identified with *persona*. We are not at all concerned here with this later development except to observe that, since it is the interpretation current today, it has led astray the thinking of many with regard to Milton's understanding of the Trinity; and it serves to emphasize that Milton, like many other Protestants, returned to the earliest tradition and built his system on it. Also to be noted is the fact that his Christianity squares in its conception of substance and essence with that of the earliest important Latin writer, Tertullian, as well as with Aristotle's original philosophical definitions. Milton was certainly aware of Tertullian's position, for during the course of the argument in *Of Prelatical Episcopacy* he makes a very good summary of some of the ideas which I have presented. Tertullian, he says, argues for "an imparity between *God* the Father, and *God* the Sonne [that is, for subordinationism], as these words import in his Booke against *Praxeas*. The Father is the whole substance, but

---

[20] See Wolfson, p. 327. In the *Christian Doctrine*, Milton, like many other Protestants, tends to avoid using nonbiblical terms like this one.

[21] "[T]he Son of God, begotten from the Father . . . , that is, from the *ousia* of the Father." Cf. Wolfson, pp. 334 f., but Prestige speculates that "the anathema . . . against those who asserted that the Son came into existence . . . from another hypostasis or ousia, means by these last two expressions, not generic substance, but individual objective source" (p. 177).

[22] Wolfson, p. 353; for a clear summary of these complex issues see C. A. Patrides' study, "Milton on the Trinity: The Use of Antecedents," printed elsewhere in this volume.

the Son a derivation, and portion of the whole" (3. 1. 97). Milton proceeds to disagree with this conclusion. In 1641, when this pamphlet appeared, he evidently had not come to the position which he supports in the *Christian Doctrine*.

Presumably, this attitude toward the Fathers and their relationship with ancient philosophy was taught at Cambridge in Milton's day, and it would not be surprising if some of his contemporaries should show some awareness of these ideas. Ralph Cudworth knows about them, for instance, though he is not so daring in adopting them as was Milton. According to Cudworth, who was interested in showing the relationship between Platonism and Christianity, Platonists think that the Trinity have "one singular or numerical essence" — this is Stoic *ousia* — but have also "distinct singular essences of their own" — the Aristotelian first *ousiai*. Likewise "the ancient orthodox fathers of the Christian church," he observes, have thought that all of the Persons had "one common and universal essence or substance; that word substance being used by them as synonymous with essence, and applied to universals likewise, as it is by the Peripatetics, when they call a man, or animal in general, substantiam secundam, 'a second substance.' " Cudworth seems not to have studied the Fathers so closely as Milton did and thus mistakenly proceeds to generalize that they commonly distinguished *ousia* from hypostasis; others, he admits, did not distinguish the two words, and thus he judges that "hypostasis, prosopon, or person, in the Trinity, might be said in another sense, and in way of opposition to Sabellius, to have its own singular, individual, or existent essence also; and that there are thus . . . 'three singular existent essences' in the Deity, as well as . . . 'three hypostases'; an hypostasis being nothing else to them, but an existent essence." [23] This is exactly Milton's position.

In Chapter 14 of the *Christian Doctrine*, Milton returns to these distinctions; here he applies them to the union of divine and human which constitutes the Incarnation. His especial concern is with the term hypostasis, since the Incarnation has been traditionally defined as a "hypostatic union," and he concludes that in this union "*hypostasis* can signify nothing in the present case [as compared with his earlier discussion] but what is expressed in Latin by *substantia* or *subsistentia*, 'substance' or 'subsistence'; that is to say, a perfect essence existing *per se*" (15: 269). He thus reasons that "there is then in Christ a mutual hypostatic union of two natures, that is to say, of two essences, of two substances, and consequently of two persons" (15: 271). In

---

[23] *The True Intellectual System of the Universe* (London, 1845), 2: 431–32.

this argument Milton is clarifying the issue by employing *substantia* now in its more usual sense of "individual," the equivalent of first *ousia*, and not in the meaning of Stoic substratum, which it had in Chapter 5. This meaning he recognizes as being more familiar to his readers, and the distinctions which he had made earlier are not at issue here. Essence, however, as before, means an individual being. Accordingly, two individual beings or persons are united, in his view of the Incarnation, with resultant Nestorian implications.[24] Milton observes that "the opinion here given respecting the hypostatic union agrees with what was advanced relative to the Son of God in the fifth chapter, namely, that his essence is not the same with that of the Father" (15: 273).

Thus we conclude that Milton might indeed believe that he was supporting the homoousian doctrine, the heart of the Nicene Creed. For him, the Persons were distinguished as three hypostases or as three essences, both words being understood in the sense of the Aristotelian first *ousia*. He is, then, no Sabellian. Furthermore, the three are unified by having a single divine substratum, which Milton calls substance, derived from the Father; it is equivalent to the Stoic conception of *ousia* as substratum and was apparently introduced to Latin Christianity by Tertullian. He is, then, no Arian by the "Nicene" Creed of 381 which still maintains its authority in the Book of Common Prayer. In agreement with every church father beginning with one of the earliest, Justin Martyr, Milton asserted the unity of rule of the Trinity: the Son, he says, is one with the Father "inasmuch as they speak and act with unanimity" and "in love, in communion, in agreement, in charity, in spirit, in glory" (14: 211–13).[25] With an understanding of his theological vocabulary one may conclude, as he himself does at the end of his long discussion of the Son of God in the *Christian Doctrine*, that his conception of the Trinity is in agreement with the creedal statement of 381 which was generally accepted as Nicene orthodoxy in his day.

---

[24] See my discussion in "Milton on the Incarnation," printed elsewhere in this volume.
[25] See Wolfson's discussion of unity of rule, pp. 321 ff.

2. The Son in His Relation to the Father

Milton's Arianism Reconsidered

W. B. HUNTER

When in 1825 Bishop Charles Sumner published the text and his translation of Milton's long-lost theological study, the *Christian Doctrine*, the results were in a way disastrous for the reputation of the poet. Instead of being the great composer of the orthodox epic of Protestantism, Milton became in the eyes of the nineteenth century and even of our own day the heretic who advocated the belief in an unequal Trinity — a heresy originally associated with the fourth-century Bishop Arius. In the light especially of the fifth chapter of the *Christian Doctrine*, critics reread *Paradise Lost* and discovered that this same doctrine was implied in passages of the poem which had been accepted for a century and a half as entirely orthodox. The shock to critical and religious sensibilities was considerable; Milton's fame underwent an eclipse from which it perhaps has never fully recovered.[1] Although our own century may be less susceptible to disturbance from the presentation of heterodox views, much the same conception of Milton continues; all critics echo Masson's stern judgment that Milton's views of the nature of Christ "are expressly and emphatically those of high Arianism." [2]

Acceptance of the theory that Milton was an Arian implies, however, two rather strange twists in his thought. In the first place, he never supports Arius

---

[1] In *This Great Argument* (Princeton, 1941), pp. 3 ff., Maurice Kelley writes of the dismay which the publication of the *Christian Doctrine* occasioned.

[2] David Masson, *The Life of John Milton* (reprint ed. New York, 1946), 6: 823. Kelley holds that the *Christian Doctrine* "asserts Arian views on the Son of God" and that *Paradise Lost* is Arian too. Although "Milton's is not an extreme type of Arianism" in Kelley's eyes and "the theologian would perhaps find 'anti-Trinitarian' a more exact term," yet, like other twentieth-century readers of Milton, Kelley has "used the two terms interchangeably" and argues also that "Miltonists . . . should cease to question the anti-Trinitarianism of *Paradise Lost*." Pp. 6, 11 ff., 35 n. 22, and 118 n. 86.

in his works. Hardly one to hide his light under a bushel, no matter how unpopular it might be with dim-eyed contemporaries, Milton does mention Arius several times in his writings but without any suggestion of indebtedness or kinship.[3] Moreover, no contemporary biographer ever mentions the fact that Milton expressed Arian views during his lifetime, though it seems a fair assumption that had he done so the fact would have come to the attention of at least some of the poet's antagonists.

In the second place, Milton was clearly aware that his conception of the Son was unusual in the Christian tradition — his introductory remarks to Chapter 5 of the *Christian Doctrine* admit such awareness — but despite his fine training in theology he does not seem to realize that he is supporting beliefs recognized as heretical. Indeed, the book is addressed to Protestants of all denominations — "To all the churches of Christ, and to all who profess the Christian Faith throughout the world" (14: 3) — in an effort to present a united program for all communicants. Milton would have been almost incredibly naïve had he planned a worldwide Protestant movement which would consciously include one of the most famous heresies of church history — a heresy which, according to Ephraim Paget, had as recently as 1611 caused "Bartholomew Legate, an obstinate Arrian" to be burned in Smithfield and Edward Wightman to be burned at Lichfield.[4] The conclusion seems evident: in his own eyes Milton was not an Arian, even though modern judges are unanimous in branding him one.

As a matter of religious history, the relationship among Father, Son, and Spirit was long a bitterly debated issue. The theological problem involves the establishment of a valid distinction among the persons without destruction of their basic unity. Some have thought that the second and third members of the Trinity are merely two phases of the activity of a single God; this is the Sabellian heresy, which destroys any real distinction of one person from another. Others, including Bishop Arius, distinguished the Son from the Father as a subordinate entity, created in time and differing in substance from the Father.[5] Especially important is Arius' theory that the Son is gen-

---

[3] Even in the midst of the main "Arian" chapter of the *Christian Doctrine*, he casually mentions Arius, but without any sense of identification. *Works* (New York, 1931–38), 14: 293.

[4] *Heresiography, Or a Description of the Hereticks and Sectaries Sprung Up in These Latter Times* (London, 1661), p. 157.

[5] Orthodox church fathers vigorously and successfully campaigned to have all of Arius' writings destroyed. Accordingly his ideas are available to us only through statements made by his opponents, of whom Athanasius is by far the most important. This summary is taken from his *Orationes contra Arianos*, 1: 5 and 6. See also H. M. Gwatkin, *The Arian Con-*

erated "out of nothing" — ἐξ οὐκ ὄντων[6] — not from the paternal substance. Thus the Son is only a creature like the rest of the divine creation and is no more to be worshipped than is any other created entity. Nor is he coeternal with the Father.

To resolve these differences and to reunite the church, which had been weakened by them, the Council of Nicaea in 325 authoritatively affirmed that the three persons in the Trinity are of one substance. The question of equality was discussed but not authoritatively disposed of nor was that of the eternity of the three persons, though both equality and eternity have been generally accepted by Christians since that day.[7] The affirmation of the Son's origin from divine substance left no doubt in anyone's mind as to his divinity. As the Nicene Creed states, Christ is "the only-begotten Son of God; Begotten of his Father before all worlds . . . ; Begotten, not made [ποιηθέντα]; Being of one substance [ὁμοούσιον not μονοούσιον, however] with the Father; By whom all things were made."[8] The Church of England reaffirms this Creed in its Eighth Article of Religion; the Presbyterians, the other church dominant in England in Milton's time, state in the Westminster Confession of Faith that "In the unity of the Godhead there be three persons of one substance, power, and eternity. . . . The Father is of none, neither begotten nor proceeding; the Son is eternally begotten of the Father; the Holy Ghost eternally proceeding from the Father and the Son."[9]

Milton, accepting no authority other than the Bible, seems to have quite different views. Much of Chapter 5 of the *Christian Doctrine* is given over to a long argument that Father and Son differ in essence: the Son is generated by the external efficiency of the Father inasmuch as God's "external efficiency" is divided into "generation" of the Son (and presumably of the Spirit), "creation" of the universe (presumably up through the angels), and "government of the universe" (14:179). Accordingly, the Son was made of God's own nature and substance — not, as with Arius, ἐξ οὐκ ὄντων: "God

---

troversy (London, 1898), p. 7. This material is conveniently available in *A Select Library of Nicene and Post-Nicene Fathers*, 2d ser., 4.

[6] The phrase is originally from 2 Maccabees 7:28.

[7] See the discussion by Harry A. Wolfson in *The Philosophy of the Church Fathers* (Cambridge, Mass., 1956), 1: 217 f.

[8] This is the translation found in the Book of Common Prayer. Its "Nicene Creed" should more accurately be known as the "Nicaeno-Constantinopolitan Creed" of 381, a revision of the statement of the Council of 325. For Milton and his audience this later creed is the authoritative one. In any case, neither statement expressly affirms the Son's eternity or the equality of the members of the Trinity, assertions which appear only in the pseudo-Athanasian Creed, which has never had any authority for Protestants.

[9] Chapter 2; see also chap. 8.

imparted to the Son as much as he pleased of the divine nature, nay of the divine substance, itself, care being taken not to confound the substance with the whole essence, which would imply, that the Father had given to the Son what he retained numerically the same himself" (14: 193); or as *Paradise Lost* says of the Son, "in him all his Father shone / Substantially express'd" (3. 139 f.). But we are not to infer that the Son is "co-essential with the Father . . . ; otherwise the Father and the Son would be one person" (14: 187). The Son so generated is the agent for creation, not the ultimate cause (14: 205). Since Father and Son differ in essence, they cannot be equal: they are "not only not co-essential, but not co-equal" (14: 211); God could not "beget a co-equal Deity, because unity and infinity are two of his essential attributes" (14: 311). Furthermore, the begetting must have taken place within the limits of time and so was not eternal (14: 189 and 309). Following the Gospel of John, Milton holds that "the Son existed in the beginning, under the name of the logos or word, and was the first of the whole creation" (14: 181). Nothing necessitated this generation: it "arose from no natural necessity" in the Father (14: 185) but "of his own free will. . . . For questionless, it was in God's power . . . not to have begotten the Son" (14: 187). The results are two different divine beings, one only "as they speak and act with unanimity" (14: 211) as well as "in love, in communion, in agreement, in charity, in spirit, in glory" (14: 213).

How then is the Son divine? "By the same right as he enjoys the title of the Word, or of the only begotten Son, namely, by the will of the one God" (14: 255). In addition, the Son has certain attributes traditionally associated with him (14: 315–43). But the Father is utterly beyond human knowledge: "to know God as he really is, far transcends the power of man's thoughts, much more of his perception" (14: 31); we may know him only indirectly in his image, his Son (14: 251, 253, 265). We may summarize that for Milton the Son is different from the Father, inferior to him, generated at the beginning of creation, but of the divine substance. This in no way derogates from the Son's incarnation as Christ nor from the traditional beliefs attached to his earthly appearance — beliefs which are considered in later chapters of the *Christian Doctrine*. In conclusion, one should observe that Milton never in any of his writings denies the divinity of the Son or even suggests such a denial.

Chapter 6 deals in a similar manner with the Holy Spirit. Milton does not know how he originated (14: 359), but considers him "as inferior to both Father and Son" (14: 377). Like the Son, the Spirit is "actually and numerically distinct from God himself [and] cannot possibly be essentially one God with him whose Spirit he is" (14: 379). Accordingly, Milton concludes that the Spirit, "inasmuch as he is a minister of God and therefore a creature, was created or produced of the substance of God [like the Son], not by a natural necessity, but by the free will of the agent, probably before the foundations of the world were laid, but later than the Son, and far inferior to him." He adds that there may be some difficulty in distinguishing Son and Spirit (14: 403).

Now as anyone who has made a close study of the *Christian Doctrine* is only too well aware, Milton there claims and faithfully follows just one source — the Bible. This book he considers to be the only sure guide for faith; he accordingly weights down his work with thousands of quotations from it to prove his points. Objective though his method seems to be, he twists the meaning of verses to suit his own preconceptions — preconceptions which any student of the book will readily admit are present. Whence these preconceptions about the Trinity? According to Edward Phillips, Milton used Wolleb and Ames, two compilers of Protestant compendiums, as his model in the treatise;[10] but they do not support his apparently Arian views. Thus Ames is quite orthodox in holding that "The same essence is common to the three subsistences" and Wolleb that "the persons of the Godhead are subsistences, which have the whole essence of God, but differ by incommunicable properties."[11]

Elsewhere in England, antitrinitarianism was indeed not dead in Milton's own day. Masson has shown that such men as Thomas Webb, Paul Best, John Biddle, Samuel Richardson, and John Goodwin were active in supporting this thesis during the mid-1640's.[12] But these are relatively unimportant writers who never achieved any real intellectual leadership. Biddle (or Bidle) may be taken as typical. He holds that a supreme created Holy Spirit exists, supreme "by way of excellency only. . . . In like manner . . . there is one *made* Lord by way of Excellency only, which is Jesus of Nazareth, who after he had been crucified by the *Jews*, was raised up from the Dead, and exalted to the right Hand of God, and by him made Lord and Christ."[13] Biddle is like Mil-

---

[10] In Helen Darbishire, *The Early Lives of Milton* (London, 1932), p. 61.

[11] William Ames, *The Marrow of Theology*, trans. John D. Eusden (Boston, 1968), p. 88, and John W. Beardslee, *Reformed Dogmatics* (New York, 1965), p. 40.

[12] Masson, 3: 157 f. I should add here that Martin Larson's attempt to trace Milton's conception of the Trinity to Servetus (*PMLA* 41 [1926]: 891–934) does not seem convincing. Servetus' ideas are easily available in *The Two Treatises of Servetus on the Trinity*, trans. E. M. Wilbur, in *Harvard Theological Studies* 16 (1932).

[13] John Bidle, *A Confession of Faith Touching the Holy Trinity* (1648), p. 2, reprinted with separate pagination in *The Faith of One God, Who is Only the Father; and of One Mediator between God and Men, Who is Only the Man Christ Jesus* (London, 1691).

ton in asserting that the members of the Trinity differ in essence: Christ "must either have the same Essence in number, or a different one. Not the same Essence in number, for then he will not be equal with God in Essence, but the same; for Equality must be in respect of two things different at least in number, otherwise it will not be Equality, but Identity. . . . If Christ hath an Essence different in number from that of God, it must needs also be inferiour thereunto, there being no Essence equal to his" (pp. 5–6). But the differences from Milton are far greater: the Spirit was present at creation but Christ was not (p. 5); the Word is really the Spirit and Christ was not divine before his birth (p. 11); Christ is the interpreter of God's will and nothing more (pp. 16–17).

II

But affinities do occur between Milton and some of his contemporaries at Cambridge — men who have more than once been accused of Arianism. Henry More and Ralph Cudworth in particular tried to reconcile the Christian Trinity with a trinity once of immense importance to Christians but now practically forgotten: that of Platonism.

For Platonism had its trinity too, which has interested Christians in many stages of their history. The origins of this trinity are lost to us — certainly it can be deduced from Plato's dialogues only by the most violent wresting of meaning. One of the earliest statements of the principle with direct concern for Christians is to be found in the pseudo-Platonic Epistle 2: "Now I must expound [the nature of 'the First'] in a riddling way. . . . The matter stands thus: Related to the King of All are all things, and for his sake they are, and of all things fair He is the cause. And related to the Second are the second things; and related to the Third the third. About these, then, the human soul strives to learn, looking to the things that are akin to itself, whereof none is fully perfect. But as to the King and the objects I have mentioned, they are of quite different quality." [14] One can hardly say that this constitutes a very definite statement about anything; but it does assert that there are three original causes in the universe, which are related to each other. It is a trinity of sorts. And it is sufficiently vague that almost any extension of meaning may be read into it.

From the time of Numenius (second century A.D.), regardless of the precise form taken by the various interpretations of this trinity, all agreed in the

---

[14] *Timaeus and Epistles*, trans. R. G. Bury (London, 1929), 312 E.

basic inequality of its members. Plotinus (205?–270) presents the theory in its complete form, but it appears in one shape or another in the writings of every Neoplatonist. In his *Enneads* this trinity is the One (το ἕν), Mind (νοῦς),[15] and Soul (ψυχή). The One, which is unknowable,[16] overflows or emanates into Mind, which in turn emanates into Soul in a descending series. Such an emanation is eternal, like the orthodox Christian view of the generation of the Son. But it is not willed; part of the nature of the One is to emanate Mind and Soul, as well as ultimately lower orders (*Enneads* 5. 1. 6). These lower emanations desire to return to higher ones, and all seek reunion with the One. This desire for return to the source of all being is as central to Neoplatonism as is the emanative descent. As Proclus writes, "all things proceed in a circuit, from their causes to their causes again. There are greater circuits and lesser, in that some revert upon their immediate priors, others upon the superior causes, even to the beginning of all things. For out of the beginning all things are, and toward it all revert." [17] Iamblichus gives further details: "there is one God . . . immoveable, and abiding in the solitude of his own unity. For neither is the intelligible connected with him, nor any thing else; but he is . . . father alone, and is truly good. For he is something even greater and prior to this, is the fountain of all things, and the root of the first intelligible forms. But from this one deity, the God who is sufficient to himself unfolds himself into light. For this divinity, also, is . . . prior to essence, and the principle of essence. For from him entity and essence are derived; and hence, also, he is denominated the principle of intelligibles. . . . Other leaders preside over the fabrication of visible natures." Thus the "demiurgic intellect," the "curator of truth and wisdom," descends "into generation" and leads "the power of

---

[15] No really satisfactory translation is at hand for this term. MacKenna uses the awkward *intellectual principle* in his translation of the *Enneads*; Inge uses *Spirit* in his *Philosophy of Plotinus*, 3d ed. (London, 1948), but this unfortunately suggests the third rather than the second member of the Christian Trinity. E. R. Dodds in his translation of Proclus' *Elements of Theology* (Oxford, 1933), uses *intelligence*. English writers in the seventeenth century were generally satisfied with *mind*.

[16] For Plotinus' main discussion of the relationship of the three "Persons" of the Neoplatonic trinity, see *Enneads*, 5. 1. Besides being quite unknowable, the One is, as Proclus says, utter unity as well: "Every manifold is posterior to the One." Dodds notes that "this proposition demonstrates that the Absolute Unity . . . is completely transcendent in the sense of being uninfected by plurality." *Elements*, Prop. 5 and note, p. 191. Milton's God is likewise in the final sense unknowable (*Works*, 14: 31) and utterly unified: "nothing can be said of the one God which is inconsistent with his unity, and which assigns to him at the same time the attributes of unity and plurality" (14: 51).

[17] *Elements*, Prop. 33. In *Paradise Lost* Milton states that after the Last Judgment "God shall be All in All" (3. 341; see also 5. 469 f.), an idea elaborated in the *Christian Doctrine* (*Works*, 16: 367). Though the Christian source is 1 Cor. 15:24–28, the idea is identical with the Neoplatonic "return."

occult reasons into light." [18] In conclusion, two important considerations must be stressed with regard to the Neoplatonic conception of the entire creation, visible and invisible: it is both timeless and unwilled, quite unlike the Christian conception of the visible creation based on Genesis.[19]

Now these three powers or entities of the Neoplatonic trinity may be found (by those who wish to find them) in other Platonists. Two of these writers are especially important to Christianity: Hermes Trismegistus (thought by many in the seventeenth century to be the true pagan originator of the whole revelation but actually a group of writers active in the third century A.D.) and Macrobius (late fourth century A.D.). Much earlier, though he is not a true Neoplatonist, is the Platonizing Jew Philo, but he will be treated separately.

As has been observed, the second person of the Plotinian trinity is *Nous*, not the *Logos* of St. John. Hermes is the main Neoplatonist to express the trinity with the term *Logos* (taken from the Stoics or from Philo) instead of *Nous*. In the *Hermetica* the First God or the One reveals himself in light; "from the Light there came forth a holy Word [*Logos*], which took its stand upon the watery substance [of the creation]; and methought this Word was the voice of the Light." Poimandres explains that the light is "Mind, the first God, who was before the watery substance which appeared out of the darkness; and the Word which came forth from the Light is son of God." [20] Toward the end of the passage occurs a hymn to God: "Holy is God the Father of all, who is before the first beginning. . . . Holy art Thou, who by thy Word hast constructed all that is." [21] In Hermes, then, the Christian could find a Neoplatonic trinity whose second person was quite similar to St. John's Logos.

Macrobius furnishes a description of the Neoplatonic trinity which is in some ways similar to the Christian and which also offers a good summary of the pagan trinity as it was typically treated: "God, who both is and is called the First Cause, is alone the beginning and source of all things which are and

---

[18] *On the Mysteries of the Egyptians, Chaldeans, and Assyrians*, trans. Thomas Taylor (Chiswick, 1821), pp. 301–2.

[19] Cf. Dodds' note in *Elements*, p. 290. But with regard to the eternal generation of the Son the similarity is striking.

[20] *Hermetica*, ed. and trans. by Walter Scott (Oxford, 1924), 1: 117. Scott notes (2: 24) that the writer has hypostatized the Logos, as had Philo. Later in this Libellus it is expressly paralleled with the Demiurgos–Nous of the Platonists (cf. 1: 119, and 2: 32). The parallels with Milton are obvious, but they can be matched in many other writers.

[21] *Hermetica*, 1: 131. I have capitalized *Word* although Scott argues that it is not hypostatized here (2: 70). But in the seventeenth century one could hardly read the passage with other than Christian meaning.

which seem to be. He, in a bounteous outpouring of his greatness, created [*creavit*] from himself Mind. This Mind, called *nous*, as long as it fixes its gaze upon the Father, retains a complete likeness of its Creator, but when it looks away at things below creates from itself Soul. . . . Soul, creating and fashioning bodies for itself — on that account the creation, which men who really know about God and Mind call *nous*, has its beginning in Soul — out of that pure and clearest fount of Mind from whose abundance it had drunk deep at birth, endowed those divine or ethereal bodies, meaning the celestial sphere and the stars which it was first creating, with mind." Then, "since Mind emanates from the Supreme God and Soul from Mind, and Mind, indeed, forms and suffuses all below with life . . . and since all follow on in continuous succession, degenerating step by step in their downward course, the close observer will find that from the Supreme God even to the bottommost dregs of the universe there is one tie, binding at every link and never broken. . . . This discussion of Soul," he concludes, "embraces the opinions of all who are known to have made pronouncements about the soul." [22]

Many Christian fathers, whether they were Arians or not, were influenced by these and other expositions of the Neoplatonic trinity. St. Augustine, for instance, admits that he came to Christianity by way of "certain books of the Platonists" and quotes sentences which parallel the doctrines of the two trinities (excepting always the Christian Incarnation).[23] Just how much influence the Neoplatonic theory had upon the contemporary Arius and his followers is difficult to say. The two systems are similar in their graduated scale of divinity. But the Neoplatonic trinity is eternal and derived from the substance of the One; the Arian begins in time and its second person is created out of nothing. The Neoplatonic is not willed; the Arian is willed. Inge observed that "Platonism, if it identifies the Logos-Christ with Noûs, and the Holy Spirit with the universal Soul, cannot maintain that the three persons are co-equal." [24] Long ago Cory noted that this "spurious Platonism" regarding the Trinity is "intimately connected" with the heresy.[25] Ultimately back of it, as

---

[22] *Commentary on the Dream of Scipio*, trans. William H. Stahl (New York, 1952), pp. 143–46. The fact that Mind is described as created and not eternal should be noted. In several other details Macrobius' ideas are analogous to those of Milton: cf. the origin and destiny of the soul (pp. 124–25; Milton, *Works*, 15: 239, and my own "Milton's Materialistic Life Principle," *JEGP* 45 [1946]: 74). Milton's Limbo of Vanities (*Paradise Lost*, 3. 440 ff.) may owe something to the *Commentary*, p. 126. Macrobius' description of creation, p. 182, is similar to Milton's lines in *Paradise Lost*, 7. 234 ff.

[23] *Confessions*, trans. E. B. Pusey (New York, 1950), 7: 9.

[24] *Plotinus*, 2: 210.

[25] Isaac P. Cory, *Ancient Fragments*, 2d ed. (London, 1832), Introduction, p. li.

Gwatkin correctly emphasized, was rationalism: Arianism "was almost as much a philosophy as a religion. It assumed the usual philosophical postulates, worked by the usual philosophical methods, and scarcely referred to Scripture except in quest of isolated texts." By considering the Trinity from the point of view of rationality rather than dogma, it consequently arrived at the conception of an unequal Trinity, which "forms a descending series separated by infinite degrees of honour and glory, not altogether unlike the Neoplatonic Triad of orders of spiritual existence extending outward in concentric circles." [26]

III

Before we consider how the seventeenth century interpreted these matters, we must turn back to Philo, who was undoubtedly the most important conveyor of Platonism to the earliest Christian movement. The Philonic God, it must be observed first, is quite unknowable (like the Neoplatonic One and like Milton's): as Wolfson summarizes, Philo's "God cannot be apprehended by any man, not only as an object of sense but even as an object of intelligence." [27] Next, following Plato, Philo accepted the reality of a world of intelligibles. When God determined upon the visible creation, he "first fully formed the intelligible world . . . and then, with that for a pattern, the world which our senses can perceive." [28] The "intellect" of the intelligible world Philo does not call *Nous*, as the later Neoplatonists excepting Hermes would, but *Logos*: "the universe that consisted of ideas would have no other location than the Divine Reason [θεῖον λόγον] which was the Author of this ordered frame" of the later-created, visible universe.[29] The substitution of *Logos* for *Nous* was of major importance for the development of the Christian conception of the second person of the Trinity, since the Logos is central in the Prologue to the Gospel of John. In Philo, then, God thinks the ideas of the intelligible world; the Mind of God is termed the Logos and it is at this stage "identical with the essence of God" and does not exist as a separate entity.[30] But the ideas leave the mind of God and take on an external existence as the intelligible world, no

---

[26] Gwatkin, *The Arian Controversy*, pp. 20, 26.

[27] For the exposition of Philo's ideas I follow Harry A. Wolfson, *Philo* (Cambridge, Mass., 1948). He discusses Philo's transcendent God at 2: 119, giving an extended argument and observing that this conception is new in the history of western philosophy and religion.

[28] "On the Creation," 4, in *Works*, trans. F. H. Colson and G. H. Whitaker (Loeb, 1929), 1: 15, 17. See also Wolfson, *Philo*, 1: 226 ff.

[29] "On the Creation," 5, in *Works*, 1: 17; cf. Wolfson, *Philo*, 1: 230.

[30] Wolfson, *Philo*, 1: 231.

longer identical with his essence. The Mind which embraces this intelligible world thus also comes into existence as an entity separate from God; Philo continues to call this separated Mind by the same name that it had when it was part of the divine essence: the Logos. The Logos, then, has in Wolfson's analysis of Philo two stages of existence: a first one, uncreated and from eternity, when it exists only as God's thought (not as a person), and a second one when it is generated as God externalizes his thought into an intelligible world. Philo often speaks of the Logos as "created," though sometimes he says that it is "eternal." [31] It is eternal in that it had so existed as a property of God. When it enters its second and external state as an entity it is properly said to be created. As such, it "is eldest and most all-embracing of created things." [32] The Logos is made not from God's substance but from nothing (ἐξ οὐκ ὄντων).[33]

Although Philo's two-stage conception of the Logos is little known today, it was unquestionably a central consideration in the effort of early Christians to establish just what they meant by the Trinity before the Council of Nicaea. Omitting the question of whether it guided the author of the Gospel of John in his opening imitation of Genesis, one can easily demonstrate that many of the earliest church fathers — the so-called Apologists — follow Philo in his consideration of a two-stage Logos. Indeed, Wolfson finds the influence of Philo on every writer from Justin Martyr to Clement of Alexandria and Lactantius, all of whom seem to have identified the Johannine and Philonic Logos and interpreted the former in terms of the latter.[34] Tertullian, for instance, whose thought Milton often follows, asserted that "before all things God was alone." Yet "even then God was not without reason or what is called Logos. But 'as soon as it pleased God' to create the world, He 'put forth the Logos himself.' It is this proceeding of the Logos from God that constitutes 'the perfect nativity of the Logos.'" [35] Accordingly, Tertullian takes "In the beginning was the Word" to refer to the emanation or generation by which the Word entered its second stage of existence and became a person separate from the Father.[36] In the same way the church father Hippolytus argues that "God

---

[31] Wolfson, *Philo*, 1: 234 f.

[32] "Allegorical Interpretation," 3: 61, in *Works*, 1: 419.

[33] *Philosophy of the Church Fathers*, 1: 293, 586.

[34] 1: 192.

[35] *Adversus Praxeam*, 5 and 7, as cited in Wolfson, *Philosophy*, 1: 195. For the entire passage see *The Ante-Nicene Fathers*, 3.

[36] *Adversus Praxeam*, 5 and 7; Wolfson, *Philosophy*, 1: 198. See also Bishop George Bull's uneasy consideration of Tertullian's orthodoxy in his *Defence of the Nicene Creed* (Oxford, 1851), 3: 10.

subsisted 'alone' and had 'nothing contemporaneous with himself' and 'beside Him there was nothing,' " although he had his reason — that is, the pre-existent Logos. Then, by an act of will, God manifested the Logos in time; this manifestation means that God "begot the Logos" and through him created everything.[37]

Did God freely will the creation of the Logos when it came to exist in its second stage? Philo asserts that "the Logos together with the intelligible world came into their second stage of existence prior to the creation of the world by the will of God." [38] The same interpretation appears in the early Fathers, Tertullian, for instance, arguing that the generation of the Logos took place "as soon as God willed (*voluit*) to put forth into their respective substances and forms the things which he had planned and ordered within himself." Similar quotations can be found in Justin Martyr, Tatian, Theophilus, Hippolytus, and Clement of Alexandria.[39] Milton obviously follows this conception throughout the *Christian Doctrine* as well as in *Paradise Lost*. Thus "The generation of the Son . . . arose from no natural necessity. . . . For questionless, it was in God's power consistently with the perfection of his own essence not to have begotten the Son" (14: 185, 187). Or more generally in *Paradise Lost*, God asserts that "Necessity and Chance / Approach not mee, and what I will is Fate" (7. 172 f.).

A final point of some concern is the distinction between *begetting* and *creating*. Milton seems to confuse these and similar terms deliberately when he says that "God of his own will created [*creavit*], whether he generated [*generavit*] or produced [*produxit*], the Son" (14: 192); likewise the Holy Spirit "was created [*creatum*], that is, produced [*productum*]" from the divine substance (14: 402). But Milton is being neither vague nor devious: his willingness to use these various words as synonyms stems from the fact that the Greek words for "beget" and "create" are actually identical, though some writers tried to distinguish them by a single ν: γεννητός and γενητός.[40] This is a clear example of the inadequacy of the early theological vocabulary to distinguish an important issue. For, in modern terminology, if Christ is "begotten" he should be worshipped as God; if he is "created" he is merely one

---

[37] *Contra Haeresim Noetim*, 10; Wolfson, *Philosophy*, 1; 194. The entire passage is in *The Ante-Nicene Fathers*, 5.

[38] As summarized in Wolfson, *Philosophy*, 1: 223.

[39] *Adversus Praxeam*, 6; Wolfson, *Philosophy*, 1: 224.

[40] Cf. the discussion in G. L. Prestige, *God in Patristic Thought* (London, 1956), pp. 135 ff. Even Athanasius had difficulty with these homophones.

other created being and it would be heretical for any Christian to worship him. Milton, however, knew what he was doing when he deliberately used those synonyms. His thought here was guided by the fact that both Son and Spirit are derived from the divine substance and are thus themselves divine. As Aristotle had observed, "man begets man"; that is, "everything that is produced is something produced from something and by something, and that the same in species as it." [41] Thus the divine Godhead would generate from itself another divinity.

So much for the Philonic two-stage Logos and some of its implications for early Christians who were trying to understand the opening of the Johannine gospel.[42] One should notice, however, that "while the exponents of the two-fold theory could speak of the Logos as eternal, they could not speak of the generation as eternal; the generation as conceived by them had a beginning." [43] It must be stressed that this two-stage Logos did not make any sense in the later-developing Neoplatonism. There Mind first emanated in one unchanging stage from eternity. Probably it was Neoplatonism which thus led Origen and Irenaeus to develop the theory of an eternal, single-stage generation of the Logos, the theory which Christians generally hold today.[44] According to this theory the generation of the Logos "is as eternal and everlasting as the brightness which is produced from the sun," as Origen asserts.[45] Accordingly he argues against the view that "there once was a time when He was not the Son [for] there never was a time when He was not." [46] In this view the Logos never existed merely as an idea in God's mind — an existence which implies denial of separate individuality. Nor was there a moment of its generation in time. "In the beginning," at the opening of the Fourth Gospel means "from all eternity," as Theophilus had interpreted it.[47] Under

---

[41] *Metaphysics*, trans. W. D. Ross, 1032a25 and 1049b27–28. See Wolfson's discussion in *Philosophy*, 1: 289 ff. Milton also believed that God generated the universe from his own substance. For the differences which he found between God's external efficiency which produced the Son and that which made the material universe, see Adamson's study, "Milton and the Creation," reprinted in this volume as "The Creation."

[42] It should be noted that this argument does not depend upon Wolfson's interpretation of Philo. See his *Philo*, 1: 239, for other opinions. But Wolfson's is clear, cogent, and an excellent basis for understanding the patristic writers.

[43] Wolfson, *Philosophy*, 1: 200.

[44] Wolfson, *Philosophy*, 1: 198 ff.

[45] Origen, *De Principiis*, 1. 2. 4; Wolfson, *Philosophy*, 1: 201. For the entire passage see *The Ante-Nicene Fathers*, 4.

[46] Origen, *De Principiis*, 4. 4. 1; Wolfson, *Philosophy*, 1: 201 f.

[47] *Ad Autolycum*, 2: 22; Wolfson, *Philosophy*, 1: 197. For the entire passage see *The Ante-Nicene Fathers*, 2.

the impact of the single-stage theory the earlier twofold one slowly disappeared from Christian thought.

With this intellectual background of Neoplatonism and the philosophy of Philo as adopted by the early Christian fathers, it will be instructive to examine the teachings of Arius to see just what his heresy meant in the early years of the church. The historical fact is that in the early church there were various conceptions of the Trinity. Arius had the fortune, or misfortune, to precipitate the issue and to force its resolution through the first of the ecumenical councils, that of Nicaea.

Among the choices available to him in the interpretation of the Trinity was, of course, that of the Apologists which has been outlined above as a development from Philo. Arius followed it in part: he refused to accept the idea that the Logos has been eternally generated. Instead he utilized the twofold theory which had been so widely accepted down to Irenaeus and Origen. Second, like Philo, he argued that in so producing the Son the Father had acted at a point in time of his own free will. It is not surprising that many have judged all of the Apologists to be Arians in that they generally stand with Arius on both of these points (neither was condemned at Nicaea). But third, again like Philo but now in sharp disagreement with these Christian fathers, Arius argued that the Logos was created by God from nothing (ἐξ οὐκ ὄντων) and was thus merely part of creation in general. Like Philo's Logos Arius' Son was thus not truly God: "the Logos is not true God; though it is called God, yet it is not true God, but, by participation of grace, as all others, it is called God only in name." [48] As a consequence of this point, the spiritual difference between Father and Son became insurmountable; the whole concept of a triune God had disappeared. As Athanasius observes of Arianism, "The substances of the Father and the Son and the Holy Spirit are separate in nature, and estranged and disconnected, and alien, and without participation of each other." [49]

So with this third assertion the fat was in the fire. It is small wonder that the early church reacted violently. All of Arius' opponents joined to agree that the Logos had not been created *ex nihilo*. The reactions to the other two points named above — the willed generation made in two stages — are interesting and instructive. Because neither involved questioning the divinity of the Logos, neither was declared anathema. We have already seen that the

---

[48] Athanasius, *Orationes contra Arianos*, 1: 6; Wolfson, *Philosophy*, 1: 586 f.

[49] Athanasius, *Orationes*, 1: 6; Wolfson, *Philosophy*, 1: 244.

Apologists from Justin Martyr through Lactantius had accepted the two-stage theory of the Word, with an implied unequal Trinity in many of the Fathers as in Philo and Plotinus. But the theory was not banned in these early councils: it is recognized now as subordinationism.[50] Gradually the single-stage theory prevailed, though as has been shown it was a later development.

Arius' consideration that the divine will was free produced many arguments. Some righteous Christians, in order to oppose anything savoring of Arianism, tended to deny the activity of the divine will with regard to the production of the Logos, which they held had been generated from eternity. At its extreme this would become exactly the position of the Neoplatonists: Plotinus asserts just such a determinate and eternal emission of Mind from the One. But Christians dared not go quite so far toward a God bound by necessity; instead they developed the theory that it is simply the divine *nature* to beget the Logos from eternity.[51] Even so, many Fathers, such as Eusebius, Gregory of Nyssa, Irenaeus, and Origen, agreed with Arius' statement that the Logos "came to be by the Divine will," despite the fact that they bitterly opposed him on the idea that the Logos is generated ἐξ οὐκ ὄντων. Thus both the two-stage Logos theory and the limitation upon the divine freedom entirely escaped condemnation by the early church.

A last question concerned the generation of the Holy Spirit. In Tertullian and Origen and many other writers the Father generates the Son and the Son the Spirit — as One generates Mind, which generates Soul in Plotinus. But the Council of Constantinople agreed (in its "Nicene" Creed) that the Spirit "proceedeth from the Father." It is interesting to note that Milton deliberately remains silent about the matter (14: 357–59).

The distinction of the persons on a graded scale, as has been presented, does not mean in any sense that the Trinity does not act and think as a unit. The Logos is indeed distinct from the Father in number, but his thoughts must, of course, be the same as those of the Father. This view, established as early as Justin Martyr from Aristotelian terminology,[52] was held by Christians of all shades of opinion. The Fathers considered that in the exercise of their different wills all members of the Trinity would act as a unit: the Trinity is a unity of rule. Such diverse writers as Origen, Basil, and Augustine affirm this

---

[50] See Prestige's discussion, chap. 7.

[51] See e.g. Athanasius, *Orationes*, 3: 60; Wolfson, *Philosophy*, 1: 227 ff.

[52] See Wolfson, *Philosophy*, 1: 310.

doctrine;[53] as Milton writes, the Father and Son "are one, inasmuch as they speak and act with unanimity" (14: 211).

IV

Finally, the seventeenth century. Many of the intellectual leaders at Cambridge University, where Milton received his education, turned to Platonism as a means of interpreting their Christian beliefs; interested in a universal religion, too, they found in these pagans ideas which they eagerly equated with Christian ones in order to show the universality of the Christian revelation which long antedated (though in a confused and obscure way) the revelation of the New Testament. Thus according to Cudworth, one of this group, the revelation was first made "amongst the Hebrews . . . , and from them afterwards communicated to the Egyptians and other nations." He does not find it surprising that this early trinity was not identical with that formulated by the Nicene Council, since "this mystery was gradually imparted to the world, and that first but sparingly to the Hebrews themselves . . . but afterwards more fully under Christianity." [54] Cudworth and his contemporaries hopelessly confused Platonism proper with the later development which we know as Neoplatonism; almost everyone in the seventeenth century argued freely from either source as though they were quite synonymous, to the helpless amazement of the modern student. It is not surprising, however, to discover them using such pagan sources to illuminate the difficulties of the Christian dogma.[55]

Thus in 1642 and again in 1647 Henry More, a Cambridge fellow, published poems which implicitly or explicitly state the similarities between the two systems. Instead of the Platonists' One–Mind–Soul trinity, More uses the terms Ahad, Aeon, and Psyche in his *Psychozoia*. In an address "To the Reader" he points out the "correspondencies betwixt the Platonick Triad, and diverse passages of Scripture. . . . Take in the whole Trinity, you shall find a strange concordance and harmony betwixt the nature of each Hypostasis in

---

[53] Wolfson, *Philosophy*, 1: 313–59.

[54] Ralph Cudworth, *The True Intellectual System of the Universe* (London, 1845), 2: 313–14.

[55] Even Sir John Suckling noted the parallel. Regarding the Trinity, he wrote, "I observe in those great lovers and lords of reason, quoted by the fathers, Zoroastes, Trismegistus, Plato, Numenius, Plotinus, Proclus, Amelius, and Avicen, that when they spoke of this mystery of the Trinity, of which all writ something, and some almost as plainly as Christians themselves, that they discussed it not as they did other things, but delivered them, as oracles which they had received themselves, without dispute." From "A Discourse of Religion," in *The Poems, Plays, and Other Remains*, ed. W. C. Hazlitt (London, 1874), 2: 256.

either of their order." [56] In Stanza 4 of Canto 1 he names Plato and Plotinus as the sources of genuine Platonism, supported by Pythagoras, Hermes Trismegistus, and the Chaldean Oracles — "all which time hath tore / But Plato and deep Plotin do restore." Stanzas 8 and 9 go on to state that "*Ahad* of himself the *Aeon* fair / Begot, the brightnesse of his father's grace. . . . This is that ancient *Eidos* omniform, / Fount of all beauty." [57]

But Ralph Cudworth deserves recognition among the group for having presented the clearest (if by no means the most succinct) account of Christianity in Platonic terms. Chapter 4 of his *True Intellectual System of the Universe* is almost entirely given over to an elaborate history of the Platonic movement and a labored reconciliation of it with Christianity. The basic theory — or delusion — from which he worked was that the true Christian Trinity had been revealed to Moses and via him to Plato. Later Platonists were then responsible for its adulteration, although in support of his thesis he is forced to quote almost entirely, of course, from Plotinus and other late Platonists. Thus he finds that some Neoplatonists consider the third person to be the *anima mundi*, which can hardly correspond to the Christian Holy Spirit, but decides that Plotinus, Aemelius, and Porphyrius had the true notion of the Third Person. [58] Yet even Porphyrius had gone astray in declaring that Mind was "self-begotten" — which the Christian Son was not — and "by way of natural and necessary emanation" — which cannot harmonize with the Christian conception of a God exercising free will (2: 371).

In his "Platonic" statement of the Christian Trinity, Cudworth generally follows Plotinus, calling in at the same time various other Neoplatonists and church fathers to witness to the different details of the scheme. Thus he admits that the Platonic trinity is one of subordination of the second and third members: the "fundamental principle of their theology [is] that there is but one Original of all things . . . from whence all other things whatsoever,

---

[56] From the 1647 edition. In 1642 he had argued that "the platonists, the best and divinest of Philosophers, and the Christians, the best of all that do professe religion, do both concur that there is a Trinity." Both editions of "To the Reader" make extensive and detailed comparisons between the two trinities.

[57] In his notes on this canto, More observes that "*Ahad, Aeon, Psyche,* the Platonic Triad, is rather . . . the Divinity . . . than the Deity." From the "one indivisible unmovable self-born Unity" come "Wisdome, Intellect, *Aeon, On,* or *Autocalon,* or in a word, the Intellectual world." One can sympathize with Paul Shorey's comment in *Platonism Ancient and Modern* (Berkeley, 1938), p. 40, upon "the imperturbable self-assurance of the Neo-Platonic type of mind — the almost comic innocent serenity with which these 'babe-like Jupiters,' in Emerson's phrase, . . . sit on their clouds and from age to age prattle to each other and to no contemporary." Or perhaps he would prefer Dodds' epithet of the "Wissenschaft des Nichtwissenwerthan," *Elements,* p. ix.

[58] 2: 347–49. His "authority" for the latter statement is Proclus.

whether temporal or eternal, created or uncreated, were altogether derived. And therefore this second hypostasis of their trinity, since it must accordingly derive its whole being from the first . . . must of necessity have also an essential dependence upon the same; and consequently, a gradual subordination to it." [59] Mind is accordingly different in its being from the One (2: 391), and this difference and inferiority give difficulty to the Christian interpreter (2: 395). Moreover, the second person must receive its essence from the first: "the second [must] needs derive its whole essence from [the first], and be generated after another manner, namely, in a way of natural emanation" (2: 400). Cudworth admits that the persons differ in essence: "notwithstanding must it be acknowledged, that [the Platonists] nowhere suppose each of these three hypostases to be numerically the very same, or to have no distinct singular essences of their own; this being, in their apprehensions, directly contradictious to their very hypothesis itself" (2: 431–32); but he goes on to argue that *substance* in this context is "synonymous with essence"; accordingly the Trinity possess the same substance but differ in their hypostases or persons (2: 432).

Another difficulty with the Christian interpretation of the Platonic trinity is the role to assign the second or third persons in creation. Plato's Demiurge of the *Timaeus*, who created the universe, was identified with Mind by some and with Soul by others. Cudworth considers that "according to the genuine and ancient Platonic doctrine, all these three hypostases were the joint-creators of the whole world" (2: 388). Or the Soul is "That which doth actively display, and produce into being, what was virtually or potentially contained in the first; and ideally or exemplarily in the second" (2: 393).

Cudworth was on safer ground when he argued that the Platonic trinity is eternal, although the theory of emanation seemed to him to imply a beginning in time and some Platonists, such as Macrobius, so interpreted it (2: 374). But the majority agree that this emanation is a timeless process, without beginning or end, and Cudworth makes much of this fact in equating the two trinities. Accordingly, the only real differences that he discovers are those of equality and identity of essence: he quotes with approval the observation of Cyril of Alexandria that "There would have been nothing at all want-

---

[59] 2: 399; see also p. 390. As George Rust observes in *A Letter of Resolution Concerning Origen and the Chief of His Opinions* (London, 1661), p. 16: "There seems such a necessity of nature that all Effects and Productions whatever, whether *voluntary* or *emanative*, should decline something from the supereminent Excellency of the Cause and Producer, that it is scarce possible to keep our mindes from thinking but that the Rule holds also in the *Divine Emanations*."

ing to the Platonic trinity for an absolute agreement of it with the Christian, had they but accommodated the right notion of co-essentiality or consubstantiality to their three hypostases" (2: 434). Accordingly, he can argue that "though some of the latter Platonists have partly misunderstood, and partly adulterated that ancient Cabala of the Trinity . . . , yet did Plato himself, and some of his genuine followers (though living before Christianity) approach so near to the doctrine thereof, as in some manner to correspond therewith. . . . First, in not making a mere trinity of names and words . . . but a trinity of hypostases, or subsistences, or persons. Secondly, in making none of their three hypostases to be creatures, but all eternal. . . . Lastly, in supposing these three divine hypostases . . . to be essentially one divinity. From whence it may be concluded, that as Arianism is commonly supposed to approach nearer to the truth of Christianity than Plotinianism, so is Platonism undoubtedly more agreeable thereunto than Arianism; it being a certain middle thing betwixt that and Sabellianism, which in general was that mark the Nicene council also aimed at" (2: 409).

As a result of Cudworth's intense interest in Platonism, we are not surprised to find him interpreting the generation of the Logos as a single-stage manifestation, produced from eternity but not *ex nihilo*. As he remarks, "Arius maintained, the Son or Word [was] a creature, made in time . . . of a different essence or substance from the Father" (2: 439). Instead he urges Athanasius' views: "Christ was the Son of God, and not from nothing . . . ; the Son was out of the substance of God, thereby to distinguish him from all created beings" (2: 440–41). But the fact that the Neoplatonic trinity was produced without will but as a necessary emanation is a fact with which Cudworth seems not to have come to real grips. He does apparently accept, with some hesitation and some indecision, the inequality inherent in the pagan trinity as acceptable for a "Christian Platonist."

The issue has frequently been raised as to whether this kind of Platonizing of the Trinity was really the Arian heresy. With the immense experience behind him of editing a number of Neoplatonic works, the Jesuit Dionysius Petavius, or Denis Petau (1583–1652), was vigorously arguing just this point in the 1640's.[60] Cudworth simply answers that "Petavius (though otherwise learned and industrious) was herein grossly mistaken," for "Arius was no Platonist at all" (2: 372). He adds that "the chief ground of Petavius' mistake . . . was his not distinguishing betwixt that spurious trinity of some

---

[60] See his *De Trinitate*, 1. 8.

Platonists" and the genuine one.[61] Instead, he tries to show that "Arius did not so much Platonize, as the Nicene fathers and Athanasius" (2: 389). Cudworth correctly argues that such a "gradual subordination of the second hypostasis to the first, and of the third to the first and second" can be found in the Apologists whose views were presented above: Justin Martyr, Tatian, Tertullian, Clement, Origen, and Lactantius (2: 417). We have seen that he can be justified in this view.[62] He can accordingly conclude that "the ancient and genuine Platonic trinity was doubtless anti-Arian, or else the Arian trinity anti-Platonic" (2: 458).

Should one then consider Cudworth (and, by implication, many of his fellow Platonists at Cambridge) to be involved in formal heresy in this view of the Trinity? These divines themselves certainly considered themselves orthodox, describing the true Trinity of early Christianity, for which they found authority in church fathers and in reason. But the argument, begun in the seventeenth century, is not dead yet. In 1666 Samuel Parker, for instance, believed correctly that the entire doctrine of a Neoplatonic trinity originated long after Plato and is not central to his philosophy. He strongly questions too that Plato received his "theological theories" from Moses, even though everyone else agrees that this belief is true. Instead, "The first Author of this mistake seems to have been *Ammonius of Alexandria* . . . who being both a Christian and a Platonist, & lighting upon these *Spurious Books*, in which the *Platonick Notions* and *Christian Articles* were blended and reconciled" took over the idea.[63] Later opponents made even stronger charges, as when Dean Inge observes that Cudworth's "equation of the Neoplatonic divine hypostases with the Christian Trinity not only fails, but involves the writer in formal heresy." [64] On the contrary, Ernst Cassirer judges that "the Cambridge Platonists are neither deists nor, as their adversaries constantly charged them with being, Arminians, Arians, or Socinians. They are plain religious moralists." [65]

Milton's place in the scheme of the Trinity which has been outlined should be clear. In many ways his views agree with those of Cudworth and the Cam-

---

[61] 2: 374 f. See also his editor Mosheim's long note to the passage.

[62] Cudworth is quite well aware too that Philo is somehow related to the question. See, e.g. 2: 316, 320, etc.

[63] *A Free and Impartial Censure of the Platonick Philosophie* (Oxford, 1666), pp. 93, 109.

[64] *The Platonic Tradition in English Religious Thought* (London, 1926), p. 58.

[65] *The Platonic Renaissance in England*, trans. James P. Pettegrove (Austin, Texas, 1953), p. 38.

bridge men. There is, of course, no trace of the Neoplatonic One–Mind–Soul terminology in the *Christian Doctrine* — and there could not be because of the nature of the treatise. But the Son and Spirit are clearly degenerating emanations differing in degree from the Father and "created, whether generated or produced," from his substance. Milton, in common with all Christians, rejects the origin of the Logos ἐξ οὐκ ὄντων — whether it be the Philonic or the Arian. In doing so he avoided the real charge of heresy which could be brought against him. On the other hand, he departed from Neoplatonism and from the Cambridge group in rejecting certain of their teachings.

First, unlike Plotinus, he held that the Father is completely free in willing the generation of the Logos. In this he is like Arius, but he also agrees with Philo and with most of the early Fathers of the church.

Second, and of extreme importance, he returned to the two-stage conception of the Logos which had been put forward originally by Philo and then had been accepted and expounded by a highly respectable group of church fathers — among the earliest writers of the Christian church. We may surmise that Milton returned to them with the principle which has always motivated the thinking of puritan Protestantism: the desire to establish church doctrines and practices as close as possible to those of the most primitive Christian church. Accordingly, we may discover that the Logos which he describes in the *Christian Doctrine* exists in two different manifestations—the Philonian two-stage Logos — though this fact seems to have been overlooked before. The treatise actually describes these two manifestations.

Milton divides God's "efficiency" into "internal" and "external." God, that is, may be active within himself or outside himself. His "internal efficiency" is "that which is independent of all extraneous agency." This "internal efficiency" Milton denominates as God's "decrees." The latter may be either "general" or "special." We are not concerned here with his "general" decrees except to note that they have been decreed "from all eternity" (14: 63). But we are concerned with his "special decrees," and Milton observes that "the first and most important is that which regards his Son, and from which he primarily derives his name of Father. . . . It appears that the Son of God was begotten by the decree of the Father" (14: 89). Thus Chapter 3 of the *Christian Doctrine*.

At the beginning of Chapter 5, "Of the Son of God," Milton begins a consideration of God's "external efficiency, or the execution of his decrees." Under this head occurs "generation," and under it "in pursuance of his decree [he] has begotten his only Son." Moreover, this generation "must be an external efficiency" (14: 179). Now clearly these two passages are describing two very different activities of the Father: the decree regarding the Son in Chapter 3 is a "special internal efficiency," whereas the external activity in 5 is an "external efficiency." Milton, it seems, is following the theory which Wolfson has called the "two-stage" instead of the more traditional but later "one-stage." He has perfectly good ecclesiastical authority for this view, as has been shown. One may even argue that the decree concerning the Son or Logos of Chapter 3 has existed in a sense, though not hypostatized, from eternity, though Milton does not say one way or the other. The depiction of the character of Sin in *Paradise Lost* is suggestive in this context. As has often been remarked, Milton deliberately paralleled his holy Trinity with the unholy one fathered by Satan. Sin apparently is conceived as undergoing a "two-stage" existence in parallel with that of the Logos: she exists as an idea in Satan's mind and then at a moment in time springs from his head as a real being (2. 755–58).[66]

Thus the various "Arian" passages in the *Christian Doctrine* and *Paradise Lost* fall into place as continuations of a tradition which antedates even the Council of Nicaea. It seems that we may positively assert that Milton was not an Arian.[67] Subordination as such has not been branded heterodox, though it is not the view of the Trinity found most widely today — or in the seventeenth century for that matter. Indeed, Milton expressly states that his interpretation of the Son agrees with traditional ones. He concludes the chapter on the Son in the *Christian Doctrine* by asserting that his views represent "the faith proposed to us in the Apostles' Creed" — though it must be confessed that this Creed is almost entirely silent on the subjects which Milton has discussed. His point is merely that there is no contradiction between his ideas and the tenor of the Creed. More interesting is his statement at the beginning of this last paragraph that his views of the Son are traditional: "Such was the faith of the saints respecting the Son of God; such is the tenor of the celebrated confession of that faith" (14: 353). Although so far as I know the "fidei celebrata confessio" has never been identified, Milton must surely mean the "Nicene" Creed of the Prayer Book, which was indeed an expression of

---

[66] Again Tertullian (*Adversus Hermogenem*, 3) offers a suggestive parallel: "There was, however, a time when neither sin nor the Son was." Cf. Wolfson, *Philosophy*, 1: 586 n.

[67] Philip Schaff, perhaps alone among nineteenth-century scholars, reaches the same conclusion. Milton, he says, cannot properly be termed an Arian; his system of ideas is "totally different" from that of Arius. *History of the Christian Church* (New York, 1867), 2: 640 n.

the "faith of the saints." There is good evidence that this creed was looked upon as a confession,[68] and in Milton's context it is difficult to imagine any other formal statement which he would have had in mind. It affirms neither the equality of the persons of the Trinity nor the eternal generation of the Logos. With regard to the anathematized ἐξ ὀυκ ὄντων Milton stands with all other orthodox Christians.

Like his Cambridge contemporaries, Milton was doing his best to present a statement about the Trinity which would harmonize with reason, with a historical and respected philosophy, with the utterances of the primitive Christian church which have always been held in high respect by most Protestants, and above all with the Bible. These seventeenth-century thinkers were grappling with ideas, not with dogma; and they refused to agree blindly with Christian assertions no matter how venerable if they were not supported by biblical texts and reason. As Cassirer observes, in their stress upon a reasonable approach to religion, "The Cambridge thinkers are very far from that kind of rationalism which becomes prevalent in the eighteenth century in the systems of English deism." Milton places perhaps more emphasis upon the Bible as authority, but he must to some degree be included in the group. Creeds alone did not suit his needs. To arrive at an understanding of the most difficult mystery of Christianity, the Trinity, he relied upon scriptural authority interpreted in the light of patristic and philosophical formulations presented by reason. For, as Henry More wrote, "Take away *Reason* and all Religions are alike true." [69]

---

[68] Hooker so names it, *Ecclesiastical Politie*, 5: 52; see also *DNB* s.v. Confession 2. 7.

[69] Cassirer, pp. 30, 84. The last quotation is from More's "General Preface" to *A Collection of Several Philosophical Writings* (London, 1662), p. vi.

Milton's "Arianism"

J. H. ADAMSON

After Professor Maurice Kelley's unequivocal statement in *This Great Argument* that "*Paradise Lost* is an Arian document," [1] scholars generally consented to call Milton an Arian [2] until an article by Professor William B. Hunter shifted the burden of proof. [3] I should like to provide some supporting evidence for Mr. Hunter's thesis, and one qualification.

When examining any poet's thought, one must carefully consider the imagery in which that thought is embodied; for a poet, in contradistinction to a metaphysician, employs symbol rather than abstraction as a vehicle for the expression of his meaning. In a consideration of Milton's views on the nature of the Trinity, the symbols are significant for an additional reason, for in the long Athanasian–Arian controversy, it was quite literally by his metaphors that a disputant most clearly revealed his position. The development of these characteristic metaphors requires some explanation.

The Christian identification of Jesus as Son of God with the Divine Logos posed some difficult problems for early Christian thinkers. Any logical formulation of the concept seemed to require the sacrifice of some belief which Christians were unwilling to surrender. Pagans found no difficulty in a subordinationist concept, but the passionate monotheism inherited by Christianity from Judaism was the basis of a reaction against subordinationism. If the

---

[1] *This Great Argument* (Princeton, N.J., 1941), p. 122. For a discussion of the various views, see especially n. 86, p. 118. Cf. Kenneth Muir, *John Milton* (New York, 1955), pp. 164–65.

[2] Although Mr. C. S. Lewis defends Milton as being more orthodox than has generally been thought, he nevertheless says, "Milton was an Arian." *A Preface to Paradise Lost* (London, 1946), p. 84.

[3] "Milton's Arianism Reconsidered," reprinted in this volume.

Christ were an inferior deity, he was not to be worshipped. This dilemma gave rise to two tentative solutions, both of which were ultimately rejected.

Sabellius, in his desire to maintain the absolute unity of God, postulated that the Father, Son and Paraclete were really three manifestations or modes of the one Divine Being; they were merely different names given to the one essence. He did not hesitate to assert what the logic of his position called for, that the Father suffered when Jesus died on the cross. From this particular tenet came the name Patripassians by which disciples of Sabellius were frequently known in the West. They were also referred to as Sabellians and Modalists.

The other important formulation, that of Arius, also arose from the need to maintain the unity and absolute oneness of Deity. Arius, however, maintained that Christ was created like any other creature, that he was raised through merit to Godhood and worshipped at the Father's command. It was especially around these two formulations that controversy raged, and the solution finally came in the rejection of both of them in favor of the semantic paradoxes of the Athanasian creed.[4]

But from the very beginning nearly all of the Fathers accepted a common set of metaphors which expressed a particularly close relationship between the Father and the Son. There are three metaphors in particular which appear continuously in patristic writings from the time of Justin Martyr through Athanasius: sun and radiance (or torch and fire), a fountain and its stream, or an archetype and its image. Thus Origen says that the generation of the Son "is as eternal and everlasting as the brilliancy which is produced from the sun."[5] These images seem to be the most characteristic expression in the writings of Athanasius and he returns to them again and again in his opposition to the Arians. The Logos, he says, is the image of the Father, an image which from the beginning was mirrored in the Divine Mind; he is as fire from a torch, as light from radiance, as a stream from a fountain.[6]

It is precisely in these metaphors that the conceptual content of Athanasius' thought can be most clearly separated from that of Arius, for the latter

---

[4] The Athanasian Creed was a relatively late solution, the main elements of which were Augustinian. See Adolph Harnack, *History of Dogma*, trans. Neil Buchanan et al. (Boston, 1899–1901), 4: 134.

[5] *The Writings of Origen*, 1, trans. Frederick Crombie, *Ante-Nicene Christian Library*, 10 (Edinburgh, 1869): 22, 24.

[6] *St. Athanasius, Select Works and Letters*, ed. Archibald Robertson, *Nicene and Post-Nicene Fathers*, 2d ser. (Grand Rapids, Michigan, 1953), 4: 311, 314, 315, 321, 400–1, *et passim*. Cf. Harnack, 4: 31, n. 3.

denied the validity of these metaphors and refused to accept their implications. Thus Harnack says, "The images of the source and the brook, the sun and the light, the archetype and the type, which are almost of as old standing in the Church as the Logos-doctrine itself, are here discarded." Arius, says Harnack, by his rejection of these metaphors indicates his rejection of the essential connection of the Logos with the Father, a connection which Athanasius and the other early Fathers had insisted upon. In short, Arius rejected an emanationist theory altogether.[7]

But the old Athanasian metaphors (which are also found in Plato and Plotinus), anathema to Arians, are Milton's constant and unchanging symbols for the Godhead. His finest statement occurs in the Invocation to Light in Book 3 of *Paradise Lost* which begins with the Logos metaphor.

> Hail holy Light, offspring of Heav'n first-born,
> Or of th' Eternal Coeternal beam [3. 1–2][8]

It should be remembered that in the writings of the Alexandrian fathers and in many of the Neoplatonists, light is the particular symbol of the Logos, the Divine Reason. Thus Henry More, Milton's coeval at Christ's College, says, "The highest manifestation of that Light created in the First day, being the face of *Jesus Christ*, the *Heavenly Adam* . . . the *divine Intellect* as it is communicable to humane Souls." [9] Arius had held that the Son was created in time, that there was a time when he was not, but Milton has embodied in his metaphor the idea common to the Neoplatonists, to Philo, and to the Greek fathers that the Logos or Divine Reason was with the Eternal in the beginning as radiance has always emanated from the sun, that Thought (or Logos) is related to the Mind of God as splendor is related to a luminous body. The Son is the "Bright effluence" which emanates from the "bright essence increate." (3.6).[10]

---

[7] Harnack, *History of Dogma*, 4: 39–42, esp. 41.

[8] All quotations from *Paradise Lost* are taken from Merritt Hughes' Odyssey Press edition.

[9] "Conjectura Cabbalistica," *A Collection of Several Philosophical Writings of Henry More*, 4th ed. (London, 1712), p. 209.

[10] This passage in *Paradise Lost* appears to be a contradiction of *De Doctrina Christiana*, where Milton denies the eternal generation of the Son (*Works*, 14: 181, 183, 189, 191). There are two possible explanations: Either Milton did not understand the metaphor and its historical implications, or he changed his position on this point between the writings of *De Doctrina* and *Paradise Lost*.

It seems that he did understand the implications of the metaphor for he says, "We cannot form any conception of light independent of a luminary . . . ." (*Works*, 15: 31). He goes on to say that this does not mean that the light and the luminary are the same or even equal. In *PL* he continues to subordinate the Son to the Father, but he also makes him a "Coeternal beam." It appears then, that on this point, he did change his mind.

As the Invocation continues, Milton employs the second common Athanasian metaphor, that of fountain and stream.

> Or hear'st thou rather pure Ethereal stream,
> Whose Fountain who shall tell? before the Sun,
> Before the Heavens thou wert, and at the voice
> Of God, as with a Mantle didst invest
> The rising world of waters dark and deep. [3. 7–11]

The Fountain of which no man can tell is, to change the metaphor, the Cloud of Unknowing, the Divine Darkness of the mystics. From that fountain streams the Divine Reason, the Mediator which to some degree reveals the Unknowable to the creature.

As the scene unfolds, the third familiar metaphor from the early Fathers appears, that of archetype and image.

> on his right
> The radiant image of his Glory sat,
> His only Son . . . . [3. 62–64]

I think it is a safe generalization to say that Milton never conceives of the Godhead except under these traditional symbols. When the angels praise the Father and the Son, they sing of the "Fountain of light" and then of the "Begotten Son, Divine Similitude,"

> In whose conspicuous count'nance, without cloud
> Made visible, th' Almighty Father shines. [3. 385–86]

Possibly the climactic use of Athanasian imagery occurs in Book 6 when the Father commissions the Son to destroy the powers of darkness.

> He said, and on his Son with Rays direct
> Shone full, he all his Father full exprest
> Ineffably into his face receiv'd. [6. 719–21]

It appears, then, that Milton continuously images the Trinity in terms of the Athanasian metaphors that Arius had rejected; Milton's thought, as expressed in these metaphors, is unquestionably emanationist. When we remember further that Arius had declared the Son to be created *ex nihilo* and recall that Milton, on the other hand, maintained that "God imparted to the Son as much as he pleased of the divine nature, nay of the divine substance itself, care being taken not to confound the substance with the whole essence," [11] it seems clear that the term *Arianism* cannot be accurately applied to the Miltonic doctrine of the Trinity.

---

[11] *Works*, 14: 193. Milton denied the entire idea of creation *ex nihilo* and consequently could not have agreed with Arius that the Son was created in that fashion. Even so he

So much for the supporting evidence. I now turn to the one qualification of Mr. Hunter's thesis that seems to me appropriate. I believe that Mr. Hunter is correct in finding an ultimate source of Milton's views on the Trinity in the long tradition of Platonic and Neoplatonic theories and particularly in the "trinitarian" discussions of Philo Judaeus. But I think also that he does not sufficiently recognize that it was the early Greek fathers who were central to the thought of the Cambridge Platonists and other liberal thinkers of the seventeenth century, including Milton himself; that it was these Fathers who provided the nexus between biblical Christianity and Alexandrian Neoplatonism. There is little point in looking for the relatively minor differences which partisans may wish to find in the Neoplatonist and Christian Platonist speculations on the nature of the Trinity. Of greater importance is the remarkable similarity of such theories. Nor is this similarity surprising. All of the Alexandrian fathers accepted one of the principal contentions of Philo, namely that all Greek learning ultimately derived from Moses.[12] Such an attitude obviated the surly antagonism toward Greek philosophy manifested by some of the Latin fathers and made it somewhat irrelevant whether one quoted Proclus or Clement of Alexandria.

In Milton's time, especially in his later years, there was a wide dissemination and assimilation of Greek learning, both classical and patristic. The humanists of all nations were turning to the Greek Fathers for support in arguments over such questions as free will and universal salvation. Calvinists, on the other hand, rejected Greek theology far more violently than had the church of Rome. Calvin said that "the Greeks beyond all others . . . have exceeded all bounds in extolling the ability of the human will . . . ." In fact, he said, all the Fathers but Augustine had been so aberrant in their treatment of the subject of grace and free will "that nothing certain [could] be learned from their writings." [13]

In contrast to the incessant denunciations of the Calvinists stands the statement of Henry More, the Cambridge Platonist, that Origen "was surely

---

makes a distinction between the Son and the rest of creation that is quite foreign to Arius' formulations: "For to Adam God stood less in the relation of Father, than of Creator, having only formed him from the dust of the earth; whereas he was properly the Father of the Son made of his own substance" (*Works*, 14: 187). For a summary of Arius' views, see Harnack 4: 15 ff. Arius said that the Son had only a relative knowledge of the Father. Cf. Milton's lines above.

[12] See "Questions and Answers on Genesis," trans. Ralph Marcus, in *Philo*, Supp. 1, *Loeb Classical Library* (Cambridge, Mass., 1953), 3. 5 (p. 188); 4. 152 (p. 434). Cf. H. A. Wolfson, *Philo* (Cambridge, Mass., 1947), 1: 140–43.

[13] *Institutes of the Christian Religion*, trans. John Allen (London, 1813), 2. 2. 4; 2. 2. 9.

the greatest Light and Bulwark that ancient Christianity had. . . ." [14] Another humanist, Milton's one-time schoolmaster, Alexander Gill, said, "Ah, blessed Origen! hath thy too much charity been blamed so long?" [15] Lancelot Andrewes expressed a similar attitude: "His name is Jesus Christ, half Hebrew, half Greek . . . so sorted of purpose to show Jews and Greeks have equal interest in him." [16] Hugo Grotius, whom Milton as a young man "was very desirous of seeing," and whose drama, *Adamus Exul*, seems to resemble *Paradise Lost* more closely than do any other of the hexameral writings, said that the Augustinian articles in the Protestant confessions did not sufficiently consider the views of the Fathers of the first four centuries. [17]

This widespread revival of interest in Greek thought and Greek theology directly affected the trinitarian issue, for in the earliest ages all the Greek fathers were subordinationists. As Eugene De Faye has said, no one of that time could have been anything else because the entire Logos doctrine arose from the need for a Mediator, subordinate in some way to the Unknowable. [18] The crucial issues which led to an abandonment of subordinationist doctrine had not then arisen.

The spread of Greek learning and the kind of influence it must have exercised on minds like Milton's can perhaps best be illustrated by a consideration of Ralph Cudworth's *The True Intellectual System of the Universe*. Cudworth, like Milton, was a student at Cambridge, and he later became master of Milton's own college. His work was published in 1678, eleven years after the appearance of *Paradise Lost*.

Cudworth is tremendously impressed by the "wonderful correspondence" between Platonic theories of the Trinity and the later formulations by the Greek fathers. [19] Not that he thinks the Platonic and Christian theories to be identical. Rather, he remains unsatisfied with the Platonic treatment of the third person of the Godhead. Still, he wishes to emphasize the positive similarities. For example, neither the Platonic nor the Christian trinity is a trinity of mere words or notions; thus both escape the Sabellian heresy. [20]

---

[14] "The Immortality of the Soul," *Philosophical Writings*, p. 116.

[15] *Sacred Philosophie* (London, 1635), Art. 1, p. 18.

[16] *Ninety-Six Sermons*, ed. J. P. W. (Oxford, 1841–43), 1: 27.

[17] See A. W. Harrison, *Arminianism* (London, 1937), p. 65.

[18] *Origen and His Work* (London, 1926), pp. 102–3. The *Catholic Encyclopedia*, s.v. "Fathers," says that "to our amazement" the early Greek apologists taught that the Son had a "distinct being" from the Father.

[19] Cudworth (London, 1845), 1: Preface, xliii. See also 2: 340, 386, 410, 427 ff.

[20] Cudworth, 1: xliii; 2: 340, 342.

Similarly, and more important for this discussion, both avoid the Arian heresy (2: 342). Cudworth did not use the term "Arianism" loosely. He believed that the essence of Arius' thought had been accurately captured by Dionysius Petavius as follows: ". . . that the Father was the only eternal God, and that the Son, or Word, was a creature made by him in time, and out of nothing . . . ." Cudworth insists that neither Plato nor Plotinus would ever have denied the eternity of the "second hypostasis," nor would any other true Platonist ever have done so. In this, they were one with Athanasius (2: 372, 373–74). Anyone who affirms the significance of the Logos metaphor, according to Cudworth, also affirms the eternity of the Word, for the persons of the Godhead can no more exist without one another "than original light can exist without its splendor, coruscation or effulgency" (2: 384). It is clear to Cudworth that Plato expressly disagrees with the doctrine of Arius but is in harmony with the formulations of the Nicene Council (2: 386).

Although the Platonists taught the uncreated nature and the eternality of the Word, Cudworth is uneasily aware that they also taught a doctrine of subordinationism. Such a doctrine, he thought, was implicit in the Logos metaphor, for radiance must draw its being from original splendor; therefore, in some sense it is dependent upon it and subordinate to it (2: 392–93). This doctrine, says Cudworth, however startling, was nevertheless the doctrine taught by "the generality of Christian doctors, for the first three hundred years after the apostles' times . . . ." He names, and rightly, Justin Martyr, Athenagoras, Tatianus, Irenaeus, Tertullian, Clement of Alexandria, Origen, Gregory Thaumaturgus, Dionysius of Alexandria, Lactantius and many others as early Christians who held subordinationist views. He cites Lactantius to illustrate this subordinationism, and the passage he chooses embodies the Logos metaphor. "Both the Father and the Son is God; but he as it were an exuberant fountain, this as a stream derived from him: he like to the sun, this like to a ray extended from the sun" (2: 417). Nor does it surprise Cudworth to find this correspondence in trinitarian thought between the Platonists and the early Fathers, for he is all but certain that much Greek thought came originally from Moses and was preserved and transmitted in the Hebraic *Cabbala*.[21]

Cudworth concludes this part of his argument with a specific disavowal of Arianism which is, he says, the same as "Pagan polytheism and idolatry" because both introduce the worship of the creature along with that of the

---

[21] Cudworth, 1: 20–21; 2: 151.

Creator (2: 446). However, this disavowal did not shield him from angry charges of Arianism, but his accusers use the term loosely to describe anyone who departs from orthodox trinitarian theology; it simply becomes a rather common form of name-calling.[22]

Another interesting work which illustrates the relation of the trinitarian controversy to the revival of Greek theology is Jean Le Clerc's *The Lives of the Primitive Fathers*, written in 1696 and translated into English in 1701. Le Clerc, incidentally, was well acquainted with Cudworth's work. His book contains, according to the subtitle, "an Impartial account of their LIVES AND WRITINGS: With their several opinions about the Deity of Christ. Which may give some Light to the late Disputes concerning the Trinity." His own final opinion seems to be that of Cudworth and Milton, "that the *Orthodox* place not the Unity of God in the *Numerical Unity* of the Divine Essence, but in a *Specifick Unity* of Distinct and Equal Essences and in a perfect Agreement of Wills." [23]

The point could be demonstrated at length, but perhaps one more significant example will suffice. The Calvinist Theophilus Gale charged Hugo Grotius with "rank *Socinianisme* and *Arianisme*," which, he said, were "foisted into the Primitive Churches by Origen . . . ." [24] Grotius' heresy, according to Gale, was that he made Christ a "second cause," which is also what Milton and Cudworth did. But so did the Logos metaphor which was emanationist in its implications as well as in common understanding.

From the polemic, one fact emerges: those who embraced subordinationist doctrine cited the Greek fathers in support of it. Those who considered that doctrine heresy condemned the Greek fathers for initiating it. Both sides considered the Greek fathers responsible for it.

Thus, while the ultimate source of Milton's trinitarian thought, indeed of Christian trinitarian thought itself, lies in the Neoplatonic writers, I think that neither he nor his contemporaries thought of themselves as having derived their thought from such sources. Rather they believed that they had rediscovered in the early Greek fathers the original and therefore true doctrine of the Trinity. Neoplatonism was thought of as a remarkable correspondence, a support, but not a source. If Greek learning indeed derived from Moses, then the striking similarity of Greek and Christian thought was under-

---

[22] Cudworth, "An Account of the Life and Writings of Ralph Cudworth, D.D.," 1: xvi f.
[23] (London, 1701), p. 255.
[24] *Court of the Gentiles* (Oxon., 1669–77), Part 3, Preface, sig. b2ᵛ.

standable; even if one did not hold for such a derivation, however, the Logos doctrine could sufficiently account for "common notions" inasmuch as the faculty of reason implanted in all men is the indwelling Logos which must inevitably, when rightly used, lead men to similar conclusions.

In 1882 portraits of various worthies were placed in the twenty-one lights of the west oriel of Christ's College. In this series, William Perkins is the last Calvinist. He is followed, among others, by Milton, More and Cudworth.[25] The general movement of mind from Perkins to Cudworth was also a movement from a Latin to a Greek theology. And it is out of this movement that Milton's trinitarian thought arose.

---

[25] John Peile, *Christ's College*, University of Cambridge College Histories (London, 1900), p. 32.

Milton and Arianism

C. A. PATRIDES

Ingemuit totus orbis, et Arianum se esse miratus est.

ST. JEROME, *Dial adv. Lucif.*, XIX

A curious aspect of the ever-continuing discussion of Milton's theology is the readiness of most scholars and critics to speak of Milton as an "Arian." This phenomenon is by no means of recent origin; its history goes back to the years immediately following the discovery, in 1823, of Milton's *De Doctrina Christiana*, when it was decided that the "Arianism" of the treatise is reflected in *Paradise Lost* in a "plain and unequivocal" manner.[1] Yet the general acceptance of Milton's reported Arianism did not set in until Maurice Kelley issued his substantial study of *De Doctrina Christiana* as a "gloss" upon *Paradise Lost* (1941) and concluded that the poem is, like the treatise, "an Arian document."[2]

My intention here is not to question the propriety of grafting a theological treatise upon a poem, or to argue that the considerable differences between the two have been ignored. I propose rather to investigate the extent to which Milton may be correctly termed an Arian, less in order to caution my peers against hasty generalizations than to cast some light on the reasons for Milton's resolution to swim against the current of tradition, aware though he was that the remorseless deep might in the end close over his head.

---

[1] Thomas Keightley, in H. McLachlan, *The Religious Opinions of Milton, Locke and Newton* (Manchester, 1941), p. 25.

[2] *This Great Argument* (Princeton, 1941), p. 122.

I

Though the actual doctrines of Arius have been preserved only in the works of his opponents,[3] the degree of unanimity among the latter is such that scholars have had no difficulty in reconstructing the essence of Arianism.[4] Considered out of context, at least one of the ideas advanced by Arius and welcomed by Milton is orthodox enough: the conception of creation as an act of God's free will.[5] Beyond this, however, Milton diverges from every one of the Arian tenets. Eight specific differences are readily apparent:

1. Central to the philosophy of Arianism is an uncompromising monotheism, best summed up in Arius' conception of God as "alone ingenerate, alone everlasting, alone unbegun, alone true, alone having immortality, alone wise, alone good, alone sovereign" (μόνον ἀγέννητον, μόνον ἀΐδιον, μόνον ἄναρχον, μόνον ἀληθινὸν, ἀθανασίαν ἔχοντα, μόνον σοφὸν, μόνον ἀγαθὸν, μόνον δυνάστην).[6] Starting from this premise, Arius went on to affirm that God is utterly incommunicable and absolutely isolated from his entire creation, whether physical or spiritual, animate or inanimate. Milton, on the other hand, asserted God's direct involvement in both the origin and the history of the created order. The universe, he maintained, was produced not *ex nihilo*

---

[3] The principal sources of Arianism are: Athanasius, *Orationes contra Arianos*, esp. 1. 5–6, 9 (*Patrologia graeca* [*PG*], 26: 20–24, 28–29) and *De synodis Arimini et Seleuciae*, 15–16 (*PG*, 26: 705–12); Epiphanius, *Adversus haereses*, 69 (*PG*, 42: 201 ff.); and the ecclesiastical histories of Socrates, 1. 5 ff. (*PG*, 67: 41 ff.); Sozomen, 1. 15 ff. (*PG*, 67: 904 ff.); and Theodoret, 1. 1 ff. (*PG*, 82: 884 ff.). Extracts from a number of these works are available in *A Source Book for Ancient Church History*, Joseph C. Ayer, ed. (New York, 1913), pp. 300–9, and *A New Eusebius*, ed. J. Stevenson (New York, 1957), pp. 340–52, 375–76. Most of the commentators cited in the next note are given to generous quotations, esp. Harnack.

[4] Among the most competent expositions of Arianism are: William Bright, *The Age of the Fathers* (London, 1903), 1: 56–66; Louis Duchesne, *Early History of the Christian Church* (London, 1912), 2: 100–2; F. J. Foakes-Jackson, *The History of the Christian Church*, 7th ed. (New York, 1924), pp. 299–303; Henry M. Gwatkin, *Studies in Arianism*, 2d ed. (Cambridge, 1900), pp. 20–28; Adolph Harnack, *History of Dogma*, trans. E. B. Speirs and James Millar (London, 1898; reprint ed., New York, 1958), 4: 14–20; J. N. D. Kelly, *Early Christian Doctrine*, 2d ed. (London, 1960), pp. 226–31, 281–82; B. J. Kidd, *A History of the Church to A.D. 461* (Oxford, 1922), 2: 14–16; Arthur McGiffert, *A History of Christian Thought* (New York, 1932), 1: 247–48; H. R. Mackintosh, *The Doctrine of the Person of Jesus Christ* (Edinburgh, 1912), pp. 176–77; T. E. Pollard, "The Origins of Arianism," *Journal of Theological Studies*, n.s. 9 (1958): 103–11; J. Tixeront, *History of Dogmas*, trans. H. L. B. (St. Louis, 1914), 2: 24–28; J. W. C. Wand, *The Four Great Heresies* (London, 1955), ch. 2; Harry A. Wolfson, *The Philosophy of the Church Fathers* (Cambridge, Mass., 1956), 1: 585–87, 593–94.

[5] 14: 62, 64, 72, 186, 192, 402, etc. I have used the edition of *De Doctrina* by James H. Hanford, trans. Charles R. Sumner, in *The Works of John Milton*, gen. ed. F. A. Patterson (New York, 1931–38), 14–17.

[6] Athanasius, *De syn.*, 16, and Epiphanius, 69. 7; trans. John Cardinal Newman, *Nicene and Post-Nicene Fathers*, 2d ser. (New York, 1892), 4: 458. Cf. Gwatkin, p. 23; Harnack, p. 15; Kelly, p. 230; Mackintosh, p. 176; Pollard, pp. 104–5; Tixeront, p. 25.

but *ex Deo*,[7] which in turn argues that God's virtue was "propagated," "diffused," "extended" throughout the order circumscribed by the Creator. In *Paradise Lost*, God's "putting forth" of himself during the act of creation — anathema to the Arians — is equally explicit:

> Boundless the Deep, because I am who fill
> Infinitude, nor vacuous the space.
> Though I uncircumscrib'd myself retire,
> And put not forth my goodness, which is free
> To act or not .... [7. 168–72]

2. Before the advent of time, Arius further maintained, God "begat" (="created")[8] the Son, of whom it must be properly said that "there was once when he was not" (ἦν ποτε ὅτε οὐκ ἦν).[9] The Son was produced not of the Father's divine nature, but out of nothing (ἐξ οὐκ ὄντων).[10] The two Persons, in fact, are utterly alien and dissimilar in substance or essence (ὁ Λόγος ἀλλότριος μὲν καὶ ἀνόμοιος κατὰ πάντα τῆς τοῦ Πατρὸς οὐσίας καὶ ἰδιότητός ἐστι),[11] and totally unequal in every respect, even glory (ἴσον, οὐδὲ ὅμοιον οὐχ ὁμόδοξον ἔχει [ὁ Πατὴρ]).[12] The Son may indeed on occasion be termed "God," but this is merely a nominal concession ([ὁ Υἱὸς] λέγεται ὀνόματι μόνον Θεὸς);[13] in reality, he is not "true God" (ἀληθινὸς Θεὸς).[14] In contrast, Milton rejected this entire scheme, even though he agreed in principle that "there was once when the Son was not." I am not suggesting that we overlook either Milton's repeated denials that the Father and the Son are of the same essence (*essentia*),[15] or his flat affirmations that "there is in reality

---

[7] *Works*, 15: 20, 22.

[8] The Arians consistently equated "begotten" with "created." Milton, however, recognized two interpretations of "begotten": one literal, in connection with the Son's generation; the other metaphorical, in connection with his exaltation (*Works*, 14: 180). In *Paradise Lost*, 5. 603, the word "begot" is subsequently explained as referring to the Son's exaltation (5. 663–64). See further note 35 below.

[9] This favorite Arian phrase is cited by Theodoret, 1. 2, but esp. by Athanasius, *De syn.*, 15, and *C. Ar.*, 1. 5, 12–13, etc. Consult further: Bright, p. 60; Duchesne, p. 100; Foakes-Jackson, p. 299; Gwatkin, p. 24; Harnack, p. 16; Kelly, p. 228; Kidd, p. 15; McGiffert, p. 248; Mackintosh, p. 177; Pollard, p. 106; Tixeront, p. 25. The orthodox formula, probably invented by Origen, was: "there is no [i.e. time] when He was not" (οὐκ ἔστιν ὅτε οὐκ ἦν); see Henry Bettenson, ed., *The Early Christian Fathers* (London, 1956), note, p. 320.

[10] Ath., *C. Ar.*, 1. 5; cf. *De syn.*, 15; and further: Duchesne, p. 100; Kelly, p. 228; Wolfson, p. 586; and Hunter (note 37 below), *passim*.

[11] Ath., *C. Ar.*, 1. 6; cf. *De syn.*, 15; Socrates, 1. 6; Theodoret, 1. 5; and further: Bright, p. 60; Duchesne, p. 100; Harnack, pp. 15, 17; Kelly, p. 228; Mackintosh, p. 177; Wand, p. 42.

[12] Ath., *De syn.*, 15.

[13] Ath., *C. Ar.*, 1. 6.

[14] Ath., *C. Ar.*, 1. 5, 6, 9; and further: Harnack, p. 18; Mackintosh, p. 177; Wolfson, pp. 586–87.

[15] *Works*, 14: 208, 210, 214, 220, 252, 254, 310, 312, 338, 350; 15: 272.

but one true independent and supreme God" [16] and, further, that "the essence of the Father cannot be communicated to another Person." [17] Yet it is imperative to appreciate the relative nature of these statements, since Milton also stated, just as categorically, that the Son participates in the Father's substance (*substantia*),[18] that indeed "God imparted to the Son as much as he pleased of the divine nature [*divina natura*], nay of the divine substance [*divina substantia*]" [19]—in brief, that although the Son is not the supreme God (*summus Deus*), he is none the less God (*Deus*).[20] In *Paradise Lost*, interestingly enough, Milton disagrees even with the views he set forth in *De Doctrina Christiana*; for while the treatise consistently maintains that the Father and the Son are not equal (*non aequalibus*),[21] in the poem we find the Father stating that the Son is

> Thron'd in highest bliss
> Equal to God, and equally enjoying
> God-like fruition. [3. 305–7]

Subsequently the Son is said to occupy the seat of "high collateral glorie" (10. 86). In all these instances, we observe, the poem's affirmation of the equality between the Father and the Son has no parallel in *De Doctrina Christiana*, and still less in the dicta of Arius.

3. The "God-like fruition" just cited is one of the numerous metaphorical statements ventured in *Paradise Lost* by way of emphasis on the close relationship existing between the Father and the Son. As Milton must have known, Arius himself had scrupulously avoided the use of metaphors, while St. Athanasius resorted to them with marked enthusiasm, aware as he was that metaphors used in connection with the Father and the Son are bound to testify to their relationship ("where the Father is, there is the Son, and where the light, there the radiance").[22] Students of Milton need not be reminded of the images that light up Book 3 of *Paradise Lost*,[23] though it is perhaps pertinent to note that *De Doctrina Christiana* is nearly devoid of imagery.

---

[16] *Works*, 14: 197; cf. 200, 208.

[17] *Works*, 14: 223.

[18] *Works*, 14: 186; cf. 330.

[19] *Works*, 14: 193. The Father's *essentia*, he states further on, is only *distincta* or *altera* from the Son's (14: 336, 350).

[20] *Works*, 14: 202, 312; 15: 262. Cf. 14: 267, 272, 276, 330, and esp. 267.

[21] *Works*, 14: 50, 190, 210, 310, 328, 342; 15: 4.

[22] *C. Ar.*, 2. 41; the same metaphor is elaborated further in 3. 4.

[23] It has been suggested that the "Holy Light" invoked in Book 3 was meant to be identified with the Son of God; if so, *Paradise Lost* is even further removed from Arianism — as well as from *De Doctrina*. See William B. Hunter, Jr., "The Meaning of 'Holy Light' in *Paradise Lost* III," reprinted in this volume as "Milton's Muse."

4. Whereas Arius maintained that the Father is both invisible and ineffable to the Son (ἀόρατος and ἄρρητος),[24] Milton took great pains to assert the extremely close communion between the two Persons.[25] The New Testament, it should be noted, specifically maintains that the Son "knows" the Father (Matt. 11: 27), that he is "in the bosom of the Father" (John 1: 18), that he is "the brightness of His [Father's] glory, and the express image of His person" (Heb. 1: 3). Arius, in the highly eclectic manner that characterized his approach to the Bible, for obvious reasons elected to disregard this evidence. Milton, in contrast, not only noticed the relevant verses, but on their basis concluded that the Son is the *effulgentia* of the Father.[26] This "effulgence" appears in *Paradise Lost* twice. To the angels, the Son is

> of all Creation first,
> Begotten Son, Divine Similitude,
> In whose conspicuous count'nance, without cloud
> Made visible, th' Almighty Father shines,
> Whom else no Creature can behold; on thee
> Impresst th' effulgence of his Glory abides. [3. 383–88]

Later the Father addresses the Son as the

> Effulgence of my Glory, Son belov'd,
> Son in whose face invisible is beheld
> Visibly, what by Deity I am. [6. 680–82]

The Son's ability to "see" the Father is stressed on yet another occasion:

> the Father . . . unfolding bright
> Toward the right hand his Glory, on the Son
> Blaz'd forth unclouded Deity. [10. 63–65]

In turn, the Son reflects the Father in "all" things "fully" (3. 139–40, 225; 5. 720; 6. 720, 736; 7. 196; 10. 65–67) and indeed "ineffably" (6. 721).

5. According to Arius, the Son of God was expressly produced in order to create the universe and time "out of nothing." [27] Milton disagreed in three respects. First, as we have seen, he rejected the idea of the world's creation *ex nihilo*; secondly, he asserted time's existence in eternity prior to the crea-

---

[24] Ath., *De syn.*, 15, and *C. Ar.*, 1. 6, 9; Socrates, 1. 6; and further: Harnack, p. 18; Kelly, pp. 228–29; Tixeront, p. 26.

[25] Even the angels are said to be permitted to see the Father "as far as they are capable of enduring His glory" (15: 33). Milton does not even hint at the notion of Arius that the Son does not know himself (Ath., *De syn.*, 15; *C. Ar.*, 1. 6).

[26] *Works*, 14: 192, 198, 336, 340, 402.

[27] All authorities; and further: Bright, p. 60; Foakes-Jackson, p. 299; Harnack, pp. 15, 18; Kelly, p. 228; McGiffert, pp. 247–48; Mackintosh, pp. 176–77; Tixeront, p. 25.

tion of the world;[28] and finally, he did not hold that the Son was "begotten" specifically with a view to the creation of the world.

6. Whereas Arius maintained that the Son is, like all rational creatures, mutable and indeed peccable ($\tau\rho\epsilon\pi\tau\grave{o}s$ and $\dot{a}\lambda\lambda o\iota\omega\tau\grave{o}s$),[29] Milton vehemently denied that he may be regarded as in any way liable to change (*mutabilis*).[30]

7. Whereas the Arians shattered the unity of the incarnate Son with their affirmation that he assumed a body without a soul ($\sigma\hat{\omega}\mu a\ \ddot{a}\psi\upsilon\chi o\nu$),[31] Milton maintained that the Christ Jesus was "very man" in both body and soul.[32]

8. Whereas Arius was of the opinion that the Holy Spirit does not partake of the Son's substance, and still less of the Father's ($\dot{a}\mu\acute{\epsilon}\tau o\chi o\acute{\iota}\ \epsilon\dot{\iota}\sigma\iota\nu\ \dot{a}\lambda\lambda\acute{\eta}\lambda\omega\nu$ $a\dot{\iota}\ o\dot{\upsilon}\sigma\acute{\iota}a\iota\ \tau o\hat{\upsilon}\ \Pi a\tau\rho\grave{o}s\ \kappa a\grave{\iota}\ \tau o\hat{\upsilon}\ \Upsilon\acute{\iota}o\hat{\upsilon}\ \kappa a\grave{\iota}\ \tau o\hat{\upsilon}\ \dot{a}\gamma\acute{\iota}o\upsilon\ \Pi\nu\epsilon\acute{\upsilon}\mu a\tau os$),[33] Milton asserted that the Third Person, though inferior to both the Father and the Son, was none the less also "begotten" of the substance of God (*ex substantia Dei*).[34]

II

Not long ago the Nolloth Professor of Christian Philosophy at Oxford reminded us of the necessity "to recognize the logical complexity of Christian claims before we argue about them." [35] As much may be urged on behalf of Milton, whose specific claims in *De Doctrina Christiana* and *Paradise Lost* have been distorted by our readiness to brand them as merely "Arian." Hence my present effort to "gloss," as it were, the tenets of Arius as contrasted to those of Milton, for this way, I think, we will be in a better position to appreciate Milton's orthodoxy no less than his heterodoxies.

---

[28] *Works*, 15: 34.

[29] Ath., *De syn.*, 15, and *C. Ar.*, 1. 5, 9; Socrates, 1. 6; Theodoret, 1. 2; and further: Bright, pp. 60–61; Duchesne, p. 100; Foakes-Jackson, p. 299; Kelly, p. 229; McGiffert, p. 248; Pollard, p. 106.

[30] *Works*, 14: 308.

[31] Bright, p. 65; Gwatkin, pp. 25, 27; Harnack, p. 19; Kelly, p. 281; Tixeront, p. 27; Wolfson, p. 594. Recently William P. Haugaard has wondered whether Arius actually held this view ("Arius: Twice a Heretic?" *Church History* 29 [1960]: 251–63); none the less, tradition normally ascribed the idea to him, and Milton would have had no reason to think otherwise. Cf. Erasmus, *Exposition . . . of the Comune Crede* (London, 1533), sig. 12¹: "Arrius . . . giue[s] to Christ the bodye of a man and taketh frome hym the soule of man."

[32] *Works*, 15: 276; Milton's opinion is directly related to his view of the "whole man" (15: 40).

[33] Ath., *C. Ar.*, 1. 6.

[34] *Works*, 14: 402.

[35] Ian T. Ramsey, *Religious Language* (London, 1957), pp. 160 ff. At this point Professor Ramsey discusses the controversial term "only-begotten" ($\mu o\nu o\gamma\epsilon\nu\grave{\eta}s$, unigenitus); but see further J. F. Bethune-Baker, *The Early History of Christian Doctrine*, 5th ed. (London, 1933), pp. 195–96, and C. H. Turner's exposition of the traditional equation $\dot{a}\gamma a\pi\eta\tau\grave{o}s$ $=\mu o\nu o\gamma\epsilon\nu\grave{\eta}s$, in " 'Ο Υἱὸς μου ὁ ἀγαπητός," *Journal of Theological Studies* 27 (1926): 113–29. See further note 8 above.

Yet it may well be argued that Milton's subordination of the Son to the Father is different from the Arian heresy only in degree, certainly not in kind. In a way, this is true enough; yet I must insist that in this case the difference in degree is of fundamental importance — it is the difference, indeed, between Christianity and mythology. For the Arians, in denying that the Son is similar to the Father in any way, denied also the historical basis of the Christian faith; while Milton, in asserting that the Son was created *ex substantia Dei* and is himself God, asserted also the fundamental Christian claim that the Incarnation is the central event in history, marking the entrance into the world not of any fantastic "body without a soul" totally alien from God, but of God himself. Milton had plainly recognized, as did the early Christians before him, that Arius had in effect reduced Christianity from a historical religion to a pseudo-philosophical mythology.

Milton's reported "Arianism" has also led us astray in at least two other respects, both extensions of claims peculiar to Protestantism. One is the professed effort of Protestants in the sixteenth and seventeenth centuries to revert to the "pure" doctrines of the early church; the other is their constant appeal to the Scriptures as the sole rule and guide in matters of faith. In *De Doctrina Christiana* — but not, I think, in *Paradise Lost* — the two claims fuse in an impressive and well-nigh unique manner. The early Fathers are invoked by name quite frequently;[36] but even when they are not named, they still form the general background of the treatise: for the "source" of Milton's subordination of the Son to the Father is not the Arian heresy but the widespread "subordinationism" of patristic writers prior to the Council of Nicaea.[37] At the same time, of course, Milton made generous use of the Bible; indeed, if we are to believe his own claim, *De Doctrina Christiana* was erected solely on the Word of God (*solo Dei verbo*).[38] To be sure, we may suspect that his further claim that "no mention is made in Scripture" of the mystery of the Trinity[39] is mistaken. None the less, as a curiosity, I may subjoin the considered opinion

---

[36] For example, in connection with his traducianist views, Milton claimed the support of Tertullian, Apollinarius, Gregory of Nyssa, and Augustine (15: 42). The latter is cited two more times (15: 48, 194), but not as enthusiastically as Milton was wont to do in his earlier works.

[37] As far as I can judge, the first to suspect that Milton "seems to approach" the subordination of early Christianity was George W. Whiting, "The Father to the Son," *Modern Language Notes* 65 (1950): 193. Lately, J. B. Broadbent has accurately referred to Milton as a "subordinationist" (*Some Graver Subject* [London, 1960], p. 155). But full credit for the first study of the theological background of *De Doctrina* belongs to William B. Hunter, Jr., "Milton's Arianism Reconsidered." This study is further supported by J. H. Adamson. Both essays are reprinted in this volume.

[38] *Works*, 14: 216; cf. 16: 267: "The rule and canon of faith is Scripture alone."

[39] *Works*, 15: 263.

of the late Kenneth E. Kirk, Bishop of Oxford, that the biblical evidence concerning the Trinity is "singularly disconcerting." [40] As the distinguished Swiss theologian Emil Brunner also observed, "Certainly, it cannot be denied that not only the word 'Trinity,' but even the explicit idea of the Trinity is absent from the apostolic witness to the faith." [41] Could it be that Milton's several claims require a reappraisal after all? [42]

In pleading for a reappraisal, I plead also, and specifically, against the persistent attempts to regard *Paradise Lost* as "a poem written by an Arian and containing Arian views" — a thesis lucidly restated in 1961 by Mr. Kelley, though presently accompanied by the intimidating warning that scholars denying his theory "must indeed be considered incompetent." [43] The danger we all face in resisting Mr. Kelley's views is real enough, if only because the threat issues from an eminent authority on Milton; yet despite the risk involved, I feel obliged to insist that the application of the term "Arian" to Milton distorts his views and confounds the important differences between "subordinationism" and the Arian mythology. In this light, is it unreasonable to call for a serious reconsideration of Milton's theological views? Among them, after all, is the problem — curiously disregarded to date — that *De Doctrina Christiana*, in asserting the participation of the Son and the Holy Spirit in the *substantia* of the supreme Father, actually upholds tritheism. Was Milton aware that in rejecting the triune God of orthodoxy as well as the incommunicable God of Arius, he had in fact espoused three Gods? At what stage in his development was this curious conclusion attained? Perhaps before the composition of *Paradise Lost*, so that the poem's affirmation of the co-equality between the Father and the Son represents an effort to "correct" the treatise's denial of that co-equality? But if so, why was not the treatise corrected as well? The problems are obviously complex, and the solutions far from easy. But an excellent beginning has been made, and so there is hope.

---

[40] "The Evolution of the Doctrine of the Trinity," in *Essays on the Trinity and the Incarnation*, A. E. J. Rawlinson, ed. (London, 1928), p. 199.

[41] *The Christian Doctrine of God*, trans. Olive Wyon (London, 1949), p. 205.

[42] In one case those claims have been accepted at their face value, with illuminating results; see George N. Conklin, *Biblical Criticism and Heresy in Milton* (New York, 1949).

[43] Maurice Kelley, "Milton's Arianism Again Considered," *Harvard Theological Review* 54 (1961): 195–205. This reply to Mr. Hunter's study (see note 37 above) disregards the impressive evidence marshalled to demonstrate the continuity of subordinationist views to the seventeenth century, and appeals instead, quiet irrelevantly, to the traditional "educated English usage" of the term "Arian" — a usage in evident need of revision. In addition, replying to Mr. R. M. Frye (*God, Man, and Satan* [Princeton, 1960], pp. 75–76), Mr. Kelley maintains that Milton's "Arianism" is clearly evident in *Paradise Lost* as well, and rests his case on the identification of "God" (in *PL*, 8. 295–451) as the Father. But in that instance "God" is, as likely as not, the Son (cf. *PL*, 3. 375, 385–87; 6. 680–82) — or, alternatively, the Godhead (as I argue in "The Godhead in *Paradise Lost*: Dogma or Drama?," reprinted in this volume). For a further restatement of Mr. Kelley's thesis, see his "Milton and the Trinity," *Huntington Library Quarterly* 33 (1970): 315–20.

The Godhead in *Paradise Lost:*
Dogma or Drama?

C. A. PATRIDES

μία μὲν οὖν ἡ τῆς ἀληθείας ὁδός· ἀλλ᾽ εἰς αὐτήν, καθάπερ
εἰς ἀέναον ποταμόν, ἐκρέουσι τὰ ῥεῖθρα ἄλλα ἄλλοθεν.

CLEMENT OF ALEXANDRIA, *Stromata*, 1. 5

De Doctrina Christiana, Milton's celebrated theological treatise, was discovered in 1823 and published two years later. Within a short time it became fashionable to regard Milton as an Arian, and this tradition has persisted to our own day. Recently, however, William B. Hunter, Jr., has investigated the matter more closely.[1] His conclusion, based on a reasonable study of the course of Christian dogmatics, is that *De Doctrina Christiana* asserts no characteristically Arian tenets, but rather leans on the "subordinationism" current throughout the period prior to the Council of Nicaea and revived in modified form by the rationalists of the later Renaissance. My own excursions in the same direction have confirmed this conclusion in nearly every respect; indeed, I venture to suggest — not impetuously I trust — that we cannot revert to the innocent days when any deviation from trinitarianism was cheerfully equated with Arianism.

In the state of innocence, the fate of *De Doctrina Christiana* had affected the fortunes of *Paradise Lost* as well. Sir Herbert Grierson, for example, was persuaded that "a skilled theologian" could "easily detect" the Arianism

---

[1] "Milton's Arianism Reconsidered," and J. H. Adamson, "Milton's 'Arianism'," reprinted in this volume. For constructive criticism of my own contribution, I am indebted to Professors Wayne Shumaker and Ernest L. Tuveson of the University of California at Berkeley, and particularly to Professor I. T. Ramsey of Oriel College, Oxford.

of the epic; E. E. Kellett was of the opinion that *Paradise Lost* is, quite simply, "an Arian poem"; while Maurice Kelley, in the most alarming statement of all, declared that the poem is "an Arian document."[2] Against these and similar views one could easily set Hunter's arguments, revising them only so far as might seem necessary to render them applicable to *Paradise Lost*. But such a course would assume that Milton's treatise was the blueprint for his epic — an assumption with grave implications, and hardly flattering to its author. For my part, I am persuaded that while much of *Paradise Lost* is "substantially expressed" in *De Doctrina Christiana*, the latter's "subordinationism" is not necessarily present in the poem. In this preliminary study, I hope to demonstrate that in *Paradise Lost* the unity of the Godhead is not impaired; for the most part, indeed, Milton does not seem to distinguish between the Father and the Son.

I

Since Hunter has already shown that divergences from trinitarianism do not inevitably lead to the Arian heresy, I need not cross swords at this point with those who think *Paradise Lost* "an Arian poem." But even the few critics who have denied the presence of Arian tenets in the poem have not been altogether correct in their approach. We may consider the most perceptive of these critics, Arthur Sewell, who has — wisely, I think — called our attention to a number of statements in *Paradise Lost* that are diametrically opposed to the ideas set forth in *De Doctrina Christiana*.[3] Of the numerous instances he cites, the most striking are two: one is Milton's observation that "all" the Father is "Substantially expres'd" in the Son (3. 139–40); the other, the Father's statement that the Son is "Equal" to him, "equally enjoying / Godlike fruition (3. 306–7) — while *De Doctrina Christiana* explicitly states that the two Persons are "not equal," still less consubstantial or coessential ("there is certainly no difference between the related adverbs 'essentially' and 'hypo-

---

[2] Grierson, *Cross Currents in English Literature of the XVIIth Century* (London, 1929), p. 253; Kellett, *Reconsiderations* (Cambridge, 1928), p. 133; Kelley, *This Great Argument* (Princeton, 1941), p. 122. See further Mr. Kelley's replies to Hunter and Adamson (previous note), in "Milton's Arianism Again Considered," *Harvard Theological Review* 54 (1961): 195–205, and "Milton and the Trinity," *Huntington Library Quarterly* 33 (1970): 315–20. James H. Sims's endeavor to clarify the controversy in "*Paradise Lost*: Arian Document or Christian Poem?" *Études Anglaises* 20 (1967): 337–47, is less than satisfactory.

[3] Arthur Sewell, *A Study in Milton's Christian Doctrine* (London, 1939), pp. 85–108. Almost the same passages discussed by Sewell are listed consecutively by Sister Miriam Joseph, "Orthodoxy in *Paradise Lost*," *Laval Théologique et Philosophique* 8 (1952): 252–54.

statically' ").[4] In *Paradise Lost* the Son is what Milton twice describes him as being: "the filial Godhead" (6. 722; 7. 175) — that is to say, the filial manifestation of the Godhead, distinct as a Person in that he sits specifically at the right hand of the Father, yet "imbosomd" in the Paternal Being (5. 597), the "Assessor" of his Father's throne (6. 679), the "full" expression of the Father in "all" things (3. 225; 5. 720; 6. 720, 736), and the occupant of the seat not of subordinate but of "high collateral glorie" (10. 86).

Such specific evidence is to be welcomed. But where does it lead us? Does it automatically argue the co-equality of the Father and the Son? Not necessarily; for later God has this to say:

> [I] am alone
> From all Eternity, for none I know
> Second to mee or like, equal much less. [8. 405–7]

These lines might well be viewed as a flat contradiction of the Father's earlier statement that the Son is "Equal" to him. Sewell himself noticed the discrepancy, and was disturbed; so much so that this "difficult" passage forced him to the conclusion that "Milton's views were developing as the poem was being written." A possibility indeed. But were we to accept it, would not the unified artistic composition that is *Paradise Lost* be shattered into a series of fragments? The impairment of Milton's epic for the sake of a critical theory is not one which I would attempt without at least some reflection on the serious consequences.

Alternatively, could we perhaps reject the dogma altogether and accept merely the "drama"? Irene Samuel has phrased this possibility rather forcefully: "we have incautiously misconstrued as dogma what Milton intended as drama."[5] But such a position is not without certain serious disadvantages. Besides disregarding Milton's evident interest in matters of doctrine, there is also a reversion to that convenient heresy again. "Doubtless," we are told, "Milton's Arianism made it possible for him to handle the council in Heaven as a dramatic dialogue between speakers more easily, with less conflict between what he saw as dramatically desirable and what he felt as doctrinally

---

[4] *The Works of John Milton* (New York, 1933), 14: 210, 220. I am grateful to Dr. John Carey of Keble College, Oxford, for supplying the translations here as well as *infra* (note 6). Dr. Carey is presently translating *De Doctrina Christiana* for the Yale edition of the *Complete Prose Works of John Milton*, gen. ed. Don M. Wolfe (1953 ff.).

[5] Irene Samuel, "The Dialogue in Heaven: A Reconsideration of *Paradise Lost*, III, 1–417," *PMLA* 72 (1957): 601–11. For an interesting extension of Miss Samuel's thesis, and a firm rejection of my own, see Stella P. Revard, "The Dramatic Function of the Son in *Paradise Lost*: A Commentary on Milton's 'Trinitarianism,' " *JEGP* 66 (1967): 45–58.

correct, than a trinitarian might." The fragmentation of *Paradise Lost* persists, I fear, in this theory as well; for while earlier Sewell had questioned the artistic unity of the epic, now its dramatic unity is dismissed all too lightly. Might not the matter and the manner be wedded after all?

I do not intend to suggest that my own theory is the decisive solution to the problem. But as a first step toward that solution, we might find it useful to consider that the distinction between the Father and the Son in *Paradise Lost* appears only during their verbal exchanges, while as soon as the "dialogues" are terminated, and particularly when we encounter the Godhead in action beyond the confines of heaven, the distinction between the two Persons is arrested abruptly. This technique satisfies, I hold, both the drama and the dogma: the drama, in that the artistic demands of the narrative are met through the fascinating "consultations" of the two Persons within the Godhead; and the dogma, in that the distinction between the Father and the Son is neither permitted to lapse into total separation — which would be polytheism — nor retained once we progress beyond the immediate area circumscribed by the Empyraean.

II

The first two books of *Paradise Lost* might not seem relevant to this inquiry. But I should like to observe one peculiarity: Satan's consistent refusal to speak of the Son of God, even though it was the latter's exaltation that had infused in him a "sense of injur'd merit" and led to the rebellion in heaven. Equally strange are two of the numerous references to the War in Heaven. One is Mammon's recollection of "the fierce Foe" who "pursu'd us through the Deep" (2. 78–79); the other, Belial's memory of the havoc effected by "Heav'n's afflicting Thunder" (2. 166). We observe that neither Mammon nor Belial names the Son — who was, nevertheless, precisely the one who routed the rebellious angels and anon pursued them to the crystal wall of heaven. Might we not conclude that the fallen angels' failure to speak of their archenemy argues that, for them at least, the Father and the Son are not differentiated? Should this be so, this further conclusion might suggest itself: that the distinction *was* introduced by Milton for dramatic purposes, although in the end it is the one God with whom he is concerned.

In isolation, I grant, my argument might seem, and perhaps is, no argument. Yet it is related to three specific events in *Paradise Lost* — not any of the "dialogues" indeed, but the three occasions when Milton depicts God as acting, in one capacity or another, *outside* heaven. With the dramatic element well-nigh absent, it is instructive to observe how the poet strives to preserve the unity of the Godhead intact.

The first event is the creation of the world (Book 7). At the outset, the distinction between the two Persons persists. The Father appoints the Son as Creator:

> thou my Word, begotten Son, by thee
> This I perform, speak thou, and be it done:
> My overshadowing Spirit and might with thee
> I send along, ride forth, and bid the Deep
> Within appointed bounds be Heav'n and Earth. [ll. 163–67]

Next, the newly appointed Creator prepares to leave the Empyraean:

> the Son
> On his great Expedition now appear'd,
> Girt with Omnipotence, with Radiance crown'd
> Of Majesty Divine, Sapience and Love
> Immense, and all his Father in him shone. [ll. 192–96]

But it is *not* the Son who actually departs; it is the triune Godhead:

> Heav'n op'n'd wide
> Her ever-during Gates, Harmonious sound
> On golden Hinges moving, to let forth
> *The King of Glory in his powerful Word*
> *And Spirit* coming to create new Worlds. [ll. 205–9]

Even more significant is the fact that once we cross the gates of heaven into Chaos, there is no mention of "the Son" *at any time*. The Creator, in fact, is indiscriminately endowed with the names and titles appropriate to any one Person within the Godhead. Thus he is referred to as "th' Almighty" (1. 339), "th' Omnific Word" (1. 217), and "the Spirit of God" (1. 235). But most frequently — no less than sixteen times — he is called by the general name often applied to the Father: "God." [6] The distinction sets in again when the creation of man necessitates the traditional "consultation" in heaven; but after the address of the Father ("Let *us* make now Man in *our* image" [1. 519]), Raphael at once resumes the references indicative of the

---

[6] 7. 232, 243, 249, 259, 261, 263, 282, 304, 331, 336, 337, 346, 352, 387, 391, 450; cf. 8: 234. In *De Doctrina Christiana* Milton argues at length that "the name 'God' is, by the will and permission of God the Father, not infrequently bestowed even upon angels and men, (how much more, then, upon the only begotten Son, the image of the Father)" (*Works*, 14: 244). Even so, there are subtle differences between the treatise and the poem — for example, in *Paradise Lost* the name of God is consistently "bestowed" only upon the Son; and in *De Doctrina Christiana* Milton has pointedly refused to "bring into my argument all that play-acting of the persons of the godhead" (p. 196).

unity of the Godhead ("in *his* own Image *hee* / Created thee" [ll. 526–27]). At the conclusion of the sixth day, "the Creator" surveys the new world and pronounces it "good." Then, back within heaven, the distinction reappears:

> at the holy mount
> Of Heav'n's high-seated top, th' Imperial Throne
> Of Godhead, fixt for ever firm and sure,
> The Filial Power arriv'd, and sat him down
> With his great Father, for he also went
> Invisible, yet stay'd (such privilege
> Hath Omnipresence) and the work ordain'd. [ll. 584–90]

We conclude that the creation, ordained by the Father and executed by the Son, was carried out by the single entity constituting the Godhead.

In Adam's account of his charming exchanges with the Creator (Book 8), we should not expect the first of men to distinguish between the Father and the Son. To him the "Presence Divine" is simply "God" — the "Author of this Universe," "Heav'nly Maker," "Creator," "Almighty," "Supream of things," "infinite," "absolute," "One." What the "Presence" has to say is, naturally, far more noteworthy. I quoted the "difficult" statement earlier:

> [I] am alone
> From all Eternity, for none I know
> Second to mee or like, equal much less.

That the speaker here cannot possibly be the Son is obvious: the speech is couched in the absolute terms appropriate only to the Father. On the other hand, the "Presence" cannot be the Father either; as Sewell rightly perceived, the lines contradict the earlier assertion that the Father and the Son are co-equal. We would be unwise, I think, to argue that the statement assigned to the "Presence" was written so much later that Milton was unaware of its discrepancy with the earlier passage — or, if aware, made no effort to correct either one. There was no need for a correction; for the "Presence Divine" amiably chatting with the first of men is neither the Father nor the Son, but God, addressing Adam in the unity of the Godhead.

There remains to consider the third pertinent event in the poem, God's last appearance in action beyond the confines of heaven. The occasion is the sentence passed on Adam and Eve (Book 10). The task is specifically assigned by the Father to the Son:

> whom send I to judge them? whom but thee
> Vicegerent Son, to thee I have transferr'd
> All Judgment, whether in Heav'n, or Earth, or Hell. [ll. 55–57]

But no sooner does the Son abandon the Empyraean than the pattern we have been tracing is repeated. Exactly as it happened during the act of creation and the exchanges with Adam, so here all references to him as "the Son" cease instantly. In accordance with his new role, he is specifically termed the "gracious Judge" (l. 118), the "mild Judge and Intercessor" (l. 96), "both Judge and Saviour" (l. 209). Most significantly, however, he is called — no less than five times — "God" (ll. 90, 97, 101, 111, 171), and once even "the Lord God" (l. 163). Needless to say, as soon as the visit to Eden is terminated and God repairs to heaven, Milton reverts, as usual, to the "dramatic" distinction between the Father and the Son.

Thus did the author of *Paradise Lost* endeavor to avoid a possible conflict between "what he saw as dramatically desirable and what he felt as doctrinally correct." His eminent success is not surprising; for if on occasion we tend to regard the worlds of poetry and dogma as separate, he saw them always as two hemispheres "cramp'd into a *Planisphere.*"

3. The Son in His Relation to the Universe and Man

The Creation

J. H. ADAMSON

A poet of the Logos is by definition a poet of the creative powers, for through-out its long history beginning with the pre-Socratics the Logos theory was an attempt to explain the cosmos. The Logos itself was either the explanation, or else the agent, of the creative process and certain images of the ordered creation began to be associated with the Logos, images of light, music, dance and harmony.

More than any other Christian poet, John Milton was a singer of the Logos; we would expect, therefore, that his creation scene would be especially meaningful for him and that he would endow it with unusual power and imaginative grandeur. That it is so endowed is at least partly owing to the fact that Milton chose a philosophical theory of creation which was peculiarly suited to a poetic mind, the *ex Deo* theory. This theory, which asserts that God created the world out of himself rather than from "nothing" or from some external coexistent matter, has been interpreted by scholars in widely differing ways. Some have considered it materialistic pantheism; others have seen it only as a slightly distended orthodoxy.[1]

None of these discussions, however, have sufficiently recognized that there is an ancient and honorable Christian tradition of the *ex Deo* theory, and that

---

[1] The two works which have influenced me most, although my conclusions differ from both, are A. S. P. Woodhouse's article, "Notes on Milton's Views on the Creation: The Initial Phases," *PQ* 28 (January 1949): 211–36, and an unpublished dissertation in the archives of Widener Library by John Palmer Reesing, "Milton's Philosophical View of Nature." I am much indebted to Mr. Reesing's lucid and reasoned discussion of the problem. In addition, I have familiarized myself with the literature in the field, especially a series of articles by William B. Hunter, Jr., and the writings of Walter Clyde Curry, Maurice Kelley, Denis Saurat, and others.

this theory has certain logical or psychological corollaries which Milton seems consciously to have accepted. It is important, therefore, to know how this theory arose, who its proponents were, and what it meant to those who accepted it.

There were three theories of creation available to Milton.[2] Aristotle held the view that the universe of form and matter had eternally existed. This theory made possible an attractive and reasonable theory of evil: the combination of form and matter was always imperfect; all that was chaotic or painful in the universe could be ascribed to that fact.

This attractive theory was rejected by Philo Judaeus, however. A passionate monotheist, he could not conceivably admit that anything existed outside of God and coeternally with him. Plato, he believed, had been instructed by the Mosaic teachings and had correctly taught that the universe was created in time.[3] Philo differed from Plato in affirming that God created not only the forms but also the *prima materia* which, together with the forms, made up the universe.[4]

Inevitably, then, the question arises, from what did God create the first matter? Where did it come from? This question, as far as I know, Philo never raised. The early Christian fathers did raise it. They followed Philo in his insistence that no "thing" in the universe could be prior to or coeternal with God. Like Philo, they taught that all that exists was created by Deity, who alone is self-existent. When the question arose as to what the first matter was created from, Origen replied that it was made from nothing, and he cited the Book of Maccabees, "God made all these things when they did not exist," in support of his position.[5] *Ex nihilo*, then, at least as early as Origen, became the standard Christian concept and ultimately, after some helpful opposition from the Gnostics, it achieved the status of dogma.[6]

Dean Inge once remarked somewhat sharply that the *ex nihilo* theory is often "ignorantly ridiculed" by persons who seem to believe that God took some "nothing" and made it into a universe.[7] Milton ridiculed it for precisely that reason,[8] but, if mitigation is necessary, he was by no means the first to do

---

[2] H. A. Wolfson, *The Philosophy of Spinoza* (Cambridge, Mass., 1934), 1: 298.

[3] H. A. Wolfson, *Philo* (Cambridge, Mass., 1947), 1: 316, 295.

[4] Ibid., 1: 305 ff.

[5] *The Writings of Origen*, trans. Rev. Frederick Crombie, *Ante-Nicene Christian Library*, 10 (Edinburgh, 1869), 1: 77.

[6] W. R. Inge, *The Philosophy of Plotinus* (London, 1918), 1: 145.

[7] Ibid.

[8] *The Works of John Milton*, ed. F. A. Patterson (New York, 1931–38), 15: 17 (hereafter cited as *Works*).

so. Both Hasdai Crescas and Spinoza, in refuting the *ex nihilo* theory, attack what they imply to be the common conception of it, namely that *nihil* is a subject out of which the world is made. Both insist that the term rightly means only that there was no "thing" outside of God from which he made the world.[9] Dean Inge also believes that this is what the concept means, and he cites from Augustine: "When we say that He made it out of nothing, we mean that there was no pre-existent Matter, unmade by Himself, without which He could not have made the world." [10] M. Gilson says that Aquinas so construed the theory and that it was never intended to mean anything more. "It is certain that nothingness is not the original matrix whence all creatures spring; being can only issue from being . . . all essence is derived from the Divine essence." [11] It seems clear enough that the *ex nihilo* theory is primarily a negative theory; it denies the Aristotelian position, but takes no affirmative position of its own about the nature of creation. There may be little to be said for the logic of this position, but it had the inestimable advantage of being orthodox.

There was a third theory which was not particularly rational or orthodox. It was, however, poetically conceived, and it is the one Milton chose. It was the theory advanced by Plotinus of creation *ex Deo*, a theory dominated by the metaphor of the sun and its radiance. As the sun poured out an eternal stream of light, so the Uncreated Essence overflowed with life which penetrated down into all levels of being. Having reached the lowest level, it turned again and, yearning for its source, traveled back through the levels of being until it once more reached the Divine.

In formulating this theory, Plotinus denied the age-old Greek duality of matter and spirit, postulating instead a metaphysical monism. Unlike the Stoics, however, Plotinus was careful not to attribute materiality or corporeality to God.[12] There is, he said, no "real" distinction between soul or form on the one hand and body or matter on the other. That which is Form in relation to something below it may be Matter in relation to that which is above it, for *omnia sunt diversis gradibus animata*.[13] Whether this distinction avoided pantheism or not became a subject for much heated discussion.

---

[9] Meyer Waxman, *The Philosophy of Don Hasdai Crescas*, Columbia University Oriental Studies, 17 (New York, 1920), pp. 154–55.

[10] *Plotinus*, 1: 145. The citation is from *Ad Orosium*, 1–2.

[11] Etienne Gilson, *The Philosophy of St. Thomas Aquinas*, trans. Bullough and Elrington, 2d ed. (Cambridge, 1929), p. 140.

[12] There is some doubt as to whether Zeno himself was not something of a dualist, but Cleanthes and Chrysippus were generally believed to be materialistic pantheists and complete necessitarians.

[13] Inge, *Plotinus*, 1: 136–44, 210.

The first influential Christian to posit a theory of *ex Deo*, as far as I know, was the fourth-century Greek father, Gregory of Nyssa. Gregory begins with the assumption, derived, he says, from the Scriptures, that all things have their being in God. He realizes that his opponents will ask, "if material existence was in Him, how can He be immaterial while including matter in Himself?" [14] In reply Gregory attempts to bridge the gap between the immateriality of God and the materiality of creation by suggesting that a wish actualized may become a substance.[15] Here he seems to be adopting the Platonic and Philonic device of positing an Idea or Thought between the Uncreated and the creation, a Logos in other words. Actually the various theories of the Logos were attempts to bridge such a gap; the fantastic hierarchies of the Gnostics, for example, were gradations separating the One and the many. But even an infinite series of gradations can never really explain how the Uncreated passed into creation, as Spinoza realized, and he consequently denied the Logos and all other mediating agencies, maintaining that extended substance was an attribute of God himself. Although there are many differences between the metaphysical monism of the Christian *ex Deo* tradition and that of Spinoza, the denial of the Logos and mediation is the principal one.

Gregory apparently realized that his first device had not really solved the problem. He therefore attempted a further solution, brief and unelaborated, but imaginative and rational. That which we call body, he says, is really a collection of various attributes, and, he continues, "not one of those things which we attribute to body is itself body; neither figure nor colour, nor weight, nor extension, nor quantity, nor any other qualifying notion whatever; but every one of them is a category . . . ." [16]

Thus, with the transformation of the "attributes of body" into "categories," Gregory has also transformed the all too solid flesh into a series of abstractions. He then continues his logical analysis. No single category, he says, can make a body. Rather body is a combination of categories, and nothing can combine categories except a thinking mind. The Deity, he says, is such a thinking Mind and therefore is capable of producing the "thinkables" whose mutual combination generates for us what we refer to as the substance of a

---

[14] *Gregory of Nyssa*, trans. William Moore and Henry A. Wilson, *A Select Library of Nicene and Post-Nicene Fathers*, 2d ser., 5 (Grand Rapids, Mich., 1945) : 413.

[15] Ibid., p. 458.

[16] Ibid.

given body.[17] Thus Mind or Logos, in a rather novel and interesting way, is again used to mediate between the Divine Essence and the created world.

Gregory's tentative and cautious espousal of the *ex Deo* theory was not nearly so influential as its unqualified assertion by pseudo-Dionysius, who was destined to have more influence on medieval thought than anyone except the very giants among the Fathers such as Augustine and Jerome. Until nearly the eighteenth century, this anonymous writer was known to most of the Christian world as Dionysius the Areopagite and was almost universally believed to have been a convert of St. Paul and the first bishop of Athens.[18]

Pseudo-Dionysius taught that the Godhead "contains and is the Ultimate Reality of all particular beings." And he elaborated the idea in the rhapsodic and repetitive style that characterizes his work. "It [the Uncreated Essence] is the life of all things that live and the Being of all that are, the Origin and Cause of all life and being through Its bounty which both brings them into existence and maintains them." [19] He specifically affirmed that in God all principles and all causes existed, including the material one. On this last point, the inclusion of the material cause in Deity, Aquinas, always highly respectful toward Dionysius, found it necessary to disagree, as all proponents of the *ex nihilo* theory were bound to do.[20]

Dionysius exerted little influence in the West until Scotus Erigena made his work available to the scholarly world in a Latin translation in the ninth century. Erigena himself was tremendously stimulated by pseudo-Dionysius and from his writings constructed a system into which he incorporated large elements from the writings of Origen, Gregory of Nyssa, and Augustine.[21]

Erigena postulated God as the ultimate Unknowable source of all things. The Logos for him, as for Philo, was not only a personage but also the aggregate of the Ideas in the Divine Mind and contained, therefore, the series of primal causes. In this manner the Logos mediated between the Unknowable and the creation.[22] Erigena accepts the fact that creation is *ex nihilo* if he is allowed to define the term. His definition is both ingenious and unorthodox.

[17] Ibid., pp. 458–59. Gregory is here on the threshold of a theory of appearance and reality which suggests those of some relatively modern Idealists.

[18] Modern scholars agree that this writer was a fifth-century Syrian monk; his work seems to be directly influenced by Proclus, whom he quotes a good deal.

[19] *Dionysius the Areopagite on the Divine Names and the Mystical Theology*, trans. C. E. Rolt (London, 1920), p. 56.

[20] Cf. Wolfson, *Philosophy of Spinoza*, 1: 302.

[21] Henry Bett, *Johannes Scotus Erigena* (Cambridge, 1925), pp. 164–65.

[22] George John Blewett, *The Study of Nature and the Vision of God* (Toronto, 1907), p. 297.

The formula *ex nihilo*, he says, does not mean that creation is from nothingness (*ex nihil nihilo*) but rather that it is from "no thing." There is only one Being that is not a thing or object, that exists within and of itself, and that is God. Creation, *ex nihilo*, therefore, when rightly understood means creation *ex Deo*. Erigena's definition rests on a concept of *nihil* as that which surpasses all finite understanding and therefore may be said to be *not*. *Nihil* does not mean mere privation of existence.[23]

After Erigena, there are many thinkers in the Christian tradition who, despite individual variations, taught a metaphysical monism based on a theory of creation *ex Deo*. The great name in the later tradition is Meister Eckhart, that towering genius among the medieval mystics. Eckhart was influenced both by Erigena and pseudo-Dionysius.[24] From Eckhart the basic concepts of metaphysical monism flowed in a broad stream into Christian thought through such disciples as Tauler and Suso. Jacob Böhme's thought largely derives from these sources and not, as is popularly supposed, directly from heaven. Among Catholic churchmen by far the most significant thinker in this tradition was Nicholas of Cusa, a disciple of both Erigena and Eckhart. Giordano Bruno professed a great debt to Nicholas, whom he called "the divine Cusanus."[25]

Such then is the tradition of *ex Deo* thought, a tradition inextricably linked with the mystical thinkers of the great Western religions. The theory of *ex Deo* has been attacked on the grounds that it is both illogical and unorthodox. The principal logical difficulty it offers is a formidable one. If matter emanated from God, why should it prove refractory? And if matter were not refractory, how could the imperfections of creation be accounted for without attributing them to Deity? Milton considers the problem in the chapter on creation in *Of Christian Doctrine*. He points out that this same difficulty inheres in the *ex nihilo* theory. "For what difference does it make, whether God produced it in this imperfect state out of nothing, or out of himself?"[26] In either case, it seems to Milton, one must account for evil in a uni-

---

[23] See Johannis Scoti Erigenae, *De Divisione Naturae* (Monasterii Guestphalorum, 1838), Bk. 3, paragraphs 20–23. Cf. Blewett, p. 288, n. 1, and Wolfson, "The Meaning of *Ex Nihilo* in the Church Fathers, Arabic and Hebrew Philosophy, and St. Thomas," in *Medieval Studies in Honor of J. D. M. Ford*, U. T. Holmes and A. J. Denomy, eds. (Cambridge, Mass., 1948), p. 357.

[24] See *Catholic Encyclopedia*, s.v. "Eckhart." Cf. Rufus Jones, *Studies in Mystical Religion* (London, 1923), p. 224.

[25] For a sketchy treatment but one which defines the tradition and suggests sources, see Bett, *Erigena*, ch. 5, "The Influence of Erigena upon Later Times."

[26] *Works*, 15: 23.

verse ruled by an omnipotent God. His own solution, which is not elaborated or argued at any length, is that once matter had emanated it became mutable and therefore subject to taint. It also became subject to the enticements of the devil,[27] he says, which may explain, in part at least, the visit of Satan to Chaos in *Paradise Lost* and the resultant league between the two.

The *ex Deo* theory has been considered unorthodox for two reasons: it is allegedly pantheistic and also it is incompatible with trinitarian dogma. In the first charge, that of pantheism, there has traditionally been much inconsistency. For example, Erigena's teaching was condemned by the Synod of Valence in 885, a judgment that is still upheld by the church. On the other hand, Nicholas of Cusa, a cardinal, has been generally vindicated even though, as Henry Bett says, there is "a striking parallel between the whole system of the Cardinal and that of the Scot . . . ." [28] Cusanus defended the orthodoxy of his emanationist position simply by asserting that although all was from God, yet God, in a mysterious manner, transcended all — a statement that appears in Erigena and many others, a statement that is really one of the basic concepts of the tradition.[29]

When one recalls that Eckhart's teachings were being condemned after his death by the Inquisition at the same time that the teachings of pseudo-Dionysius were being upheld with repressive measures, one recognizes the need to suspend judgment, to abandon, temporarily, the terms *materialism*, *pantheism*, and the others and to try to determine what the doctrine meant to those who adopted it rather than what it was called by their opponents.

Eastern and Western mystics agreed on one basic paradox: God was immanent and he was also transcendent. He contained all things but was contained by nothing.[30] In no writer is the insistence on this paradox more striking than in Erigena. As Blewett says, "on almost every page" of Erigena's writings, one can find the God who transcends absolutely and yet, at the same time, pours himself forth in the forms of nature.[31]

---

[27] Ibid., p. 25.

[28] Bett, *Erigena*, p. 192. For the influence of Dionysius and Eckhart on Nicholas of Cusa see Bett, *Nicholas of Cusa* (London, 1932), pp. 102 ff.

[29] See Evelyn Underhill's introduction to *The Vision of God*, trans. Emma Gurney Salter (London, 1928), xxv.

[30] Rudolf Otto, *Mysticism East and West*, trans. B. L. Bracy and R. C. Payne (New York, 1932), pp. 77 ff. Perhaps the central concept of Hinduism is the phrase "Brahman is Atman." Brahman is God transcendent and Atman is God immanent, and, properly understood, the two are one.

[31] Blewett, p. 286.

Nicholas of Cusa presents us again and again with the same paradox:

The being of the universe derives from God, but the being of God does not derive from the universe.

. . . All begins from God and all ends in God . . . . God is all of all that is, and yet nothing of all that is.[32]

In fact, Nicholas considered that the principles of the "coincidence of contraries," was the central truth of his system, and this truth, he said, flashed upon him with the force and power of supernatural revelation.[33]

Eckhart illustrates the same paradox. "The more God is in all things, the more He is outside them. The more He is within, the more without." [34]

We may ask then if this relation of God to the universe is pantheistic. If pantheism is defined as a belief that the sum total of "things" in the universe is equal to God, then the *ex Deo* theory is at the farthest remove from such a concept. Or if pantheism means that God is thought to be equally in all things, again, as will be shown, the *ex Deo* theorists were not pantheists. If, on the other hand, pantheism is loosely used to describe any system or concept in which the immanence of God in the universe is mystically felt and movingly uttered, then the whole mystical tradition, East and West, is pantheistic.

We come then to the question of the materiality or pantheism of Milton's *ex Deo* concept. In a sense, even the question, "Is God material?" is an absurdity to the thinkers in the *ex Deo* tradition who never weary of insisting that nothing can ever be known of God. The finite mind may consider "attributes," but must realize that these attributes are merely a finite attempt to describe infinitude. There is no thinker known to me in the *ex Deo* tradition who ever suggested that materiality was an attribute of God until Spinoza; all did maintain, however, that the Deity contained the material cause within himself. With this latter point, Milton agreed.[35] Further, the question of the materiality of God has little meaning for metaphysical monists. Thinkers in this tradition assert that we are not in a dualistic universe of body and spirit, matter and form, but rather in a monistic universe where everything that exists is a gradation of one prime matter. At the lower end of the scale are what a dualist would call material things: rocks, earth, flesh and money. At the other end of the scale are the immaterial things such as soul, spirit, and pure

---

[32] Bett, *Nicholas of Cusa*, pp. 104–5. I am quoting Bett's paraphrase.

[33] Bett, *Nicholas of Cusa*, pp. 127–28.

[34] Quoted by Aldous Huxley in *The Perennial Philosophy* (New York, 1945), p. 2.

[35] *Works*, 15: 21.

intelligence. God is neither the one nor the other; he is beyond both, above any concept that may be formed of him. But the higher end of the scale is nearer God, in a sense more like him, than the lower end. Materiality is that in the universe which has emanated farthest from its source; it is the thing most unlike God.

Milton goes to great lengths to assert the transcendence of God and preserve him from any trace of the anthropomorphic and corporeal. "To know God as he really is," Milton says in *De Doctrina Christiana*, "far transcends the power of man's thoughts . . . ." [36] His statement that "God is the primary, and absolute, and sole cause of all things" can be matched anywhere in Judaic or Christian orthodoxy. Milton never says that the substance of things existed in God but rather that "a diversified and substantial virtue" is in Deity. Milton acknowledges, as had Gregory of Nyssa, that it is exceedingly difficult to see how body emanated from spirit. [37] But he feels that it is even more difficult to believe that body originated from "nothing." [38] He then offers a suggested explanation, exceedingly simple, but one which shows again that he is attempting to avoid attributing corporeality to God. A more excellent substance such as spirit, he says, contains within itself, virtually and eminently, the inferior substance. In such a way, he continues, God or the substance of God contains within itself a "bodily power." [39] Here, it seems to me, is the clearest indication of what Milton's position really is. The words "virtually" and "eminently" were scholastic terms used to indicate that a thing possessed or contained another thing in a more perfect or higher manner than was required for a formal possession of it. Thus Aquinas states that God virtually contains all being. [40]

Duns Scotus used the terms "virtually" and "eminently" in constructing his metaphysical hierarchy of the principles of being. Scotus postulated a twofold order consisting of an order of "eminence" and an order of "dependence." In the order of eminence the final cause comes first, followed by the efficient, the formal and the material. The supreme existent, according to Scotus, as first in the order of causation, therefore "virtually" contains "the

[36] *Works*, 14: 31.

[37] The author of the *Tao Teh King* acknowledged the same difficulty. "These two things, the spiritual and material, though we call them by different names, in their origin are one and the same. This sameness is a mystery — the mystery of mysteries."

[38] *Works*, 15: 21, 23, 25.

[39] *Works*, 15: 25. It was in Mr. Reesing's dissertation that I was first made aware that Sumner had mistranslated "eminently" and had used the term "essentially."

[40] Gilson, *Aquinas*, p. 140.

totality of actuality," and it "eminently" contains the "totality of perfection." [41] Similarly, Aquinas had said that effects preexist in their causes, but he added that they exist only according to the mode of being of the cause.[42] By that he means that if an object exists in God, for example, it exists only according to the mode of God's being, not according to its own mode of being. I think it would be a reasonable simplification of the matter to say that "virtually" and "eminently" were terms devised to indicate the possibility of a higher thing containing a lower without in turn being contained by it. When Milton says that spirit virtually and eminently contains matter, he simply means that spirit is a higher cause and thus, in a higher manner, contains the lower cause in itself, even as God "virtually and eminently" contains all things within himself.

Again when Milton says that there is a "bodily power" in the substance of God, he is not saying that God is corporeal. Gregory of Nyssa had said that a wish actualized may become a substance. Probably no man was less capable by nature and training of making subtle metaphysical distinctions than Jacob Böhme; consequently both More and Cudworth accused him of teaching that God had a body. But such a sympathetic and able scholar as Dr. Hans Lassen Martensen sees clearly that when Böhme says that Nature is contained in God, he does not also mean that God is contained in Nature. Dr. Martensen readily admits that one may find pantheistic implications in Böhme, but he believes that what Böhme is trying to say is that it is not matter, but rather an "energetic potency" that is in God, and this potency is the *fons originis* of matter.[43] Böhme's "energetic potency" and Milton's "bodily power" are two ways of saying the same thing. Gregory of Nyssa believed that from God, whose nature is that of thought or spirit, a material world could come.[44] Milton, too, believed that God was spirit "in his most simple nature," and that the creation was a "species of external efficiency." [45] There would seem to be little difference in the two views.

Proponents of the *ex Deo* theory in Christianity, in Judaism or Islam would have considered it an impossible sacrilege to attribute corporeality to God. At most it could be maintained only that they did so without realizing it.

---

[41] C. R. S. Harris, *Duns Scotus* (Oxford, 1927), 2: 69–72.

[42] Gilson, *Aquinas*, p. 137.

[43] *Jacob Böhme*, trans. T. Rhys Evans (London, 1885), p. 173.

[44] Cf. Blewett, p. 311.

[45] *Works*, 14: 41; 15: 3.

Spinoza, it must be emphasized, was the first to make extended substance an attribute of God; but before doing so, he found it necessary to refute the idea of a Logos and all other mediators between the Unknowable and the created world. For the very function of these mediatorial agents was to bridge the chasm between God and matter without involving God in materiality. Far from denying the Logos, Milton made it the central doctrine of his theology, and there is no indication that he had any intention of positing extended substance as an attribute of God. On the contrary, when he lists the attributes of God, Milton names only immaterial ones: truth, spirit, immensity, infinity, eternity, immutability, incorruptibility, omnipresence, omnipotence, and unity.[46] According to Milton, even the Logos, who is of the substance of God, cannot be of the essence, for that would mean that a change had occurred, that Deity had emptied itself or had been altered.[47]

The attribution of extended substance to Deity is, in fact, the most characteristic and original feature of Spinoza's philosophy. To attribute such a view to Milton would entail an important change in the current views of history of philosophy and would require substantiation, but the fact is that Milton specifically avoided stating or implying such a view. His creation scene, it seems to me, is based on an emanationist theory that a potency existed in God, and that the potency was made actual, somehow, through the process of emanation.[48]

But as far as the *ex Deo* theory was concerned, it appears that the more profound Christian minds were less worried about its pantheism than they were about its incompatibility with orthodox trinitarian views. Although Plotinus was the schoolmaster who brought Augustine to Christ, the great bishop nevertheless completely rejected the most characteristic Plotinian teaching. "For, Thou didst not make heaven and earth out of Thyself; otherwise, it would have been equal to Thy Only-begotten Son, and in this way to Thee . . . . And, apart from Thee, there was nothing else from which Thou

---

[46] *Works*, 14: 41–51.

[47] *Works*, 14: 187, 193, 313, 343.

[48] In taking this position, I am aware that I disagree with the formidable authority of Mr. Woodhouse. I believe that the crucial difference between his view and mine is that he, in my judgment, does not recognize the fact that Spinoza attributed extended substance to Deity only after he had denied the mediators, including the Logos, the very function of which was to keep God from involvement in corporeality. Further, the fundamental argument Milton advanced against trinitarian views was that if the Logos were of one Essence with God, his emanation would indicate a change in Deity, which Milton would by no means allow. A man who would stick at this point would hardly be likely to make matter, the most mutable of all existences, a part of God.

mightest make them, O God, one Trinity and Threefold Unity. Therefore, Thou hast made heaven and earth out of nothing." [49]

The *ex Deo* theory postulates a hierarchical order of life emanating from God; the first emanation in this order was the Logos, the metaphysical light and the first Form. But Augustine cannot accept hierarchical excellence as the only difference between the Logos and creation. He insists rather on a complete separation between them because, according to trinitarian theory, the Father and the Son are one essence. On the other hand, those Christians who held subordinationist views, as Milton did, would find no insuperable theological difficulty in the theory.[50]

The question remains as to whether Milton really belongs to the *ex Deo* tradition, or whether he more or less fell into a similar position without realizing it. One might even question whether a mystical philosophy, extending over many hundreds of years and expressed through varying religious traditions, can be coherent enough to be said to have a defined position. Mr. George N. Conklin has denied that Milton belongs to a defined traditional theory. "Milton's position, despite the similarities of Plato, Lucretius, Philo, Eriugena, Servetus, Gerson, Ibn Ezra, Fludd, Böhme, and others is uniquely his and was independently derived from his exegetical conclusions alone. No precise parallel can, in fact, be found between Milton's conception of the creation and that of any other." [51]

---

[49] Augustine, *Confessions*, trans. Vernon J. Bourke, Fathers of the Church Series (New York, 1953), 12. 7. 7.

[50] Whether Milton was a subordinationist has, of course, been argued.

[51] George N. Conklin, *Biblical Criticism and Heresy in Milton* (New York, 1949), p. 67. In a footnote to this assertion, Mr. Conklin states that Milton's doctrine of creation *ex Deo* is unique in two ways: first, in its teaching that God is unwilling or, properly speaking, unable to annihilate any created thing and, second, the fact that Milton was the only one to derive his doctrine "solely from the first verb of the Bible." However, the doctrine of God's inability to annihilate created beings is, as will be shown, a commonplace of the *ex Deo* tradition. The second point also will not withstand close scrutiny. Professor Wolfson tells us that "the very starting point" of all Talmudic interpretation is the idea that any biblical text worthy of serious study must be assumed to have been written "with such care and precision that every term, expression, generalization or exception is significant . . . ." (see *Crescas' Critique of Aristotle* [Cambridge, Mass., 1929], pp. 24–25). Further, the Spanish Jewish scholar Ibn Ezra favored the philological approach as the "best way to arrive at the true meaning of Scripture," and his biblical exegesis, for which he was widely noted, is based principally upon the philological method. Ibn Ezra supported his denial of creation *ex nihilo* by philological argument. Isaac Husik says, "The Hebrew word 'bara,' ordinarily translated 'created,' which implies to most people the idea of *creatio ex nihilo*, Ibn Ezra renders, in accordance with its etymology, to limit, to define, by drawing or incising a line or boundary." (See *A History Of Jewish Philosophy* [New York, 1916], pp. 184, 187.) "Bara" is, of course, the first verb in the Hebrew Bible. The student of Milton will immediately be reminded of Milton's creation scene, where the Son with the golden compasses inscribes the boundary of the created world. That Milton knew Ibn Ezra cannot be demonstrated, but Henry More knew his exegesis and quotes a philological interpretation from it at some length in "Defence of the Literal Cabbala," *A Collection of Several Philosophical Writings* (London, 1662), p. 67.

I agree that Milton's view of the Scriptures was a significant factor in his acceptance of the theory. That his theory is unique, however, seems to me a dangerous statement, incapable of demonstration. Milton's treatment of the *ex Deo* theory, compared to the comprehensive and thorough treatment given it by Erigena or Cusanus, seems very sketchy indeed, the merest outline of his belief, a credo, not a system. It is thus rather difficult to compare it in great detail with one of the preceding systems. I do believe, however, that Milton's relation to the tradition may be tested by the analogy of what is known in medicine as a syndrome. That word is used to denote a situation or condition in which a group of symptoms are concurrently present, making diagnosis relatively certain. Through the centuries the *ex Deo* theory has logically or psychologically gathered around itself certain auxiliary concepts. If these auxiliary concepts can be shown in the writings of the other thinkers in the *ex Deo* tradition and if, in turn, they can be shown in the writings of Milton, it will be very difficult to divorce Milton from the tradition. For, that an original thinker such as Milton might have arrived at one or two important concepts independently is one thing; that he should have arrived at a linked group of concepts in such a way is something else.

The first postulate of the *ex Deo* theory is that God is forever unknowable and that, as a result, he can best be understood through the *via negativa*, that is, by saying and thinking of what God is not, rather than what he is. And the mystics of the *via negativa* have developed a characteristic set of images by which they express the Deity. Thus Dionysius the Areopagite says, "Unto this Darkness which is beyond Light we pray that we may come and may attain unto vision . . . ." Again he speaks of that "super-essential Darkness which is hidden by all the light that is in existent things." [52]

This image of Darkness to indicate the unknowability of God becomes a universal characteristic of the *ex Deo* tradition. It is altogether typical of Erigena that he should use the image, but refer it to a source in the Scriptures. Thus he speaks of God who *solus habet immortalitatem, et lucem habitat inaccessibilem.* [53]

Eckhart says that the Logos is the bright flowing river whose source is the "Motionless Dark," or the "Bottomless Abyss." [54] It is the same idea but a different though familiar metaphor when he says that splendor of the divine

---

[52] Rolt, pp. 194, 196.

[53] Erigenae, *De Divisione*, p. 7.

[54] Quoted by Rufus Jones in *The Flowering of Mysticism* (New York, 1939), p. 77.

light is a cloud and that "God is found on the mountain in the cloud." [55] It
is enough, perhaps, in addition to these citations, to recall the title of such a
work as *The Cloud of Unknowing*, which employs the same imagery of the
cloud on Mt. Sinai that Eckhart had used, to see how this concept of the Unknowability of God came to be imaged in a certain way. The central image of
this concept may be summed up in the statement from Dionysius that "the
Divine Darkness is unapproachable Light in which God dwells." [56]

Milton teaches, in *De Doctrina*, that to know God as he really is surpasses
man's comprehension. He follows this statement by citing from I Timothy 6:
16, a passage which Erigena was fond of: "dwelling in the light which no
man can approach unto." [57] Milton notes further that the complete unknowability of the Divine Glory is revealed by the fact that a description such as
man is capable of understanding is contained in the scriptural phrase, "mount
Sinai was altogether on a smoke," or "the cloudy pillar descended," or "the
cloud filled the house of Jehovah." [58]

The poetry reveals even more clearly Milton's use of the central images
of the *ex Deo* tradition. In the Invocation to Light in *Paradise Lost*, it is said
that God

> never but in unapproached light
> Dwelt from Eternity . . . . [3. 4–5]

The imagery of darkness appears again in the splendid lines from the
Angelic hymn.

> thee Author of all being,
> Fountain of Light, thyself invisible
> Amidst the glorious brightness where thou sit'st
> Thron'd inaccessible, but when thou shad'st
> The full blaze of thy beams, and through a cloud
> Drawn round about thee like a radiant Shrine,
> Dark with excessive bright thy skirts appear,
> Yet dazzle Heav'n. . . . [3. 374–81]

One may compare this description with John Tauler's statement, "This is the
quiet Desert of the Godhead, the Divine Darkness — dark from His own sur-
passing brightness, as the shining of the sun is darkness to weak eyes . . . ." [59]

---

[55] *Meister Eckhart*, trans. C. De B. Evans (London, 1931), 2: 130, 129.

[56] Jones, *Flowering of Mysticism*, p. 35.

[57] *Works*, 14: 31.

[58] *Works*, 14: 61. Quotations from *Paradise Lost* are from Merritt Y. Hughes' Odyssey
Press edition.

[59] Quoted by Jones, *Studies in Mystical Religion*, p. 278.

The cloud imagery, central to the writings of the *via negativa*, Milton carries through the entire epic. Only to the Son, the Divine Similitude, is God known,

> In whose conspicuous count'nance, without cloud
> Made visible, th' Almighty Father shines . . . . [3. 385–86]

In the seventh book, after the creation, "incense Clouds / Fuming from Golden Censers hid the Mount" (7. 599–600). When the Son is proclaimed Messiah in Book 5, the Father is likened to "a flaming Mount, whose top / Brightness had made invisible . . . ." (5. 598–99). Again,

> the most High
> Eternal Father from his secret Cloud,
> Amidst in Thunder utter'd thus his voice. [10. 31–33]

And again Milton indicates that the Unknowable is known only to the Logos, who in turn reveals him to man. Such revelation is the mediatorial function of the Logos.

> So spake the Father, and unfolding bright
> Toward the right hand his Glory, on the Son
> Blaz'd forth unclouded Deity; he full
> Resplendent all his Father manifest
> Express'd . . . . [10. 63–67]

But, it may be asked, was not the unknowability of God simply a commonplace of Christian theology? Certainly it was, but still one cannot fail to recognize the difference in the tendency to think of God in terms of his known attributes on the one hand and to approach by the *via negativa* on the other. It is the difference between Ames and Eckhart or Calvin and Dionysius. Because they see God in terms of darkness, the mystics of the negative way tend toward the poetic and rhapsodic in their depiction of him; the ineffable that must be expressed can only be formulated in mystical and lyrical terms. No reader of *Paradise Lost* can doubt that the *via negativa* is Milton's most inspired and continuous approach to the Deity. By this approach he preserves the sanctity and transcendence of the God who is the Cloud of Unknowing revealed only to the Son. Rufus Jones has said of Eckhart that no one has gone further "in the direction of removing all anthropomorphic traits from God." [60] His statement applies to the entire tradition and it is certainly true of the imagery of the Deity in *Paradise Lost*.

---

[60] Jones, p. 225.

A more significant auxiliary concept of the *ex Deo* theory, perhaps the most characteristic and essential one, is that of *egressus–regressus*, the theory that all which emanated from God would ultimately return to him. Plotinus conceived of a kind of cosmic convection current in which life first flowed out from the Fount of Rest descending through all hierarchies of Being and then ultimately ascending by the same degrees. The life of nature, for Plotinus, was a constant aspiration toward the higher forms of activity.[61] This Plotinian concept is brilliantly embodied in Augustine's declaration that all creation yearns toward God.

Plotinus described this cosmic systole and diastole as follows: "The procession of intelligence consists in descending to things that occupy the lowest rank, and which have an inferior nature . . . . Finally there occurs a conversion which brings them back from the lower to the higher natures." [62]

The pseudo-Dionysius accepts the emanation and return, postulating an advance along the hierarchies of being from simple to complex as life is added to mere being, consciousness is added to life, and, finally, as rationality is added to consciousness.[63] Further, according to Dionysius, as life progresses in the scale of being it comes nearer to God and increasingly participates in his perfections.[64]

Erigena, as we would expect, systematized the idea and worked out in more detail both the procession and return. He taught that all proceeds from the super-essentiality of God which can only be called Non-Being or the Unknowable. Next to the Unknowable is the Logos which, although central to his system, remains largely a metaphysical abstraction conceived to be the totality of primordial causes. These causes are the beginning of every essence and all life.[65] Descending out of these abstract and primordial causes, God may be said to "become" in the effects of those causes and is manifested in his theophanies.[66] For Erigena, the Son is part of the "forthgoing of God" and hence is a second cause, as he was for Milton. Only God is without cause.[67] Further, Erigena stated that it was not from the essence but rather from the

[61] Inge, *Plotinus*, 1: 155.

[62] *Plotinos — Complete Works*, trans. Kenneth S. Guthrie (London, c. 1918), *Enneads*, 4. 8. 7 (1: 131).

[63] Rolt, p. 25.

[64] Rolt, p. 114.

[65] Cf. Blewett, p. 287.

[66] Erigenae, *De Divisione*, p. 243.

[67] See Bett, *Erigena*, p. 25. Cf. Blewett, p. 283.

substance of the Father that the Son proceeded, a position which Milton also held.[68]

The *regressus* of all creatures to the Divine, as developed by Erigena, is of particular interest to the student of Milton. Erigena conceived of a progression up the chain of being as earthy corporeality acquired vital motion, as vital motion was transformed into sense, sense into reason and reason into soul.[69] Ultimately the lower and disparate faculties are progressively unified in higher faculties. Thus far the progression is all within the natural order. In the supernatural order, Soul is transformed into Intelligence, Intelligence into Wisdom, and Wisdom unites the purified soul with the Divine Wisdom which is the Logos. Thus the soul, through the Logos, is reunited with God.[70]

The forthgoing and return is a fundamental part of Eckhart's thought also.

Things all flow out of him as light to manifest the hidden light. . . . Herein lies proof that all things are light, the Father having poured them forth to manifest his concealment, even as all things are shown a light to light them back into themselves, those who do not choose to turn away.
. . . Know, all creatures are asking this question, they are eager for being, to find divine being; all study of the works of nature is nothing but a search, a quest for, a question about the dwelling of God.[71]

Nicholas of Cusa, who owed much to Eckhart, develops the same concept. All being begins and ends in God, he said, as motion begins from rest and ends in rest.[72]

Milton, too, develops the doctrine of the emanation and return.

> O *Adam*, one Almighty is, from whom
> All things proceed, and up to him return,
> If not deprav'd from good . . . . [5. 469–71]

In his further development of this theme, Milton shows a progression both in nature and in man more or less corresponding with that which Erigena had shown in nature as a whole. In plants, Milton says, the root comes first, motionless and dull; from it springs the green stalk which in turn produces leaves,

---

[68] *Works*, 14: 193.

[69] Erigenae, *De Divisione*, p. 591. This passage is important enough to be reproduced: "Ac *primus* erit mutatio terreni corporis in motum vitalem: *secundus* vitalis motus in sensum; *tertius* sensus in rationem; *dehinc* rationis in animum; in quo finis totius rationalis creaturae constituitur" (5. 39). Cf. *Paradise Lost*, 5. 479–87.

[70] Erigenae, *De Divisione*, p. 591; cf. Bett, *Erigena*, p. 86, and Blewett, p. 327.

[71] *Eckhart*, 2: 191, 128.

[72] Bett, *Nicholas of Cusa*, p. 105.

> last the bright consummate flow'r
> Spirits odorous breathes . . . . [5. 481–82]

Thus is shown a progression from dull matter to odorous spirits within the vegetable realm. That realm is transcended when the fruit of plants, eaten by man, is "by gradual scale sublim'd." Renaissance science taught that food generates vital heat which in turn generates the three kinds of spirits which correspond to the threefold division of the soul. At the highest level, the "intellectual" spirits, as Milton calls them, knit the material and immaterial parts of man together, some of these spirits passing over into pure intellectual substance.[73] It is by this process, according to Milton, that the soul is enabled to receive life, sense, fancy, understanding, and reason. Nor is this process confined to man and his world; it is rather universal and cosmic.

> of Elements
> The grosser feeds the purer, Earth the Sea,
> Earth and the Sea feed Air, the Air those Fires
> Ethereal, and as lowest first the Moon . . . . [5. 415–18]

Thus Milton shows the *regressus*, the yearning of all life toward the common source.

Another auxiliary concept of the *ex Deo* theory, another symptom that goes to make up the syndrome, is the theory that if all life comes from God, no being can ever be finally annihilated. One finds this concept in Plotinus and in the other thinkers in this tradition. Erigena, for example, states, "When it is said that the last enemy will be destroyed . . . this does not mean that his substance, created of God, is to perish . . . ."[74] Eckhart teaches the same thing when he says that God is not the destroyer of nature but the perfecter of it even as grace crowns nature rather than destroying it. "It is not in God," he says, "to destroy any thing that has being."[75]

Milton, in *De Doctrina*, resolutely commits himself to the same proposition. Matter, he says, "proceeded incorruptible from God; and even since the fall it remains incorruptible as far as concerns its essence." And speaking of the doctrine of *ex Deo*, he says, "I proceed to consider the necessary consequence of this doctrine, namely, that if all things are not only from God, but of God, no created thing can be finally annihilated."[76]

---

[73] E. M. W. Tillyard, *The Elizabethan World Picture* (London, 1943), p. 63.

[74] Quoted by Blewett, p. 321, from *De Divisione*, 5. 27.

[75] *Eckhart*, 2: 35–36.

[76] *Works*, 15: 23–25, 27.

There is one other auxiliary concept which the *ex Deo* theory seemed logically to suggest, a concept which was either held or implied by the thinkers in the tradition, and that is the idea of a plurality or an infinity of worlds. Erigena taught that creation was an integral part of the nature of God and that he, therefore, necessarily created. This necessity, he explained, was that which belonged to a moral nature and was therefore a "free necessity," God acting according to the necessity of his own nature.[77]

Eckhart held that creation was the eternal process of God's thought. He envisioned an infinite Deity whose essential nature is creative. In fact he said that *creare*, meaning *conferre esse*, was the principal function of Deity.[78] A doctrine of an infinite Deity whose nature is essentially creative implies an infinite creation.

Nicholas of Cusa, like Eckhart, taught that creation was a necessary consequence of the very nature of God, but that the necessity was only moral, in no way external. Nicholas' own theory of creation as a circle that begins and ends in God also implies a continuous creativity, which in turn demands a plurality of worlds.[79] It was probably his study of Cusanus that set Bruno thinking about an infinite universe.[80]

Whether Milton believed in a multiplicity of worlds is, I suppose, open to question. Certainly he "uses" a finite universe in *Paradise Lost*. Also, Adam asks Raphael what "Mov'd the Creator in his holy Rest / Through all Eternity so late to build" (7. 91–92), which implies that the creation of the earth was a unique event. God himself announces that the creation of man is for a special purpose, that of filling up the vacancy in the heavenly hierarchy created by the fall of the angels (7. 150–61). On the other hand, Milton shows unmistakable signs of dissatisfaction with the idea of a single creation. In *De Doctrina*, he raises the question of what occupied God from all eternity, and dismisses impatiently the idea that he was wholly concerned for all that time with devising the divine decrees.[81] Further, Milton is definitely attracted to the idea of a plurality of worlds, although even in *Paradise Lost* he seems wary of speculating about it. The universe, Raphael tells Adam, is large

> That Man may know he dwells not in his own;
> An Edifice too large for him to fill,
> Lodg'd in a small partition, and the rest
> Ordain'd for uses to his Lord best known. [8. 103–6]

---

[77] Bett, *Erigena*, pp. 94–96.
[78] Otto, *Mysticism: East and West*, p. 87; Bett, *Erigena*, p. 191.
[79] Bett, *Nicholas of Cusa*, pp. 110–11, 105.
[80] William Boulting, *Giordano Bruno* (London, 1914), p. 30.
[81] *Works*, 15: 3–5, 29–31.

When Satan is flying toward earth he makes his way through stars which "nigh hand seem'd other Worlds . . . but who dwelt happy there / He stay'd not to enquire" (3. 566, 570–71). Raphael does specifically suggest the possibility of life on the moon (8. 145), and the angels' hymn after the creation of the earth goes a good deal further.

> Witness this new-made World, another Heav'n
> From Heaven Gate not far, founded in view
> On the clear *Hyaline*, the Glassy Sea;
> Of amplitude almost immense, with Stars
> Numerous, and every Star perhaps a World
> Of destin'd habitation . . . . [7. 617–22]

The phrase "almost immense" may be the clearest indication of Milton's meaning. He is using the word with the full meaning of the Latin *inmensus*, so great that it cannot be measured. In *De Doctrina* Milton named immensity as one of the attributes of God. What he seems to imply is that only God is infinite and that the universe is "almost" so. It is very much like Nicholas of Cusa's statement that the universe "is infinity contracted to the relatively infinite." [82]

Few readers will fail to perceive the force of Douglas Bush's remark that "Milton's imagination responds, as no other English poet's has responded with equal power, to the conception of infinite space." [83] And Milton speculates with what seems to me imaginative conviction that this "almost immense" space is the stage for the creative activity of Deity.

Thus the description of the syndrome is as complete as I am able to make it. Other affinities of Milton for the *ex Deo* tradition will be suggested, but those I am aware of that are capable of demonstration are those which have been discussed: namely that God is the immanent ground of all things, yet wholly transcendent and best approached by the negative way; that there is a procession of all being from the Divine and a yearning to return; that all created beings, inasmuch as they are outflowings of the Divine, are indestructible; and, finally, that the creative activity of an infinite God strongly implies a plurality or infinity of worlds. To these general propositions, I think it can be shown that every thinker in the *ex Deo* tradition, including Milton, assented. Surely it is obvious that the main movement of mind in the seventeenth century was from Greek dualism, which had something of a late flower-

---

[82] Nicholas of Cusa, *Of Learned Ignorance*, trans. Fr. G. Heron (New Haven, 1954), p. 80.

[83] *"Paradise Lost" in Our Time*, 2d ed. (New York, 1948), p. 51.

ing in Descartes, to metaphysical monism and to the later Idealists. Hegel's debt, especially to Eckhart but also to Böhme, is well known, as is Spinoza's to Crescas, Moses of Cordova, and other Neoplatonists. If Milton is placed in this tradition, he may lose something of solitary grandeur, but he becomes more comprehensible when he is seen in a movement central to his age.

There is one other auxiliary concept associated with the *ex Deo* theory, another corollary of the general tradition, but one that is difficult to demonstrate. The difficulty arises not from inability to perceive it, but rather because it is a matter of tone and feeling rather than of declarative statement. For the *ex Deo* theory, more than the *ex nihilo*, emphasizes the immanence of God in creation. Thus the corollary of the *ex Deo* theory of creation is a theory of a deiform nature. Such a theory induces a feeling for the beauty manifested in all forms of life. Plotinus, Dionysius, Erigena, Nicholas of Cusa, especially Eckhart and Böhme, all have a feeling for nature that is something more than an abstract perception and appreciation of forms and colors; it tends to be "Wordsworthian" in its deep love and affinity for the living forms of nature that reveal the immanent presence of the Beautiful. For Plotinus, says Dean Inge, "the natural world, which we see with our eyes, is spiritual throughout and instinct with life . . . ." Recognizing that nature is not the Beautiful itself, but rather an image of it, Plotinus asks, "But could there be a more beautiful image?" [84]

Blewett says that Erigena had a keen eye and affection for the face of nature, and he continues, "the God who goes forth from Himself, communicates Himself, and gives rise to a universe which in the ordered scale of its existences is full of harmony and beauty and in its natural arrangements testifies of spiritual truths . . . ." [85] For those who accept the *ex Deo* theory, and for whom it is something more than an intellectual counter, the world is literally "charged with the grandeur of God." The universe created *ex Deo* is an organic universe and the finer breath of its being is divine.

Milton's contemporary Ralph Cudworth, in speaking of the mechanistic world of the seventeenth century, the creation of Descartes, Hobbes, and others, said, "They made a kind of dead and wooden world, as it were a carved statue, that hath nothing neither vital nor magical at all in it." [86] Such a universe Cudworth found "highly obnoxious" and he constructs a different

---

[84] Inge, *Plotinus*, 1: 161–62, 198.
[85] Blewett, *The Study of Nature*, p. 275, 292.
[86] *The True Intellectual System of the Universe*, ed. Thomas Birch (London, 1845), 1: 221.

one in which the earth is permeated by soul and does not subsist "alone by itself as a dead thing, but is still livingly united to [God], essentially dependent. on him, always supported and upheld, quickened and enlivened, acted and pervaded by him . . . ." [87]

With such wholly opposed conceptions of the universe — the polar opposites of the mechanistic and deiform — struggling for the possession of the minds of the age, it is unlikely that Milton could have been unaware of the conflict or that he could have viewed with any more complacency than did Cudworth the ascendancy of mechanistic materialism.

With the conflict over the nature of Nature in mind, it is interesting to read again Milton's account of the creation in *Paradise Lost.* Here rhythm, sound, and image are united in the depiction of an organic, fecund, and vital universe. Here is the Abyss with the great wings brooding over it, the fertility gods of masculine sun and feminine earth, the sexual love of man awakening cosmic echoes, the water spawning into life, the plastic and seminal earth burgeoning into ordered and harmonious forms of being, varied, intricate, vital, lovely, and mysterious.

Against the barrenness of the world of pulleys and levers, wearisome beyond utterance, against the abstract and impersonal horror of the great machine, Milton created an organic universe and a deiform nature, glowing with vitality, permeated by symbols of life and love, possessed of a beauty that mirrored the Source of its being. It is difficult not to feel that Milton's universe is both a response and an answer to the rising mechanism and materialism of his age and that his *ex Deo* theory of creation provided him with the concepts and orientations from which such a universe could be constructed. In constructing it, we may presume that he fulfilled his own needs. I believe it is not too much to say that he also met the needs of an age.

---

[87] Ibid., 1: 515.

The War in Heaven:
The Merkabah

J. H. ADAMSON

Milton was a poet of the Logos; the traditional images of the Logos such as the sun and its radiance, dance, music, song, and the harmony of the spheres are close to the artistic center of his work. There was also another and much more specialized image of the Logos which Milton employed in the sixth and seventh books of *Paradise Lost*, and that is the image of the Divine Chariot. To the Jewish mystic, after a long period of historical development, that chariot had come to symbolize the chariot of the Logos.

The image of the flaming chariot originated in a wild vision recorded in the first and tenth chapters of the Book of Ezekiel. This vision seems to have fascinated the ancient Hebrews, for the passages in which it is recorded are an exotic intrusion, quite different from the basic Old Testament writings. The vision is more likely to puzzle than fascinate the modern reader who comes to it unprepared; there is, for example, the matter of the cherubs who surround the chariot. To the casual reader that word conveys a picture of those aerodynamically unsound little creatures, the winged Cupid and Psyche of the Alexandrians. But the Hebrew *keruv* was something else entirely, a fabulous animal, a symbolic counterpart of the power and creative energy of the divinity with which it was identified.

In the vision Ezekiel saw a cloud of fire, like a whirlwind. This moving cloud had wheels, and its motive power came from four cherubim, each of which had four faces. Lightning bolts shot forth from the chariot and the entire vision was bathed in an amber light; in fact, the vehicle appears to be, in some sense, a chariot of light.

Above the fabulous beasts there is a "firmament"; above the firmament is a sapphire throne upon which is seated the likeness of a man, and it was this likeness that came to symbolize the Logos. The most remarkable thing about the chariot, according to Ezekiel, is that it moves according to the spirit (*ruach*), and he repeats this significant fact several times: the movement of all the parts of the chariot in harmony and order is somehow central to the final meaning of the vision. In all, it is a mysterious, strangely moving and complex image that cried out for mystical and metaphysical elaboration. Before analyzing Milton's use of this apparition, it is desirable to seek its ultimate source and to attempt to trace its intellectual development before Milton's time.

Ezekiel's vision had many counterparts in the art of other Semitic and Asiatic peoples. The Canaanites, Arameans and Hittites usually represented their gods as standing on the backs of animals or as seated on thrones being borne by animals.[1] This custom has led scholars to speculate that the infamous golden calves of the Israelites were not themselves deities, but rather were intended to be vehicles for that Deity whose nature was not yet fully understood. Later, in the Temple of Solomon, Yahweh was thought of as an invisible deity enthroned above two cherubim which were apparently winged sphinxes.[2]

In a remarkable study Heinrich Zimmer has explained a good deal of the mystery which has surrounded this god–animal relationship in which the animal serves as a vehicle for the god.[3] This device of god and vehicle had its origin in the Mesopotamian valley, where it can be traced back to 1500 B.C., and it may be even older. Zimmer believes that the symbol of the divine vehicle originated by analogy with the technique of picture writing in which a symbol called a "determinant" was placed beneath the pictograph to confirm its meaning. The pictograph and its determinant came to have an essential relationship; later, the god and his vehicle were similarly essentially related.

This Mesopotamian device spread westward and appears to be the origin of the Hebrew image of the chariot, but it was also exported eastward to India where its development, while having no direct influence on Milton, is nevertheless of some peripheral interest to Miltonic studies. In Hindu mythology,

---

[1] William F. Albright, *From Stone Age to Christianity* (Baltimore, 1940), p. 229.

[2] Ibid.

[3] Heinrich Zimmer, *Myths and Symbols in Indian Art and Civilization*, ed. Joseph Campbell (New York, 1962), pp. 69 ff.

Vishnu has a vehicle which is called the Garuda. This animal is usually represented with "wings, human arms, vulture legs, and a curved beaklike nose." Vishnu rides into battle on this cherub-like creature carrying "the fiery sun disk of a thousand spokes." [4] It is this weapon which he hurls against his opponent, the great serpent which, like a river, emerges from a cavern in the dark earth. In this myth the bird and serpent represent the forces of light and darkness. Milton seems to have arrived independently at some of the concepts embodied in this myth.

Of much more direct influence, however, are certain ideas which had arisen in Greek thought and which, by way of Philo and the mystical Jews, came to be part of the context of the symbolism of Ezekiel's chariot.

Many of the pre-Socratic Greeks were concerned with *logos* and, over a century or two, the word changed and developed in meaning. Although the Milesians differed among themselves, all held that there was a material substratum out of which the cosmos arose. This substratum they invested with mysterious spiritual qualities for, they said, the substance of which things were made also, in some manner, continued to shape and direct the creation. To illustrate this idea they developed a metaphor from navigation: the basic substance "steered" the universe as a pilot steers a ship. Aristotle knew this concept of the pre-Socratics and was puzzled by it. "It appears to be the originator of things, to surround and direct them . . . . And this, it seems, is the divine, for it is immortal and indestructible, as Anaximander and most of the natural philosophers say." [5]

Heraclitus gave a new and deeper meaning to the traditional pre-Socratic material. Before him, philosophers had spoken of finding a *logos* or rational explanation of the universe. Heraclitus said that the explanation was the Logos. The true Logos was not the explanation of a process but the vision of the actual process itself. Reacting against predecessors who had postulated the permanence and unchangeability of Being, Heraclitus said that change was universal, but this change occurred according to a plan. That plan was the *Logos*, a rational design, the ultimate Reality, an island of permanence in a sea of change.

Because it was still difficult, in spite of Pythagorean immaterialism, to divorce life from substance, to escape from Milesian hylozoism, Heraclitus closely identified his *Logos* with the element of fire. This fiery substance, he

---

[4] Ibid., pp. 75–76.

[5] *Basic Works of Aristotle*, ed. Richard McKeon (New York, 1941), *Physics*, 203 b 10.

said, was divine, self-moving and probably surrounded the earth like a bright, enveloping cloud. But it also penetrated the cosmos, irradiated it, and brought about its harmony and order. He too uses the metaphor of the pilot steering a ship: his *Logos* "steers" the universe. "That which is wise is one: to understand the purpose which steers all things through all things" (fr. 41).[6] This purpose constitutes a "hidden harmony" (fr. 54).

After Heraclitus, the concept of Logos was further refined by Anaxagoras, by Plato and by Aristotle. Anaxagoras has said that the *logos* of the universe was Mind (fr. 12); being unmixed with matter, it was independent of it, had complete understanding of it and complete power over it.[7] This revolutionary idea that mind rather than substance was the basic reality initially interested both Socrates and Aristotle, both of whom developed their own theories to account for rationality and order. Neither appears to have used the symbol of the pilot "steering" the universe; that metaphor lived on, however, for Numenius knows it and makes an extended elaboration of it, using Platonic terminology. For him the Demiurge is the pilot of the universe.[8]

Before Numenius, Philo Judaeus also knew and used this metaphor. Deploring the fact that weak minds had thought Moses attributed the cause of all things to fate and necessity, Philo gave what he believed to be the true Mosaic teaching. "He envisaged something else higher than and antecedent to these, a Someone who is borne on the universe like a charioteer or pilot. He steers the common bark of the world, in which all things sail; He guides that winged chariot, the whole heaven, exerting an absolute sovereignty which knows no authority but its own." [9] In another work, Philo pursues the same metaphor. "While the Word [logos] is the charioteer of the Powers, He Who talks is seated in the chariot, giving directions to the charioteer for the right wielding of the reins of the Universe." [10] In this passage, God and the Logos are compared to the warrior and the driver in a Homeric chariot. The warrior directs the driver who in turn guides the chariot of the universe.

So far the development seems clear. A very ancient image of a god and his vehicle, essentially related, came to the Hebrews from the east. Later, the

---

[6] Quotations from the pre-Socratic philosophers are taken from Kathleen Freeman, *Ancilla to the Pre-Socratic Philosophers* (Cambridge, Mass., 1962).

[7] Cf. Kathleen Freeman, *Companion to the Pre-Socratic Philosophers* (Oxford, 1959), p. 267.

[8] *Numenius*, trans. K. S. Guthrie (London, 1917), Liber 6, fr. 32.

[9] *Philo*, trans. F. H. Colson and G. H. Whitaker, Loeb Classical Library (Cambridge, Mass., 1949), 4, "Who Is the Heir of Divine Things," ¶ 60 (pp. 437–39).

[10] Ibid., 5, "Of Flight and Finding," 19 (p. 65).

theorizings of the Greeks and especially the logos metaphor were also to some extent adapted by mystical Jews. But at this point it appears that there is a lacuna, for nowhere so far as I know does Philo say explicitly that the ancient logos metaphor of a pilot steering the universe is embodied in or conveyed by Ezekiel's vision of the likeness of a man steering a chariot of light. Nevertheless in mystical Judaism, the Philonic idea of the universe as the chariot of the Logos was ingeniously adapted to the details of Ezekiel's vision. Ultimately this symbolic chariot, known by its Hebrew name of *Merkabah*, became the most sacred and secret piece of lore in all Judaic thought. And it is this same *Merkabah* which appears in *Paradise Lost* at the critical moment in the War in Heaven.

The oral traditions of Judaism are called the *Cabbala*. The tradition centered especially around two biblical events, the creation, designated by the Hebrew word *Bereshith* (in the beginning), and, as we have seen, the vision of the *Merkabah*. These oral traditions were established quite early, for the *Mishnah*, the earliest part of the Talmud, compiled by the end of the second century A.D., prohibits the indiscriminate dissemination of the doctrines of the oral tradition.[11]

Of these two biblical events and the mystical doctrines which they embodied, the *Merkabah* was considered the more sacred. It could be discussed only with one person at a time, and that person had to be capable of understanding the inner meaning of spiritual things, a sage in other words.[12] That the oral tradition was considered both sacred and significant can be illustrated by observing the attitude displayed toward it by the great rationalist of the twelfth century, Maimonides. He acknowledged that the sages had praised those who kept the mysteries of *Bereshith* and *Merkabah* and blamed those who revealed them. The same sages, he said, "have clearly stated that the Divine Chariot includes matters too deep and too profound for the ordinary intellect."[13] When he concluded his own purposely vague interpretation, he breathed a sigh of relief. "Do not expect or hope to hear from me after this chapter a word on this subject, either explicitly or implicitly, for all that could be said on it has been said, though with great difficulty and struggle."[14] It is surely relevant to recall at this point that in *Paradise Lost*, when Adam asks

---

[11] Ernst Mueller, *History of Jewish Mysticism* (Oxford, 1946), pp. 42 ff. and ch. 3, n. 1.

[12] J. Abelson, *Jewish Mysticism* (London, 1913), p. 36.

[13] *The Guide to the Perplexed*, trans. M. Friedlander, The English and Philosophical Library, 30 (London, 1885), 3: 1–2.

[14] Ibid., p. 23.

Raphael to tell him of the War in Heaven, a war that is resolved by the appearance of the Messiah in the *Merkabah* of Ezekiel's vision, Raphael tells him that not only is it difficult to reveal it to a mortal man, but also that it is perhaps not lawful to do so (5. 563–70).

Actually the vision of the chariot came to have two distinct though related meanings. One of these meanings was adapted to personal mysticism. The Jewish mystic *"felt* instinctively that the *Merkabah* typified the human longing for the sight of the Divine Presence and companionship with it." The chariot was the mystical vehicle which carried the ecstatic worshipper into the realm of essence. All mystics wished to be *Merkabah* riders.[15]

The vision of the Chariot had another significance, however, one that went beyond the idea of a personal union with the Divine. It was also an elaborate symbol for the Logos steering the universe; it signified a universal harmony of all being with the Divine Will. The details of the vision were fitted into a theory of emanation like that of Plotinus except, in Hebrew thought, it was said to have occurred in four stages,[16] harmonizing with the mystically significant fact that there were four letters in the sacred name of Jahweh. The four emanations constituted the four realms of being and these were symbolized by four aspects of the vision: the Heavenly Man, the throne, the firmament and the cherubim.

Abelson says that in general the *Merkabah* vision signified the idealized universe.[17] Such a universe might be the one preexistent in the Mind of God, untainted by evil or mutability, or it might be the future universe when the creation is restored and all things are again subject to the Creator. *Bereshith*, in other words, might signify the original creation and *Merkabah* the recreation. This is how some in the seventeenth century interpreted it, and in this view, the vision of the chariot implies a cycle of creation, consequent separation from the Divine, and finally a restoration in which the Divine Will is again all in all. Both creation and re-creation are accomplished through the Logos.

This interpretation of the Divine Chariot as the vehicle of the Logos was ideally suited to convey Milton's basic conflict of harmony against disorder, of Logos against Chaos. The significant question which must now be answered is whether such an interpretation was known in his time and readily available

---

[15] Abelson, *Jewish Mysticism*, pp. 33–35.

[16] Mueller, *History of Jewish Mysticism*, pp. 79 ff; Abelson, *Jewish Mysticism*, p. 107.

[17] Abelson, *Jewish Mysticism*, p. 97.

to him. Unless that can be established, the entire matter becomes mere speculation. I believe that it can be shown that Milton had reasonable access to
Cabbalistic interpretations.

A literate Englishman would have known something about them from Sir
Walter Ralegh's *History of the World.* In 2. 4. 5–8, Ralegh enters into his
famous digression on law. In discussing the Positive Law, he dichotomizes it
into the written law contained in the Bible and the oral law which he defines
as "the doctrine and religion of the patriarchs before the written law of
Moses, which some call Cabala." At first, he says, this unwritten law was not
concealed from anyone; it was handed down openly from the patriarchs to
their children. But later, the Jews added "the interpretation of secret mysteries, reserved in the bosoms of their priests, and unlawful to be uttered to
the people."

Later (2. 6. 6), Ralegh discusses Hermes Trismegistus whom some scholars, he says, have believed to be Moses himself. Hermes bears no resemblance
to the Moses of the Torah; but the Hermetic writings do embody the kind of
esoteric Neoplatonism found in the *Cabbala.* In 2. 6. 7, Ralegh refers to
Bereshith and *Merkabah*; the first, he says, is the "works of nature," the
second is the "works of miracle," the one is *sapientiam naturae* and the other
is *sapientiam divinitatis.*

There were also two biblical commentaries that discussed the Jewish
mysteries and both of these held a special interest for Milton. One of them
was written by John Diodati, the uncle of his closest friend; the other by Hugo
Grotius for whom Milton had a lifelong admiration. John Diodati, in "The
Analysis" of the Book of Ezekiel, chapter 1, v. 4 (page 1 of the unnumbered
pages of "The Analysis") writes,

His *consecration* to his function, by a glorious vision, which, whether it be a type of Gods
providence ruling all sublunary things (typified by the wheels) by the ministery of Angels,
(typified by the four creatures) or whether it points out Gods conduct of the Babylonish
army to destroy *Jerusalem*, I shall leave the Reader to inform himself. . . . A vision it is,
so mysterious, so difficult to be understood, that the Jewish Church, did not permit any
man to read it, untill he were thirty years of age: but no man to explain it, but only the
generall heads . . . .[18]

The interpretation of this passage by Grotius is interesting because it
shows a recognition of the relationship, to be discussed later, between *Bereshith* and *Merkabah*, and calls attention to the interpretation of Maimonides.

---

[18] *Annotations Upon the Holy Bible,* 3d ed. (London, 1651).

4. Et vidi) Visum hoc quod sequitur, מרכב id est, *currum*, vocant Hebraei, et hoc nomine
appellant secretiorem Theologiam de Deo et Angelis; sicut Physicam appellant בראשית
(*In principio*), ab initio Geneseos desumto nomine. Nolunt autem Iudaei has duas
Scripturae partes legi nisi ab hominibus prouectae aetatis.

Grotius then cites Maimonides.[19]

Both of these interpretations are vague, but they must have aroused curiosity and speculation concerning the "secret theology."

Alexander Gill, who was Milton's headmaster at St. Paul's, shows a more precise knowledge of the meaning and relationship of *Bereshith* and *Merkabah*. "And as for that glory of His, which is manifest in the creature, it shall be more wonderfull and excellent in that worke of His recreation, which the *Cabalists* call *de Mercava*, when the creature in the world to come shall be brought to glory, and be able to consider the super-excellency of His mercy and goodnesse, than it is in this worke, *de Bereshith*, or state of creation in this present world." [20]

The Cabbalistic writings particularly excited the Neoplatonic Christians of the seventeenth century because they found in them a doctrine of the Logos. They apparently believed that they could convince the Jews that this doctrine was identical with Christian theology. Herr Knorr Rosenroth, who translated parts of the *Cabbala* into Latin, predicted a mass conversion of Jewry. It was said that Pico della Mirandola became interested in the *Cabbala* for primarily the same reason.[21]

Henry More, Milton's coeval at Christ's College, with whom Rosenroth corresponded about these writings, said that if his theories on the *Cabbala* proved to be true, the restored tradition would convince Jews that Christians do not "worship the *incarnate* Logos *for nought*." [22] Further, he maintained that the Cabbalistic writings were a *"Tradition of Moses,"* and, he continued, inasmuch as "Christ is nothing but *Moses* unveiled, I think it was a special act of Providence, that this hidden *Cabbala* came so seasonably to the knowledge of the *Gentiles* . . . ." [23] More apparently failed to see that a Logos theory did

---

[19] *Annotationes in Vetus Testamentum*, ed. Vogel and Doderlein (Halae, 1775–76), 2: 247.

[20] *Sacred Philosophie* (London, 1635), Article 3, pp. 97–98. Note: In this edition, pagination starts over with Article 3.

[21] A. E. Waite, *The Holy Kabbalah* (London, 1929), p. 82.

[22] *A Collection of Several Philosophical Writings of Henry More*, 4th ed. (London, 1712), "The Preface General," xxvii.

[23] Ibid., dedicatory epistle to "The Conjectura Cabbalistica," iv, v (mis-paged as iii in this edition).

not require the adoption of the specifically Christian corollary that the Logos had been made flesh.

That the vision of the Divine Chariot was understood in the seventeenth century to be a vision of the Logos can be demonstrated with exactness from the writings of Henry More. "But the greatest Power over all hath Jesus Christ, or the Soul of the *Messias,* united with the eternal *Logos,* as is manifest from the Vision of *Ezekiel,* or the *Mercavah :* which is nothing else but a Representation of this so mighty Polity and Government of Christ, reaching from the highest Aethereal Regions, or from what the *Cabbalists* call the *Ariluthick* World to this *Asiathick* and *Terrestrial* World, in which our selves are." [24] In his *Divine Dialogues,* More again returns to an exposition of the *Merkabah.* He finds the key to the vision in the fact that the chariot is wholly obedient to the will of God[25] and then explains what the chariot is. "The Vision of the *Cherubim* or Chariot of God seen by *Ezekiel . . .* is the Pattern of the Angelical Polity over which God immediately rules . . . . Now the great design of all is, that in the fulness of time the Church upon Earth may be his Chariot as fully and commandingly as the Angelical Orders in Heaven." [26] One of the characters in the Dialogue asks who rides in the Chariot and the reply is, "The Heavenly Humanity of the Son of God. His very Title is writ in Amber . . . if you read it *Cabbalistically.*" [27] This last cryptic remark can be analyzed with some probability. In the Hebrew alphabet each letter represents a number as well as a sound. Consequently each word has a numerical value as well as a conceptual meaning. To read "cabbalistically" generally refers to the process of determining the number of a word and then finding other words which have the same numerical value. It was believed that similar numerical values were the outward sign of a mystical affinity in the words themselves. The word "amber" is the Hebrew word *Chashmal* which means "light." It is the modern Hebrew word for electricity. One of the qualities of amber, for which it was much prized in the ancient world, was the mystical light which it seemed to emanate. The numerical value of *Chashmal* is 378. The numerical value of the word *Messiah* is 358. But if the second singular possessive suffix is added to Messiah, a form rather common in Old Testament writings, the necessary points are added and the two numbers are equal. It is as if the phrases "sacred light" and "your (or thy) Messiah" had the same numeri-

---

[24] Ibid., "The Immortality of the Soul," p. 206.
[25] Second ed. (London, 1713), p. 434.
[26] Ibid., p. 433.
[27] Ibid., p. 440.

cal value and hence a mystical affinity. Or there is another possibility. The Hebrew word for God was always considered too sacred to be written and hence two "yods" were substituted for it. Each yod had a value of ten points. Hence "Messiah of God" would also equal "amber" numerically.[28]

Such then is the evidence I have been able to discover. It indicates a reasonably widespread knowledge, in Milton's time, of Ezekiel's vision as the central mystery of the Jewish tradition. It further indicates that Henry More had a precise understanding of its meaning some thirty years before the publication of *Paradise Lost*. I do not think that Milton, in his poem, attempted to work out a technically precise meaning of the vision as Henry More had done. But he must have known that from the earliest times the Logos had been imaged as the Pilot or Charioteer who governed the course of the universe. He would have seen that the Jewish mystics had interpreted the *Merkabah* as a symbolic vision of an idealized universe "steered" by the Logos. He saw that the Divine Chariot contained a vision of universal harmony which he had expressed previously through the imagery of song, music and dance.

In the War in Heaven, Satan, the dark angel, sits in a "Sun-bright Chariot." But the amber light of the Divine Chariot comes from the Sun beyond the sun. It is the "holy Light" invoked at the beginning of Book 3, and it is this metaphysical light, flaming out of the divine chariot, which destroys the forces of darkness.

When the Divine Chariot goes forth to battle, Milton first develops the theme of unity. Michael

<blockquote>
soon reduc'd
His Army, circumfus'd on either Wing,
Under thir Head imbodied all in one. [6. 777–79]
</blockquote>

The theme of unity and harmony continues as the hills that had been uprooted in battle return to their places and the scarred earth is covered with flowers. Then "one Spirit" rules all the symbols of the vision: the eyes, the wheels, the faces and each eye "glar'd lightning." In that moment of unity the powers of darkness are helpless. When the creation is obedient to the Divine Will, evil cannot exist. Only the separateness of the creature from the Creator gives evil its scope and power. One is reminded here of the *Nativity Ode*. When the universal harmony was heard, the demons fled and were overcome.

---

[28] This interpretation was pointed out to me by Professor Aharon Lichtenstein to whom I give sincere thanks.

If, as I believe, Milton's War in Heaven is an adaptation of the *Merkabah* theme, it is pertinent to enquire if he recognized the correlation between *Bereshith* and *Merkabah* as Gill, More and others had before him. Such a correlation would provide him with the kind of pattern that is one of the most characteristic features of his art.

An examination of the creation episode indicates that Milton has indeed developed a pattern. The battle in heaven is imaged as a kind of chaos; and similarly, in the Creation scene, Chaos is depicted in terms of a battle. The parallels are so close that passages might be transposed without serious loss of meaning or effect.

When the Word goes forth to create the world, he again rides in the Divine Chariot surrounded by the angels. When this host moves, the movement is spontaneous; they are guided by the one spirit within them. When the gates of heaven are opened, music is heard and, as the Word approaches Chaos, Milton employs the imagery of the battlefield. The Abyss was

> Outrageous as a Sea, dark, wasteful, wild,
> Up from the bottom turn'd by furious winds
> And surging waves, as Mountains to assault
> Heav'n's highth, and with the Centre mix the Pole. [7. 212–15]

In the War in Heaven mountains had been similarly uprooted and used as weapons. Also, when the War in Heaven raged, Milton compared it to "Nature's concord broke," that is, Chaos (6. 311). Only it was worse than war which "seem'd a civil Game" as "confusion heapt, / Upon confusion rose" (6. 667–69). And when the irresistible light shot forth from the chariot and the evil angels fell, "*Chaos* roared."

Uriel, who had witnessed the Creation, described it in imagery reminiscent of the War in Heaven.

> Confusion heard his voice, and wild uproar
> Stood rul'd, stood vast infinitude confin'd;
> Till at his second bidding darkness fled,
> Light shone, and order from disorder sprung. [3. 710–13]

In both the creation scene and in the War in Heaven, Logos, imaged as light and harmony, triumphs over Chaos, imaged as darkness and disorder.

And this is the basic pattern of *Paradise Lost.* There is an initial harmonious creation, followed by the introduction of chaos, and then a re-creation. As Satan introduced chaos into heaven, so he will later successfully introduce it into the mind of man. But the War in Heaven is also a primal analogue. As there is a triumphant Logos so there is an indwelling Logos in the mind of man which, aided by prevenient grace, can also triumph, although not without a cruel struggle which will manifest itself in the tragic history of mankind.

There is no indication that anyone before Milton had suggested that the Divine Chariot was a symbolic vehicle of war, a chariot of light, to be used against the powers of darkness. In mystical Jewish thought, it was a vision of the universal harmony. But implicit in such a vision is the counterforce. If the universe needed to be restored, something must have disrupted it and whatever it was must be overcome. As we have seen, Hindu mythology developed the idea of a primal conflict resolved when Vishnu, carried by a kind of cherub, employed the shafts of the sun against the serpent. Milton could not have known of such a development, but his artistic insight seems to have carried him in precisely the right direction. For stripped of all its mystical accretions and overburdens, of all its metaphysical subtleties, the vision of the Chariot must have been, in its earliest beginning, an imaginative symbolizing of the sun chariot upon whose daily and seasonal victories over the powers of darkness and chaos the life of the world depends.

The War in Heaven:
The Exaltation of the Son

W. B. HUNTER

I

One of the most perplexing but most important sections of *Paradise Lost* appears in Book 5, when God the Father, by whom the Son sat "imbosom'd," calls all of the angels together so that he may announce his decree that "this day" he has "begot" his only Son and has anointed him. The newly anointed Son (or Messiah, for Messiah means anointed) now appears at the right hand of the Father, who thereupon appoints him head of the angels and requires that they henceforth obey him:

> Hear all ye Angels, Progeny of Light,
> Thrones, Dominations, Princedoms, Virtues, Powers,
> Hear my Decree, which unrevok't shall stand.
> This day I have begot whom I declare
> My only Son, and on this holy Hill
> Him have anointed, whom ye now behold
> At my right hand; your Head I him appoint;
> And by my Self have sworn to him shall bow
> All knees in Heav'n, and shall confess him Lord. [5. 600–8]

The passage is central to the poem in that it is the first explicit event of the plot; from it ultimately derives all of the rest of the action of Milton's epic. But it is perplexing because the angels are already in existence to witness the begetting, whereas Abdiel shortly later declares to Satan that the newly begotten Son had himself been the instrument for their creation: neither singly nor as a group are they equal to the

> begotten Son[,] by whom
> As by his Word the mighty Father made
> All things. [5. 835–37]

Thus the newly begotten Son must have been antecedent to them.

David Masson first suggested a way out of the difficulty.[1] Milton, he thought, was distinguishing between the existence of the divine Logos or Word described at the opening of the Gospel of John, which had been in existence "in the beginning" and which had created everything, including the angels, and the recognition of the Word as Son at this later point in time. There is some evidence for this view. The lines which have been quoted from Abdiel's speech could imply that the newly begotten Son had earlier been the Word by which the Father had created everything. In his theological treatise, *Of Christian Doctrine*, Milton also argued that the Son had certainly "existed in the beginning under the name of the logos." [2] But these statements do not conclusively prove that he distinguished an earlier Word from a later Son, and the terms may be merely synonymous. Masson's argument that the "begetting" represents the recognition of the Word as Son may thus not have been alien to Milton's thought, but it does not explain for certain the passage in Book 5.

Sir Herbert Grierson went further by exploring the meaning of "beget" in this context.[3] Turning to the *Christian Doctrine*, he found that for Milton "the Father [is] said in Scripture to have begotten the Son in a double sense, the one literal, with reference to the production of the Son, the other metaphorical, with reference to his exaltation" (14: 181). The major proof text of the begetting is found in Psalm 2, which is the immediate source for *Paradise Lost* 5. 600 ff.: "Yet have I [the Father] set my King upon my holy hill of Zion. I will declare the decree: the Lord hath said unto me, Thou art my Son; this day have I begotten thee. Ask of me, and I shall give thee the heathen for thine inheritance, and the uttermost parts of the earth for thy possession. Thou shalt break them with a rod of iron." In the New Testament these verses were interpreted as metaphorically applying to the Messiah (the "Anointed"), that is, to the historical Christ. In particular, Paul and the author of Hebrews thought that when God "begot" the Son he actually had "raised up Jesus again" from the dead (Acts 13: 33); or, "being the brightness of his glory, and the express image of his person," when the Son "had by himself purged our sins," he "sat down on the right hand of the Majesty on high, being made so much better than the angels. . . . For unto

---

[1] *Poetical Works of John Milton* (London, 1882), 3: 363.

[2] *The Works of John Milton* (New York, 1931–38), 14: 181.

[3] *Milton and Wordsworth* (New York, 1937), p. 99; see also Arthur Sewell, *A Study in Milton's Christian Doctrine* (London, 1939), pp. 88–91, and Edmund Creeth, "The 'Begetting' and the Exaltation of the Son," *MLN* 76 (1961): 696–700.

which of the angels said he at any time, Thou art my Son, this day have I begotten thee?" (Hebrews 1: 3–5). But this event took place at the resurrection. Accordingly, for Milton as for other Christians of his day the passage in Psalm 2 was metaphorically referred to the resurrection of Jesus from the dead and to his concomitant exaltation. This is the "metaphorical" begetting or, as Milton writes, the Psalm applies to "his metaphorical generation, that is, to his resuscitation from the dead, or to his unction to the mediatorial office" (14: 183). Indeed, Milton argues that "begotten" refers to the Son only in this metaphorical sense (14: 191). But a new difficulty is now obvious: how can the Son be begotten or exalted as *Paradise Lost* 5. 600 ff., describes the event, exciting the revolt of the angels which took place before the creation of the world, when the begetting actually refers to Christ's resurrection from the dead at the beginning of our own millennium?

This contradiction led Maurice Kelley to argue that for once Milton's treatise on Christian dogma was not an adequate gloss for *Paradise Lost*. Purely for literary purposes Milton, he thought, needed some event to motivate the revolt of Satan and his cohorts. When he describes the begetting of the Son as he does, says Kelley in an analysis of 5. 600 ff., "Milton makes the dry and meagre bones of his theology live in the feigned image of poetry." [4] Accordingly, "without sanction or authority of his own systematic theology" Milton moved the begetting from its proper time sequence at the resurrection to one before the creation of the world. When the Father "begets" the Son he does raise him to the position of king — of King, that is, over Satan, who accordingly has adequate motivation for his rebellion. But Milton had no theological justification for this change with the result, as Kelley observes, that "*Paradise Lost* V, 603–06, therefore has no actual place in the dogma of the *De Doctrina*" (p. 105). It is purely and simply a "theological fiction."

Although it accounts for all of the facts, this interpretation of *Paradise Lost* does not adequately support the general purpose of the poem, and it may misrepresent the relationship between it and the *Christian Doctrine*. With regard to the first point, it appears to be overwhelmingly certain that Milton earnestly meant to "assert Eternal Providence, / And justify the ways of God to men." His central purpose in writing the poem was this justification with its concomitant theology. His means were literary, indeed, but his artistry was handmaiden to his theology, not the other way around. Whenever Milton writes any Christian dogma into *Paradise Lost*, he really means it, in either

---

[4] *This Great Argument* (Princeton, N.J., 1941), p. 100.

a literal or a metaphorical sense — the senses in which he read his Bible. It is impossible to overstate the high seriousness with which he confronted the religious truth of his epic subject, although this is not to argue that a modern reader must read the poem with this same emphasis.

Much the same attitude governs his composition of the *Christian Doctrine*, but he made no attempt whatever to present its dogma with artistic force. Rather the reverse. Both poem and treatise, however, are undergirded with the same theological content — Reformed, that is, Calvinistic, dogmatics, somewhat modified by Arminianism — presented in their two very different media. I have not observed any significant disagreement between them (and indeed, this is Kelley's thesis in *This Great Argument*), a fact which makes the apparent discrepancy between the treatise and *Paradise Lost* 5. 600 ff., take on unusual significance if it does indeed exist. The complete silence of the treatise upon any relationship between the begetting and Satan's rebellion may also suggest caution. For one point, such a "begetting" only for the purpose of fictional motivation would give some excuse for the rebellion in that it would picture a God who is merely petty in thus daring Satan to revolt, with great comfort to the Satanists and denigrators of Milton's God. Not only is there no support in the *Christian Doctrine* for this interpretation, but the exaltation of the Son has never been related to Satan in this way by any Christian tradition. Furthermore, to consider that Milton has the Father beget the Son by elevating him above Satan may imply to some degree the Arian view that the Son was created inferior and then raised to a superior position by divine fiat. The Arian position does nicely fit in with the motivation of Satan's rebellion (though at some expense of our respect for the Father and of the failure of the Son to possess true divinity), but I do not believe that Milton was an Arian. The purpose of the remainder of this paper is to explore what he meant by the begetting of the Son in *Paradise Lost* and to see how this meaning is basic to the War in Heaven.

II

According to Christian dogma, the Son of God exists with the Father until, at a point in historical time, he unites man's nature to his own divine nature so as to become the Jesus of history, God embodied or incarnate, true God and true man, mediator between divinity and humanity. As the man described in the New Testament, the Son obviously did not fully exercise his divine powers: he had laid aside or concealed his Godhead. This action of renunciation is called his "humiliation" whereby, according to such texts as Psalm 8:5, he was made "a little lower than the angels." The explicit statement of the humiliation is found in Paul's epistle to the Philippians 2: 6–9, where, "being in the form of God," the Son voluntarily took upon himself "the form of a servant," that is, of a man, emptying himself of his Godhead so as to appear as the Jesus of the New Testament. This "emptying" or *kenosis* began his humiliation;[5] during his entire life he remained in this humiliated state, to have it at last replaced at his Easter resurrection by a resumption of his full divinity as he assumed a new state, his "exaltation": God, Paul concludes, "hath highly exalted him, and given him a name which is above every name." Christians of all persuasions have accepted the related dogmas of humiliation and of the subsequent exaltation which have been outlined here, though with various interpretations.

Christ's mediatorial office according to Milton, who in most of these matters is quite orthodox, reveals itself in three ways: as he is prophet, priest, and king (15: 287 ff.). As prophet he has enlightened his church since the world was created. As priest he "once offered himself to God the Father as a sacrifice for sinners" (15: 291), where Milton says that "once offered" means that he did this "*virtually* [virtute] and as regarded the efficacy of his sacrifice, from the foundation of the world" — an offer "*actually* [ipso facto]" carried out later in the course of time (15: 293, 294).[6] The virtual offer is made as though he were indeed the God–man who he in fact later became. This is his metaphorical "unction to the mediatorial office." Polanus, an important Calvinist, had argued the same position: Christ, he writes, "was mediator as being *incarnandus* (about to become flesh), just as he is now our mediator as being *incarnatus* (become flesh)." From the position of divinity, this takes place outside time, for with God, "things done and to be done, present and future are in the same place."[7] This kind of thinking underlies the long section of *Paradise Lost* 3. 227 ff., where the Son virtually offers himself to atone for the sins of mankind.

---

[5] In parody Satan unwillingly undergoes a kind of kenosis when he undertakes his own "incarnation" with the serpent in order to tempt Adam and Eve in Book 9. See further the discussion of kenosis in "Milton on the Incarnation" printed elsewhere in this volume.

[6] My italics, Milton's proof text for the virtual offer is the latter part of Revelation 13. 8: "the Lamb [Christ] slain from the foundation of the world."

[7] *Syntagma Theologiae Christianae* (Hanover, 1624), 6: 27, in H. Heppe, *Reformed Dogmatics*, trans. G. T. Thomson (London, 1950), p. 452. See also the stimulating analyses of time and eternity in *Paradise Lost* by A. R. Cirillo, *ELH* 29 (1962): 372–95, and *JEGP* 68 (1969): 45–56.

Such are the mediatorial functions of the Son as prophet and priest. As king, he governs his church, says Milton, and "conquers and subdues its enemies" (15: 297), who include the world, death, the Old Testament law, sin, and Satan. His "kingdom of glory" will be made yet more manifest at his second advent (15: 301).

The realization of these three functions is accomplished in the "administration of redemption," the subject of the sixteenth chapter of the first book of the *Christian Doctrine.* This is the life of Christ itself, climaxed by his death and resurrection. Its actualization includes, as has been noted, the states of humiliation and exaltation. The exaltation of Christ for Milton (and it must not be forgotten that this is what the word "beget" metaphorically signifies for him) is "that by which, having triumphed over death, and laid aside the form of a servant, he was exalted by God the Father to a state of immortality and of the highest glory, partly by his own merits, partly by the gift of the Father, for the benefit of mankind; wherefore he rose again from the dead, ascended into heaven, and sitteth on the right hand of God" (15: 309–11). This exaltation affects "the whole of his person," that is, both the divine and human natures, Milton argues (15: 307, 315), observing that the exaltation of the divine nature was "its restoration and manifestation," whereas the human received "an accession of glory" (15: 315).[8] The exaltation, which in time occurred in a sequence beginning on Easter morning, includes for him the three distinct degrees of resurrection, ascension, and session at the right hand of God (15: 313). As its result, the Son now manifests his glory, which he had earned in part through his own merits, and he now sits manifested at the right hand of God, a synonym, Milton says, for his exaltation "to a place of power and glory next to God" (15: 313). This had been his original place of glory, to which he returns (14: 337) now fully evident as the Son.

According to the *Christian Doctrine* these changes at the exaltation took place in time only at the resurrection, when God "begot" the Son. But in *Paradise Lost* they are applied to the Son throughout the poem, long before the incarnation, which is promised for the future in Book 3 and again in Book 12. Thus at the first introduction of the Son in the poem, he is described as being "the radiant image of [the Father's] Glory" (3. 63), he is "most glori-

---

[8] In the eyes of the Calvinists, the "glory and power and majesty" of the divine nature, which had been concealed by kenosis, "is now revealed and exercised," whereas the human nature receives "an intrinsically new glory or power." Marvin P. Hoogland, *Calvin's Perspective on the Exaltation of Christ* (Amsterdam, 1966), p. 63. As Milton writes in *Paradise Lost*, the Son's "Humiliation shall exalt / With thee thy Manhood also to this Throne" (3. 313–14).

ous" (3. 139), is the glory of the Father (3. 388, and 5. 719), and so on. Apparently as the immediate result of his offer to save mankind, the paternal glory becomes visibly manifest in the Son (3. 139, 386; see also 10. 66). Likewise he is regularly pictured at the Father's right hand — from, indeed, the earliest time in the poem when the Father "begets" him, coincidentally revealing him there (5. 606). But the fullness of his Sonship is made fully manifest only at the end of the War in Heaven, when the Father says to him,

> Into thee such Virtue and Grace
> Immense I have transfus'd, that all may know
> In Heav'n and Hell thy Power above compare,
> And this perverse Commotion govern'd thus,
> To manifest thee worthiest to be Heir
> Of all things, to be Heir and to be King
> By Sacred Unction, thy deserved right. [6. 703–9]

The doctrine of Christ's merits, which the *Christian Doctrine* also applies to the exaltation (15: 311, quoted above), is an interesting one. Most orthodox interpreters of the exaltation agreed that by his death Christ had indeed merited reward without limit but that, being divine, he could not benefit from it. Accordingly, God applied the rewards of his merits to beings who could receive them and who sorely needed them: to sinful men, as Milton says in *Paradise Lost* 3. 290, and 12. 409–10. But the poet also assigns the merits to the person of the Son himself, not only, as has been shown, at the exaltation proper as it is described in the *Christian Doctrine*, but also as the Son offers to be mediator in *Paradise Lost* — his "unction to the mediatorial office" — occasioning the Father's comment that he is Son "by Merit more than Birthright" (3. 309). A few lines later he is invited to "assume / Thy Merits" (3. 318–19). In Book 6 he reigns "by right of merit" (line 43). In complementary manner, Satan deserves his "bad eminence" by his own merits, which in turn result in his own "exaltation" (2. 5, 21).

There are certain theological dangers in this doctrine of exaltation for merit as Milton applies it to the incarnate Son, for true divinity can earn nothing for itself by its own meritorious actions. Indeed, just such a view could easily lead to the heresy of adoptionism, a kind of Nestorianism, whereby the Father adopts another being as his very son because that being has, so to speak, earned the right to this position through his meritorious actions. For this reason trinitarians have generally applied Christ's merits only to human beings. But as a subordinationist who believed that, though the Son was divine and God he was subordinate to the divinity of God the Father and so could be exalted in some sense yet higher, Milton had no difficulty in accepting the application of some of the merits of the Son to himself, who accordingly was exalted, as Milton argued, in both his natures. In particular, the Godhead of the Son was fully restored to him after his humiliation and as a result of his merits was made fully manifest (15: 315). This indeed was what the Father was metaphorically doing when he begot the Son or exalted him or recognized his merit or fully manifested his glory or revealed him at his right hand in *Paradise Lost* 5. 600 ff.

Although this interpretation of the merits of Christ as applied to himself may seem strained, especially to strict trinitarians, there is a strong tradition in the Reformed Church which supports it. As a matter of fact, two opposing views have existed among the Calvinists themselves. One group argues the trinitarian belief that the merit of the divine nature applies only to others[9] (there is no problem with the merit of the human nature). But Hoogland observes that probably a majority of Reformed theologians "defend the propriety of saying that Christ not only merited our [human] exaltation . . . but also merited exaltation for Himself": by undergoing humiliation even to crucifixion he thus merited his own exaltation. As Zanchius observed in defense of this position, the idea is developed in various church fathers.[10]

To summarize, the argument to this point is that, when the Father "begot" his only Son, as *Paradise Lost* 5. 600 ff. describes the issuance of the decree, Milton interpreted the action in every respect as the exaltation of the Son. Supporting this interpretation beyond the quotations from Psalm 2, which appear in lines 600 ff., are the details of the Son's session at the Father's right hand then and thenceforth in all parts of the poem, the full revelation of his glory then and thenceforth, and the acceptance of the Son's merit for himself as well as for all mankind. And yet, according to the *Christian Doctrine*, the exaltation with all of these supporting details did not come to pass in time until long afterward, when the crucified Christ rose again from the dead. We accordingly must face again the dilemma which confronted Grierson and Kelley, intensified now by the recognition that it permeates the whole epic, even though it is most clearly posed in Book 5. Is there any way to resolve it so as to explain why Milton so deliberately confused his time sequence? Or is it indeed true that his artistry overtook and in fact for a while destroyed his theology?

---

[9] See Johannes Wollebius, *Compendium Theologiae Christianae* (1626), translated by J. W. Beardslee in *Reformed Dogmatics* (New York, 1965), p. 110. Other citations are found in Hoogland, pp. 87–89, especially quotations from Polanus, *Syntagma*, 6: 26.

[10] Hoogland, p. 89 and n. 164.

III

There is a solution for this problem which has been presented at such length, but it involves a radically new understanding of certain parts of the poem. In particular, as Milton begins his great story with the begetting of the Son in Book 5 and its immediate consequence, the War in Heaven, the reader must recognize that he is simultaneously narrating there three events from three very different points in time: first, the surface narrative of the fall of the angels, which took place before the foundation of the world; second, the defeat of Satan and his fellow devils described in the book of Revelation, which will take place at the end of time; and third and most important, the exaltation of the Son of God, which took place concomitantly with his resurrection as the incarnate God–man. All three of these events, from the beginning, middle, and end of time, are to be viewed as being simultaneously and metaphorically present in the one narrative framework. Unifying this disparate material is a single theme: the victorious exaltation of the Son of God.

In order to accept this reading, one must immediately ask, of course, how Milton could telescope time in this way. The solution has already been suggested in his analysis of the exaltation: the Son *virtually* offered himself as sacrifice, its efficacy dating "from the foundation of the world" — a sacrifice which *actually* is accomplished in the "fulness of time" (15: 293). Or in Polanus' terms, he was mediator *incarnandus* who then became mediator *incarnatus*. This is the metaphorical begetting, for as has already been made abundantly clear Milton read Psalm 2 in this way. One must recognize that the metaphor concerns not only its word "beget" but all the rest of the terminology in this Psalm, including especially the phrase "this day." Thus the Son is once begotten metaphorically or "virtually" and then again "actually."

Paradise Lost expresses this same idea, though in somewhat different terminology, building upon the contrast between time and eternity. God, of course, is eternal. Accordingly all moments of time — past, present, and future — are immediate to him.[11] Strictly speaking, he has no past, present, or future; as Polanus observed, with him "things done and to be done, present and future are in the same place," or more explicitly, "All things which become in time are said to have been in God from eternity; not by their own real essence, not by formal substance, but by knowledge and decree; not

---

[11] The point is cogently argued in Stanley E. Fish, *Surprised by Sin* (New York, 1967), pp. 30 ff.

through a formal *esse* but through the virtual *esse*." [12] But man's thinking and experience are conditioned by time, and accordingly he can conceive of events only as taking place in time. As Milton prepares to begin his story with the begetting of the Son, he first makes this point to alert his reader to his full meaning. His spokesman, Raphael, states that before the foundations of this world were laid,

> on a day
> (For Time, though in Eternity, appli'd
> To motion, measures all things durable
> By present, past, and future) on such day
> As Heav'n's great Year brings forth,

the Father announced the begetting of his Son (5. 579 ff.). Milton is saying that the begetting which is about to be described happened in eternity (Heav'n's great Year) but must be related in temporal measures of present, past, and future. For anyone dissatisfied with such abstract metaphysics, another way of phrasing the same idea is to say that Milton is describing the event by a metaphorical interpretation of time ("today" from Psalm 2), just as he is metaphorically interpreting "begot." The whole of this section of the poem is, accordingly, to be read as one enormous metaphor (indeed, in a somewhat different sense, the entire poem is one) [13] — a metaphor which has three different temporal interpretations, three different events which will later be realized in time and which collectively span all of time: the fall of the angels from heaven before the creation of the world, a second defeat of these angels at the end of the world, and the exaltation of the Son at his resurrection. All three events show him victorious over the forces of evil. How Milton means for the reader to understand them as being represented in the War in Heaven remains to be demonstrated.

First, and most obvious, is the defeat and fall of Satan and his angels which constitute the surface narrative. Though lacking explicit biblical authority, the event was generally assumed to have taken place as a way to account for Satan's activity in the serpent when he tempted Adam and Eve; Milton considered it "probable, that the apostasy which caused the expulsion of so many thousands from heaven, took place before the foundations of this world were laid" (15: 35). But the time of their fall itself did not become a

---

[12] *Syntagma* 4: 6, in Heppe, p. 141. "Virtual" is applied to the divine decrees by Polanus and Milton in exactly the same sense.

[13] See especially Jackson I. Cope, *The Metaphoric Structure of Paradise Lost* (Baltimore, Md., 1962).

formal dogma,[14] and it never attracted those amplifying theological details which Milton as a matter of fact inserted in his poem from the traditions associated with the other two metaphorical meanings. The vague theory of the fall of the angels upon which he built provided him with a strategy for the work and with a victory (and consequent exaltation) for the Son of God which would prove to be complementary to the other depictions of exaltation which he also intended in the episode.

As the Son of God overcame Satan at the beginning of time, so Milton expected him to do at the end of time. His most pertinent authority was Revelation 12, according to which John saw in heaven a woman who was pregnant. A "great red dragon" whose "tail drew the third part of the stars of heaven, and did cast them to the earth" stood before her so as to devour the child, but "she brought forth a man child, who was to rule all nations with a rod of iron," whereupon "her child was caught up unto God, and to his throne." For the metaphorically minded, here again is the exaltation of the Son (the "child"); the dragon, of course, is Satan, and the "third of the stars" which are swept down are the angelic hosts who follow him (as has long been recognized in *Paradise Lost* 2. 692; 5. 710; and 6. 156). Milton would find corroboration for this interpretation in the throne to which the child is lifted (the "holy hill of Zion" of Psalm 2. 6) and in the "rod of iron" — the same "Iron Rod" which Abdiel forecasts will "bruise and break" Satan (5. 887), as the evil angels finally came to recognize in hell (2. 327). The *Christian Doctrine* argues that this verse from Psalm 2 refers to Christ's second coming (15. 301) — that is, to the time of the book of Revelation.

After this episode John's vision continues with the scene of a war in heaven, where "Michael and his angels fought against the dragon; and the dragon fought and his angels, and prevailed not; neither was their place found any more in heaven. And the great dragon was cast out, that old serpent, called the Devil, and Satan." Then a "loud voice" from heaven announces that the "power" of Christ has come in this victory; the conquest has been made "by the blood of the Lamb" — that is, by the passion of Christ.

In these verses from Revelation Milton found authority for his general depiction of the War in Heaven as well as for some of its details.[15] As a descrip-

---

[14] Wollebius, for instance, merely admits his ignorance, *Compendium*, p. 63.

[15] Much of the supporting material is, of course, derived from other apocalyptic texts, especially Daniel and Ezekiel. See J. H. Adamson, "The War in Heaven: The *Merkabah*," reprinted elsewhere in this volume. But many phrases in the description of the fall of the angels are taken from Revelation too: Satan will be chained, *P.L.*, 6. 739, and Rev. 20: 1–2, while the saints in heaven will sing hallelujahs, *P.L.*, 6. 742–45, and Rev. 19: 3; the evil

tion of the exaltation of the Son over Satan, it had attracted theological attention long before his time, though many dogmatists thought that Michael
should be identified with the Son in his victory over Satan.[16] But Milton rejects this interpretation, both implicitly in *Paradise Lost* and explicitly in the
Christian Doctrine; in the latter he writes that Michael is leader of the angels
but that Christ alone vanquished Satan (15: 105), as he does indeed in the
poem. As will appear, Milton employs this conclusion because he intends the
exaltation proper at this point.

This interpretation of God's "begetting" or exalting the Son in some sense
at his second coming and especially the manifestation of the Son's "kingdom
of glory" at that time, which is part of that exaltation (15: 301), explains
many details of the War in Heaven, but not all of the major ones. For example,
it fails to account in any way for the fact that the War lasts for three days, a
span of time equivalent to that of the passion of Christ leading to his triumph
over death. But this triumph, as has been shown, is the central meaning which
Milton connects with the exaltation: when the Father "begets" the Son at
Paradise Lost 5. 600 ff., he is metaphorically exalting him, an event which the
Christian Doctrine says actually took place when Christ triumphed over death
and laid aside his form of a servant on Easter morning (15: 309). Accordingly, the War in Heaven must be considered yet a third time as it primarily
reflects the resurrection of the Son from death in historical time.

The first piece of evidence has already been mentioned, the three days of
battle, a time span which does not appear in any of the other biblical sources.
The period of three days, however, strongly suggests the period during which
Christ was under the power of death: from Good Friday to Easter Sunday
morning. To describe this metaphorical time by "present, past, and future,"
let us assume that in *Paradise Lost* 5. 600 ff., the Father announces to the
assembled angels that the Son is begotten on the "day" before Good Friday
— that is, on Maundy Thursday.[17] All of the angels receive the news with
pleasure, real or feigned, and spend the rest of the day in song and mystic
dance, following their regularly irregular form of life (5. 618 ff.). In Christian tradition the most important event of that day occurred in the evening,

---

angels wish to be hidden under mountains, *P.L.*, 6. 842, and Rev. 6: 16, and so on. See
the full index of scriptural parallels in James Sims, *The Bible in Milton's Epics* (Gainesville,
Florida, 1962).

[16] Wollebius, for instance, argues that "the archangel Michael is best understood as the
Son of God" (*Compendium*, p. 62).

[17] Somewhat paradoxically, from the divine standpoint the humiliation itself can be
identified with the coming exaltation, for the exaltation can be achieved only through it.

when Christ met with his disciples about a table to institute the celebration known as the Eucharist or Holy Communion, the central sacrament of Christianity. It may not be purely coincidental that the angels in heaven that same evening meet around tables, where "They eat, they drink, and in communion sweet / Quaff immortality and joy" (5. 637 f.).[18] That same night, or earlier according to some biblical accounts, Satan enters Judas, who leaves the disciples after the meal and goes to betray Christ. At the equivalent time in the poem Satan enlists the support of various angels and departs for his "Quarters of the North."

The next day, Good Friday, the biblical Christ is delivered by Pilate to the Jews, who crucify him. He dies, reaching the final depth of his humiliation, and remains under the power of death the rest of that day and through Saturday until Sunday morning. In the poem Satan incites all of the angels who have joined him, except Abdiel,[19] to fight against the Father and his newly begotten Son. The battle breaks out, Michael's forces against Satan's, and ends indecisively that Friday night, only to be renewed the next day, when it is again indecisive despite the devilish invention of cannon to produce a sort of harrowing of heaven. The entire duration of the War in Heaven exactly represents for all Christians the time while Christ was under the power of death. For some it also represents his descent into hell,[20] but Milton says that it is the final stage of his humiliation, when he "was detained in the grave," according to the *Christian Doctrine*, in both his divine and human natures (15: 307). Thus his complete disappearance during the War in Heaven; thus the utter silence of the Word, a nonparticipant during the entire course of the struggle.

---

[18] That Satan presumably participated should excite no wonder: so did Judas. In the first edition of the poem (1667) Milton had written, "They eat, they drink, and with refection sweet / Are fill'd." The revision which he made in the second edition is designed to emphasize the sacramental nature of the meal. This is not to argue, however, that angels ever literally participate in it as a sacrament.

[19] The metaphorical interpretation of the entire episode of the War in Heaven in New Testament terms suggests that Abdiel himself may represent a New Testament character — in particular St. Paul, whose career also began in association with anti-Christian forces. Abdiel's name means "Servant of God." Paul so designates himself in the first verse of his epistle to Titus. At 5. 813 ff., Abdiel emphasizes the significance of God's begetting the Son as Psalm 2 states it; Paul was the great New Testament interpreter of the same passage in Acts and was the supposed author of Hebrews. Abdiel's lines at 5. 835–45, reflect Colossians 1: 15–17 on the creative power of the Son. Paul had "fought the good fight" (2 Timothy 4: 7); Abdiel had "fought / The better fight" (6. 29–30). Further parallels appear in Sims' compilation. Finally, in his discussion of zeal in the *Christian Doctrine* (17: 153), Milton named Paul among nine biblical characters noted for this attribute. Abdiel is especially recognized as zealous too (5. 805, 807, 849, 900).

[20] For the Reformed, this "descent" is the "most profound humiliation, in which Christ was abandoned by the Father to the power and dominion of death," but he does not literally descend into hell, Heppe, p. 491.

Before the dawn of the third day, however, the Father at last addresses the Son (6. 680 ff.), into whom he now transfuses immeasurable virtue and grace. The now-manifest Son, that is, has completed the atonement; he will now throw off his humiliation to reveal his exaltation and to glorify the Father (6. 723–27). Accordingly, just as "the third sacred Morn began to shine" (line 748), the dawn of Easter morning, he ascends the chariot of deity to crush the power of Satan. It surely is not coincidental that he "ascended" — that is, was exalted — just at the mid-point of the 1665 version of the poem, a word preceded and followed by 5,275 lines (6. 762),[21] for the center of the Christian story and the physical center of the poem are identical. The Son thereupon rides forth and as a result of his exaltation he alone triumphs completely over Satan and his powers, including Sin and Death, just as Christ did at his resurrection. Finally, he returns to the Father, who receives him into glory "Where now he sits at the right hand of bliss" (6. 892).

The exaltation is thus metaphorically complete at the end of the first great episode of the poem, which ends Book 6. Accordingly, Milton may freely apply to the Son whenever he appears in subsequent portions of the work terms which had been made manifest at his exaltation — in particular, his glory, his merits, and his session at the right hand of God. But the story of the incarnation and exaltation will happen yet again, this time actually. Accordingly, the metaphorically exalted Son in 3. 227 ff., promises that he will in time literally become incarnate and atone for the sins of man by his death. As had once been metaphorically true in the War in Heaven, he will then literally "rise Victorious" as he is exalted at the resurrection, will "subdue / My vanquisher" and will "lead Hell Captive maugre Hell," binding the powers of darkness (lines 250 ff.). Finally, the story is related yet another time as a prophecy by Michael to Adam in Book 12, the conclusion to the whole poem: the incarnate Son will die, but will soon revive:

> ere the third dawning light
> Return, the Stars of Morn shall see him rise
> Out of his grave. [12. 421–23]

In this act he "Shall bruise the head of Satan" and "crush his strength" (line 430); in this victory he shall be exalted and ascend

> triumphing through the air
> Over his foes and thine; there shall surprise

---

[21] See John A. Shawcross, "The Balanced Structure of *Paradise Lost*," *SP* 62 (1965): 697. I have argued that Milton consciously tried to keep this word at the center of his revised poem of 1674, but failed because he was unaware of errors in his numbering in the 1667 Book 3. See *ELN* 7 (1969): 32–34. The defeat of Satan in the War in Heaven is also the mid-point of Revelation (12: 9).

The Serpent, Prince of air, and drag in Chains
Through all his Realm, and there confounded leave;
Then enter into glory, and resume
His Seat at God's right hand, exalted high
Above all names in Heav'n,

from whence he shall later come to the Last Judgment (12. 451 ff.). But these victories had already been metaphorically described at the end of Book 6.

One must remark that Milton shows the good angels in their fruitless battle against Satan not merely to reveal their willing submission to duty but also to show how utterly powerless they are to achieve the goal of Christ's humiliation, the satisfaction of divine justice. Paradoxically, they would have had to lose the battle (temporarily) in complete humiliation before they could be exalted in victory as he was. This is the reason for the inconclusive nature of the War in Heaven, upon which various critics have commented. But if the Son is to atone for man's sin, the battle cannot go otherwise: the good angels can neither win nor lose. As a matter of fact, its outcome is quite unimportant beside the concurrent humiliation of the Son in death, and Milton can accordingly underline some of its comic aspects. As he writes in 9. 28 ff., *Paradise Lost* is unlike other epics, which describe "Wars . . . With long and tedious havoc . . . In Battles feign'd." Rather, it is "the better fortitude / Of Patience and Heroic Martyrdom" which he expects his readers to recognize in the divine humiliation which lies beneath the surface narrative of the War in Heaven.

Such is Milton's depiction of the exaltation of the Son, a theme which in both its literal and metaphorical sense dominates the poem. The complexity and deep Christian sense of the interplay of these two ways of presenting the event, its connection in the poem of the beginning with the ending of time, its great affirmation in historical time as the Christian era began, its centrality indeed to all of the action in the poem — for all of it grows out of God's words in Book 5, "This day I have begot" — show how central the exaltation of the Son was in Milton's thinking. After the fall of the angels, as Don Cameron Allen has remarked, "For Satan and his peers, the harmonious vision is lost, and there is no miracle that will restore it." But the case is different for man, for whom "it can be won again." [22] The depiction of man's salvation through the sacrifice of the Son is an overwhelming concern in *Paradise Lost*. It is small wonder that, after the Father and Son have worked out the details of the

---

[22] *The Harmonious Vision* (Baltimore, Md., 1954), Introduction.

atonement in Book 3 and the angelic chorus has praised them for it, John Milton himself should join the choir at the conclusion:

> Hail Son of God, Savior of Men, thy Name
> Shall be the copious matter of my Song
> Henceforth, and never shall my Harp thy praise
> Forget, nor from thy Father's praise disjoin. [3. 412–15]

Milton on the Incarnation

W. B. HUNTER

Although Milton's conception of the Trinity has been subjected to extensive comment that is often hostile and in my opinion frequently mistaken,[1] the views which he supported concerning the second of the great mysteries of Christianity, the Incarnation, have been quietly ignored. One may guess at the probable reasons for this state of affairs. First, the doctrines underlying Christian orthodoxy upon this point are often obscure — obscure from the difficulty of the terminology as much as from the ideas inherent in the words. Second, Milton has been somewhat more careful than in his trinitarian statements in guarding the meaning of his poetry from charges of heterodoxy. Third, the chapter in the *Christian Doctrine* which argues this subject is briefer than the one concerning the relationship of the Son to the Father, and the arguments and conclusions are perhaps not so clearly stated. Yet as a matter of fact, though it seems to have escaped comment, Milton may even better be accused of supporting the heresy of Nestorius than he has been of supporting that of Arius. It is my purpose here to explore Milton's conception of the union of God and man which is called the Incarnation, to indicate something of the philosophical and religious background of this conception, and to show how the underlying theories permeate other areas of his thought.

At the outset it may be well to state the orthodox position. Until the time of Apollinaris of Laodicea (d. 390?), the union of God with man had been assumed in Christian discussion, but its exact mode and meaning had not been clarified. Apollinaris had the misfortune to precipitate the issue by arguing that the divine Logos had indeed entered man but only to replace the rational

---

[1] See my "Milton's Arianism Reconsidered," reprinted elsewhere in this volume.

soul. Christ, that is, had in the old psychological terminology a vegetative and sensitive nature or soul; but in place of a rational soul he had the Logos. The implication was that he was not completely man, and for denying the completeness of the Incarnation Apollinaris was quickly brought to task by the Council of Alexandria (362) and the Council of Constantinople (381).

Early in the fifth century the school at Antioch, represented especially by Theodore of Mopsuestia and Nestorius, argued the opposite interpretation, that in Christ a divine person and a human person were joined. The result was a union of the two persons, but each continued as an individual after the incarnation. This idea too was opposed vigorously by Fathers who argued that such is not a true union but only a juxtaposition of the two persons. The two extreme positions of Apollinarianism and Nestorianism (which was soon condemned by the Council of Ephesus in 431) ultimately led the church to think through the problem, to clarify its terminology, and to formulate the dogma of the Council of Chalcedon in 451. Christ, it held, is "known in two natures [not persons], without confusion, without conversion, without severance, and without division; the distinction of the natures being in no wise abolished by their union, but the peculiarity of each nature being maintained, and both concurring in one person and hypostasis." [2] In England as elsewhere this became general dogma. The second of the Thirty-nine Articles holds that the Son "took Man's nature in the womb of the blessed Virgin, of her substance: so that two whole and perfect Natures, that is to say, the Godhead and Manhood, were joined together in one Person, never to be divided." Chapter 8 of the *Westminster Confession of Faith* asserts that the Son took upon him "man's nature, with all the essential properties and common infirmities thereof, yet without sin; being conceived by the power of the Holy Ghost, in the womb of the Virgin Mary, of her substance. So that two whole, perfect, and distinct natures, the Godhead and the manhood, were inseparably joined together in one person, without conversion, composition, or confusion. Which person is very God and very man."

In general, Milton's early poems reveal no specific information about his interpretation of this mystery, though the general import of the Nativity Ode, the Passion, and the Circumcision is orthodox. *Paradise Lost* is more precise; in Book 3 the Son offers himself to God for man:

> I for his sake will leave
> Thy bosom, and this glory next to thee
> Freely put off . . . . [3. 238–40]

---

[2] Philip Schaff, *History of the Christian Church* (New York, 1867), 2: 745 f.

The Father replies that the incarnate Christ will join two natures (not two persons):

> Thou therefore whom thou only canst redeem,
> Thir Nature also to thy Nature join;
> And be thyself Man among men on Earth,
> Made flesh, when time shall be, of Virgin seed . . . .
> Nor shalt thou by descending to assume
> Man's Nature, lessen or degrade thine own.

Then, after the resurrection,

> thy Humiliation shall exalt
> With thee thy Manhood also to this Throne;
> Here shalt thou sit incarnate, here shalt Reign
> Both God and Man . . . . [3. 281 ff.]

Book 12 returns to the subject: Adam comments upon the future Incarnation, "So God with man unites" (1. 382), and Michael agrees that the Son joins "Manhood to Godhead" (1. 389). Finally, *Paradise Regained* portrays at length the incarnate Christ as he begins his ministry, though this poem contains surprisingly little direct evidence for Milton's understanding of the Incarnation. In conclusion, his poetry mirrors throughout the usual description of the incarnate Logos, presented in traditional terminology; no phrases appear which could cause any theological mischief. He had practiced much the same strategy in his treatment of the Trinity, though with somewhat less success.

In the *Christian Doctrine* Milton expressly argues his conception of the Incarnation which underlies that of his poetry, but in it the implications are anything but orthodox. Chapter 14 of Book 1, "Of Man's Restoration and of Christ as Redeemer," begins with the traditional distinction of Christ's nature as "twofold; divine and human." [3] Milton goes on to reject the early heresy of Ebionism, which had denied the existence of the Logos before the Incarnation: the Son, he says, "must necessarily have existed previous to his incarnation, whatever subtleties may have been invented to evade this conclusion by those who contend for the merely human nature of Christ" (15: 263). Adding that the mystery of the Incarnation stands next to that of the Trinity as "the greatest mystery of our religion," Milton then repeats the received view: "that two natures are so established in the one person of Christ that he subsists as real and perfect [in it] without his subsistence in the other nature; so that from two natures is made one person" (15: 264–66). He adds that this is what is called the "hypostatic union" and quotes the explanation

---

[3] *Works of John Milton* (New York, 1931–38), 15: 259. In many of the quotations from the *Christian Doctrine* I have altered Sumner's inaccurate translation.

of the Calvinist Zanchius, who had supported the orthodox interpretation: "Properly speaking, he assumed human nature, not man. For the Logos, being in the womb of the virgin, assumed human nature for itself, both forming in itself a body from the substance of Mary and creating at the same time a soul. And he so assumed that nature in himself and for himself that that nature never subsisted independently, outside the Logos" (15: 266).

It is important to understand what Zanchius was getting at in this intrauterine theology and why Milton quoted the passage. The point is that at the very moment of conception the Logos united with man's nature. Had this union taken place at any subsequent time, the "flesh" which the Logos became (see John 1:14) would have already existed as a complete human being, not merely the "flesh" or the "nature" of mankind, and thus it would have been a person. But this is the Nestorian heresy, which had insisted on the union of two persons, not of two natures within the divine person, and which Zanchius was trying to combat. He accordingly declares in another passage, "The foundation of Nestorius' whole heresy was his thinking that outside the person of the λόγος a particular person had been created and conceived by the λόγος in the Virgin's womb and had been associated with the λόγος and joined to it." [4]

But Milton will have nothing to do with this orthodox interpretation; Zanchius, he says, argues "as if one who assumes human nature does not assume man. For human nature, that is, form in matter, whenever it exists, constitutes man, deficient in no part of his essence, not even (if the words have any meaning) in subsistence or personality" (15: 266). Milton is arguing here that the Incarnation is the union between the person of the Logos and the person (not merely the nature) of man; like the Antiochenes he cannot conceive of complete humanity deprived of personality. [5] In order to emphasize his position, he rejects Zanchius' belief that the conception and the Incarnation happened simultaneously; the newly conceived Jesus, Milton implies, existed for some time (he does not say for how long) before the Logos

---

[4] H. Zanchius, *De Incarnatione Filii Dei* (Heidelberg, 1593), p. 141, as translated in Heinrich Heppe, *Reformed Dogmatics* (London, 1950), p. 419.

[5] As Theodore of Mopsuestia wrote, "it is impossible to speak of a perfect subsistence without a person . . . but when we consider the conjunction [συνάφεια] then we speak of one person and two natures," *De Incarnatione*, viii, as quoted in J. S. MacArthur, *Chalcedon* (London, 1931), p. 31. Accordingly, MacArthur adds, one subject does not "*become* the other; so in becoming man what the Logos did was to assume something." See the analysis of Harry A. Wolfson, *The Philosophy of the Church Fathers* (Cambridge, Mass., 1956), 1: 455–57.

entered him (15: 267, 271).[6] But this separate existence of the man, no matter how brief, implies that he has a human personality in addition, of course, to a human nature. Thus for Milton complete human nature cannot be separated from personality; as he argues, in the incarnate Christ there is a "union of two essences," and from this union "a single being, a single person is made" (15: 268, 270). Milton, however, understands *essence* here in terms of Aristotle's primary οὐσία,[7] that is, as the principle of individuation. Accordingly, for him this is a union of two individuals, divine and human; the human nature must have existed independently (in opposition to the orthodox views of Zanchius); otherwise the Logos could not have been made "very man" or have "assumed the real and perfect substance or essence of man" (15: 271). Accordingly Milton thinks that "the Logos was certainly made that which he assumed; if then he assumed human nature but not man, he was made human nature but not man; these two things, however, cannot be separated" (15: 268).

Now this argument of Milton is on the face of it heretical, for to the orthodox it implies mere juxtaposition of persons rather than true union; furthermore, the Logos assumed and accordingly elevated the manhood of only one man rather than the *nature* of the whole human race. Richard Hooker had already presented the argument as clearly as it may be put: "It pleased not the Word or wisdom of God to take to itself some one person amongst men, for then should that one have been advanced which was assumed and no more, but Wisdom to the end she might save many built her house of that Nature which is common unto all, she made not *this or that man* her habitation, but dwelt *in us* [cf. John 1:14]." To assume a person, on the other hand, implies Nestorianism: "If the Son of God had taken to himself a man now made and already perfected [i.e., if the Incarnation had followed by any length of time at all upon the conception, as Milton implies], it would of necessity follow that there are in Christ two persons, the one assuming and the other assumed; whereas the Son of God did not assume a man's person unto his own, but a man's nature to his own Person." Thus it happens that "The flesh and the conjunction of the flesh with God began both at one instant; his making and taking to himself our flesh was but one act, so that in

---

[6] Wolfson argues that this too is Theodore's interpretation and Nestorius' as well. See, e.g., Justinian's Second Edict: according to them "there was first a man subsistent, and then he was united with the Logos." Wolfson, 1: 454.

[7] See my discussion of first ousia in "Milton's Theological Vocabulary," reprinted elsewhere in this volume.

Christ there is no personal subsistence but one. . . . By taking only the nature of man he still continueth one person [i.e., the divine], and changeth but the manner of his subsisting." [8] Milton certainly must have known what he was doing when he flew in the face of such statements as those of Zanchius and Hooker, but he resolutely concludes that "There is then in Christ a mutual hypostatic union of two natures, that is to say, of two essences, of two substances, and consequently of two persons," adding that this union does not "prevent the respective properties [or qualities] of each from remaining individually distinct" (15: 271).

The central question, of course, is that of just how this union was accomplished, a subject upon which Milton resolutely keeps silent, admitting his ignorance (15: 271). In some sense, indeed, he views the union as one of natures, the conclusion reached at Chalcedon. For as he observes, the two natures may interchange their properties: what is written about the "Son of Man" in the Bible may actually refer to a property of the "Son of God," and vice versa. This is an ancient recognition of the ambivalence of some biblical phraseology; technically, it is a "communicatio idiomatum" or "proprietum." Such an interchange of properties, Milton says, occurs only between the two natures (not persons): "*κατ' ἄλλο καὶ ἄλλο*, as theologians express it; for in speaking of Christ the proper expression is not *ἄλλος καὶ ἄλλος*, but *ἄλλο καὶ ἄλλο*" (15: 279). Milton is following an ancient distinction of the natures which refers to them by the Greek neuter (implying nature) rather than the masculine (implying personality). Even so, inasmuch as *nature* means the same to him as *essence* (15: 269) and because he understands *essence* in the Aristotelian sense of first ousia or individual, he also concludes that two persons are involved in the union — the mode of union being the subject upon which he is unwilling to commit himself.

Further support for the argument that Milton interpreted the Incarnation in a Nestorian sense to at least some degree comes from the words which he uses to describe the union. Usually he is satisfied with the standard term *union* (*unio*), which gives no clue to any specific interpretation. But the most frequent synonym which he employs for it is *coalesce* (*coalescere*), which in general does not imply the orthodox idea of complete union but rather the Nestorian juxtaposition. As Wolfson remarks, "conjunction" and "coalescence" are the translations generally used for *συνάφεια* and *συμφυΐα*; and these words were especially appropriated by Theodore and Nestorius to indi-

---

[8] *Of the Laws of Ecclesiastical Polity* (London, 1907), 5. 52. 3.

cate their understanding of the union of the Incarnation.[9] Milton describes the hypostatic union as "hypostatice coaluere" (14: 228) or again the Son "in unam personam cum homine coalescit" (14: 312). Sometimes, indeed, he uses this word almost as frequently as *unio*: "if the divine and human nature have coalesced [coaluerunt] in one person . . . it follows that these two natures must have also coalesced [coaluisse] in one external form." Furthermore, the Son's essence "could not have coalesced [coalescere] in one person with man" without including the Father — "which is impossible" unless, Milton argues, Father and Son differ in essence (15: 271, 273). On the other hand, this argument from vocabulary is not conclusive: various orthodox writers sometimes used συνάφεια and συμφυία or their Latin equivalents to describe the union of the Incarnation. Tertullian and Gregory of Nyssa are cases in point.[10] It is difficult to determine just how much weight to give this evidence, since Milton nowhere defines what he means by *coalescere* and the theological vocabulary never became completely fixed; the word, however, is well established in Nestorian usage and his employment of it further supports the idea that Milton conceived of the Incarnation as a somewhat less close union than orthodoxy generally has permitted. It must be recognized, however, that he resolutely refused to speculate upon the final meaning of the Incarnation, preferring to accept it as a mystery.

Even so, it may be possible, through the employment of several traditional analogies, to come to some further understanding of how Milton conceived of the various kinds of union. Until relatively recent times, scientists had great difficulty in explaining how two different substances may be combined. Today the concepts of physical mixture and chemical combination explain these relationships, but these ideas were not available to Milton. Various efforts to explain the different ways in which substances may be combined appear in classical antiquity, and of course have their applicability as explanations of the mystery of the Incarnation. A convenient if late analysis of various kinds of combination appears in Boethius' theological tractate addressed to Eutyches and Nestorius upon their faulty understanding of the union of God and Man, an analysis which anyone concerned with theology in the seventeenth century would probably have known.[11]

---

[9] *Philosophy of the Church Fathers*, 1: 398 f.

[10] See Wolfson's discussion, 1: 389 and 399.

[11] *The Theological Tractates*, trans. H. F. Stewart and E. K. Rand (Loeb Library, 1918); for a more elaborate analysis, based on the original distinctions made by Aristotle and the Stoics, see Wolfson, 1: 372 ff.

In his classification of various kinds of union, Boethius first recognizes that which occurs merely by "juxtaposition" — κατὰ παράθεσιν — though such adjacent location is not really a union at all, he says, any more than when "two bodies are laid the one against the other."[12] This, of course, is the governing metaphor for the "union" of the two persons as argued by Nestorius.

Apparently similar to this "juxtaposition" is the metaphor of the dwelling of the Logos in man as in a temple, tabernacle, or house, frequently to be found in Paul and John (e.g., 1 Cor. 3: 16, 17; 6: 19; John 1: 14). Milton employs these images a number of times to express the Incarnation. Thus in the Nativity Ode, line 14, the Son "chose with us a darksome House of mortal Clay." In "The Passion," line 17, he entered his "poor fleshly tabernacle"; and in *Paradise Regained* he is "enshrin'd / In fleshly Tabernacle, and human form" (4. 598 f.). False incarnations, on the other hand, occur with the pagan gods, who "forsake their temples dim" in the Nativity Ode, lines 197 ff. Even though Milton employs the idea of an indwelling spirit so readily, however, this is not to convict him of Nestorianism in that the metaphor had enjoyed wide circulation from the earliest days of Christianity. A more significant appearance of the concept of juxtaposition appears when Satan combines with the serpent in *Paradise Lost* 9: Satan says that he will be "mixt with bestial slime, / This essence to incarnate" (lines 165 f.). After the successful temptation of Eve, the Satan–serpent union is quickly and completely separated, just as the pagan gods leave their temples in the Nativity Ode after the true Incarnation has taken place. The Satan–serpent relationship, that is, is only a Nestorian juxtaposition. The sexual union of the angels which Raphael describes seems to be a similar separate juxtaposition.

The opposite error, that of Eutyches, held that in the Incarnation the two natures were firmly united but in such a way as to produce a third being, a *tertium quid*, which differed from either. Again Boethius explains the error by means of an analogy, this time that of the mixture of honey and water which, he believed, could not be separated once it was made and which differed in its nature from that of both of its constituents.[13] This mixture is a *confusion*. Milton's understanding of the Incarnation as a union of persons cannot possibly belong with this theory of union, though he consciously employs the conception of confusion elsewhere in his depiction of Chaos, which exists "by confusion" (2. 897) as the place where the potential elements

---

[12] *Theological Tractates*, p. 93.
[13] *Theological Tractates*, p. 113.

exist "in thir pregnant causes mixt / Confus'dly" (2. 913–14). *Confusion* personified shares the throne with Chaos and Night (1. 966); the Deep in Book 10 is likewise described as being composed "of horrible confusion" (1. 472). Thus Chaos is a mixture of matter in which the distinction of each part is totally lost. In that both *confound* and *confusion* derive from the same Latin root, the "Confusion worse confounded" in Chaos (2. 996) emphasizes the inseparable nature of this mixture. In building their causeway through it, Sin and Death do not separate out the constituent elements but merely compress the confusion so that it will remain fixed. God, on the other hand, can resolve it, as Milton's description of creation in Book 7 shows.

The third and last form of union which Boethius recognizes has no name; he considers it, however, to be the explanatory analogy for proper understanding of how the union of God and Man took place at the Incarnation.[14] In this combination there is a true union, not a mere juxtaposition; but each of the combining entities continues in some sense to display its own nature: "a thing . . . is so combined of two that the elements of which it is said to be combined continue without changing into each other, as when we say that a crown is composed of gold and gems." [15] The gold and gems, that is, each keep their original natures but at the same time constitute together a single unit, the crown. One should observe that the analogy is not a very satisfactory one, for the union of Divine and Human cannot be resolved (as, of course, the constituents of the crown can be separated). Indeed, there is no significant difference between this union and a juxtaposition. One may, however, grasp something of what Boethius was driving at; implicit in his statement also is the fact that two very unequal entities (the divine and the human, the gems and the gold) are united in this "true union."

Like the conceptions of union as juxtaposition and as confusion, this third interpretation proved useful in areas outside the strict bounds of the theories of the Incarnation. Milton employs it variously. A first example appears in his understanding of the relationship between the body and soul, which God inseparably joined in Adam to produce a single individual (15: 39–41; *Paradise Lost*, 7: 524–26). This is indeed a basic analogy also found in attempts of Christians to explain the relationship of the two natures in the Incarnation: just as soul is united with body, so is the divine united with the human. Chris-

---

[14] See Wolfson's discussion of the union of "predominance," 1: 377 ff. See also Plotinus' discussion of "Complete Transfusion" (ὅλων κράσεως) in *Enneads*, 2: 7.

[15] *Theological Tractates*, p. 115.

tians generally have believed, however, that the soul is newly created and joined with the body at the conception of each individual or at some later time, and that at death it separates from the body. Accordingly, only in its earthly existence does the soul–body relationship present a sound analogy for the Incarnation.

It is instructive to see Milton's differing interpretation of the soul–body union. He accepts the tradition that the soul is the form of the body, educed from the potentiality of the matter of the body and being produced in a way analogous to that of other forms from their matter.[16] Following Aristotle, he goes on to argue that the soul — that is, the form — has no separate existence apart from the body: it does not exist independently before birth but is produced by propagation from the parents. At death it dies with the body and enters the grave with the body. Milton accordingly falls into the errors of traducianism and of mortalism, which have never held the allegiance of many Christians.[17]

Again, this kind of union is understood to exist in the union of Christians in the mystical body of Christ. As Hooker has been seen to argue, orthodox Christianity insisted that the Incarnation involved "human nature" so that all human beings may participate in the resurrection. But Milton, as has been made clear, denied that human nature in general was the object of the Incarnation, affirming instead that only one individual was involved. For him the union of the elect with the Son is accomplished by each individual rather than by the common human nature of each. Possibly this attitude accounts in part for his lack of interest in the visible church, the union of all believers in the mystical body of Christ. Instead, for him, the regenerate join directly with the Son so that ultimately they will be united with the Father and "God shall be all in all." [18] It is suggestive to observe that Milton uses the same word, *coalescere*, to define this relationship as he does for the Incarnation: "believers coalesce [coalescent] in one body with Christ (16: 2).[19]

In some ways Milton's most interesting application of this conception of union is that dealing with marriage. As Christ says (Mark 10: 8–9; cf. Matt.

---

[16] See my "Milton's Power of Matter," *JHI* 13 (1952): 551–62.

[17] See George Williamson, "Milton and the Mortalist Heresy," *SP* 32 (1935): 553–79, and my "Milton's Materialistic Life Principle," *JEGP* 45 (1946): 69.

[18] Reiterated (from 1 Cor. 15: 28) thrice in *Paradise Lost*: 3. 341; 6. 732; 11. 44.

[19] Perhaps the angels are similarly united with the Son: God ordains that they shall
Under his great Vice-gerent Reign abide
United as one individual Soul
For ever happy .... [*PL*, 5. 609–11]

19: 5–6), interpreting Genesis 2: 24, "they twain shall be one flesh: so then they are no more twain, but one flesh. What therefore God hath joined together, let not man put asunder." Like his contemporaries, Milton understood these words to mean that true marriage is an actual union of two individuals under this same analogy. From this interpretation comes some of the basic argument in his divorce pamphlets, not to speak of his understanding of the relationship between man and woman and his explanation of the cause of Adam's fall.

As has been shown, in this third kind of union the superior nature joins with the inferior nature without the entire destruction of the latter: the two constitute a single entity in which something of each survives though the superior, in this case the man, is the determining factor, just as the divine dominates the human in the Incarnation. The relationship between Adam and Eve in *Paradise Lost* must be understood as deriving from this concept of union: they are not equal (4. 296) but together make "one Flesh, one Heart, one Soul" (8. 499). She recognizes in him the higher existence and finds that her own comes to completion only in him. The various statements in the poem supporting Adam's superiority do not simply express male bias but rather reveal the true relationship of this kind of unequal union. Adam falls not because of a romantic attachment for Eve but because their union is a true one; in his last words before his Fall, "Our State cannot be sever'd, we are one, / One Flesh; to lose thee were to lose myself" (9. 958 f.), an assertion which the fallen Eve supports, who "gladly of our Union hear thee speak, / One Heart, one Soul in both" (9. 966 f.). Milton evidently intends their union with literal force. Adam feels that it cannot be broken and he accordingly joins her in sin. Despite their later bickering the union continues, for disagreement between the parties does not break it.

The same conception of marital union appears in the divorce pamphlets, where Milton argues from the idea that a true marriage (a genuine union) is not subject to separation; divorce, he believes, should be granted when the union was not actual but only apparent — a juxtaposition in Boethius' classification. In this way he was able to interpret Christ's statements forbidding divorce so that they would agree with the practices of the Old Testament. Thus he says that "mariage, *unlesse it mean a fit and tolerable mariage*, is not inseparable neither by nature nor institution." [20] Accordingly, "the place in Genesis contains the description of a fit and perfect mariage, with an inter-

---

[20] *Doctrine and Discipline of Divorce*, in *Works*, 3: 458; my italics.

dict of ever divorcing such a union; but where nature is discover'd to have never joyn'd indeed, but vehemently seeks to part, it cannot be there conceiv'd that God forbids it" (3. 2. 469). Without such a true union there has never really been a marriage and the separation should be rather "by a nullity, then by a divorce." [21]

As has been shown, Milton considered man's union with Christ to be of the same order as that of marriage. Indeed, the analogy between these two unions still appears in many marriage services. Thus, in order to explain what marriage is, Milton expressly compares the union of married partners with the union of believers with Christ. With reference to Ephesians 5 he comments, "this union of the flesh proceeds from the union of a fit help and solace. Wee know that there was never a more spiritual mystery then this Gospel taught us under the terms of body and flesh; yet nothing less intended then that wee should stick there. What a stupidnes then is it, that in Mariage, which is the neerest resemblance of our union with Christ, wee should deject our selvs to such a sluggish and underfoot Philosophy, as to esteem the validity of Mariage meerly by the flesh," a juxtaposition. Accordingly, he concludes, "none but a fit and pious matrimony can signify the union of Christ and his Church, ther cannot hence be any hindrance of divorce to that wedlock wherin ther can be no good mystery" (4. 98–100). Or again, "Mariage is a solemn thing, som say a holy, the resemblance of Christ and his Church; and so indeed it is where the persons are truly religious" (4. 126). These observations do not, however, find complete support in the *Christian Doctrine*, where Milton argues that marriage was indeed indissoluble before sin entered the world, but "after the fall [God] permitted its dissolution" (15: 173). Or again, "Marriage . . . is an union of the most intimate nature; but not indissoluble" (15: 155). Yet even here Milton holds that "God has joined only what admits of union" and partial unions are formed by other agents. Accordingly, he concludes that his "doctrine does not separate those whom God has joined together in the spirit of his sacred institution" (15: 157–59).[22]

From the analogies of soul and body, risen Christ and man, and man and woman it is clear that in these kinds of true union Milton understood that unequal entities are combined to form a new entity in which the more powerful constituent is the controlling factor but in which the less powerful continues to have some sort of existence or of individuality. This kind of union may

---

[21] *Tetrachordon*, in *Works*, 4: 106.

[22] In this chapter Milton generally avoids the word *unio*, preferring such a synonym as *necessitudo* (15: 120–22).

continue forever. Milton readily accepts these points of view even though they lead him to mortalism or to a perhaps impossibly ideal conception of marriage. There remains the application of this basic theory of union to his understanding of the Incarnation.

It seems best to admit at once that no orthodox church writers verbally support Milton's views that the Incarnation is the union of two persons rather than of two natures. Indeed, his only support comes from the anathematized Nestorian party. Theodore of Mopsuestia perhaps stands closest to Milton, and he was condemned by the Church. Thus Capitula 12 from the Fifth Council (Constantinople, 553): "If anyone defends the impious Theodore of Mopsuestia, who has said that the Word of God is one person, but that another person is Christ, vexed by the sufferings of the soul and the desires of the flesh, and separated little by little above that which is inferior . . . let him be anathema." Theodore had also compared the union of God and man in the Incarnation with that between husband and wife: "this same impious Theodore has also said that union of God the Word with Christ is like to that which, according to the doctrine of the Apostle, exists between a man and his wife," and again he is anathematized.[23] Like Milton, the school of Antioch found it impossible to conceive of a complete human nature without personality. They accused their opponents, especially the Alexandrians led by Cyril, of being unconscious followers of Apollinaris; but, being in the minority, they were damned for their stand. Nevertheless, their contribution to the history of Christianity is clear: they brought into prominence the human nature of Christ, a fact which many have tended to forget. Although Milton seems to have verbally accepted their position, there is no reference to their writings anywhere in his works. It seems probable that he developed these ideas independently from his own reading and reflection, and thus seems to have arrived unconsciously and independently at the Nestorian position, perhaps by the way he understood the nature of union. Accordingly, it is necessary to explore further his discussion of the Incarnation to see whether he views the Incarnation as a true union or as a Nestorian "juxtaposition."

As for the time when Jesus was conceived, Milton has no use for the Origenist hypothesis that the Son and his human soul were combined long before his appearance on earth. At the same time, he does not follow his own traducian theory as to the origin of Christ's soul, for this would imply that

---

[23] *A Select Library of Nicene and Post-Nicene Fathers*, 2d ser. (Buffalo, 1900), 14: 315. Theodore's antagonists implied from the man–wife analogy the continuing presence of two persons. Cf. MacArthur, p. 20.

Christ inherited the sinful soul of Adam. Rather, this generation "was super-natural" (15: 53). As has been argued, Milton implies that the conception occurred before the Incarnation proper. The Bible says that the cause was the Holy Spirit (Matt. 1: 20, Luke 1: 35), but Milton interprets these passages as referring to "the power and spirit of the Father himself" (15: 281; cf. 14: 363–65 and *Paradise Lost*, 12. 369). This construction apparently stems from Milton's subordinationist conception of the Trinity and finds its earliest expression in Justin Martyr, who held that the begetting in Mary was "the operation of the power and will of the Maker of all things." [24] The conceived baby then existed for an undetermined length of time until the Son descended to unite with him. The descent of the divine person was complete; although some have argued that the Son remained in heaven and only partially descended, Milton evidently considers that he descended entire. Thus in *Paradise Regained*, after the Incarnation has occurred, God turns to Gabriel as interlocutor in place of the Son, who had filled this position in *Paradise Lost*.

Somewhat unusual is Milton's interpretation of Christ's death. First, he accepts the fact that Christ's soul died with his body; there is nothing exceptional about this, nor is it denied by Milton's mortalism. But he goes on to argue that the Passion had affected both the human and divine elements: "not a few passages of Scripture intimate that his divine nature was subjected to death conjointly with his human." Accordingly, "God raised from the dead the whole person of the Lord Jesus" — not his human nature alone (15: 307). Milton has apparently left the safe road of orthodoxy here. The belief that the divine nature suffered and died is the theopaschite (or patri-passian) error, which asserts that the divine may indeed suffer and die. But this definition is based upon the belief that the three persons of the Trinity are one in essence; the suffering of one member involves all three. For Milton, however, their essences are not the same; thus the divinity of the Father does not in any way undergo the sufferings of the Son. Milton's clear distinction of the essences of Father and Son stands him in good stead here to remove him from the ranks of the patripassians. [25]

---

[24] *Ante-Nicene Fathers* (Grand Rapids, 1967), 1, *Dialogue with Trypho*, 241; cf. *Apology*, 1: "The power of God having come upon the virgin, overshadowed her," p. 174.

[25] In *Milton's Brief Epic* (Providence, 1966), p. 155, Barbara Lewalski observes that theopaschites and monophysites (who insisted that the incarnate Son possessed only a single nature) were really from the same tradition. She accordingly questions whether Milton was in any sense a Nestorian, suggesting rather that he was a member of the opposite or monophysite party: he had "instead moved to some variety of Monophysitism, whereby the two persons united in the Incarnation are seen to be fused or joined into one nature." I do not, however, know of any monophysite (e.g., Apollinaris or Eutyches) who asserted

On the other hand, his argument that the Son may have suffered shows clearly that Milton was not a Nestorian in at least one sense. For the Nestorians had no problem in interpreting the death of Christ in perfectly orthodox terms. Following the analogy of juxtaposition, they could observe that at death the bonds uniting the two members of the juxtaposition were severed. The man died and the God did not. Milton's understanding is that the union is far more intimate and permanent; indeed, it will continue forever. Thus in *Paradise Lost* the Father tells the Son that after death

> thy Humiliation shall exalt
> With thee thy Manhood also to this Throne;
> Here shalt thou sit incarnate, here shalt Reign
> Both God and Man . . . . [3. 313–16]

The Incarnation, that is, is a continuing union which apparently will never be dissolved. As Milton says, "after the hypostatical union of two natures in one person, it follows that whatever Christ says of himself, he says not as the possessor of either nature separately, but with reference to the whole of his character, and in his entire person, except where he himself makes a distinction" (14: 229). Later he adds that the exalted human nature "exists nevertheless in one definite place, and has not, as some contend, the attribute of ubiquity" (15: 315). This argument is addressed to the ubiquitarian conception of Christ's body as actually present in the transformed elements of the mass.

Milton provides surprisingly few details about the earthly ministry of Christ, *Paradise Regained* being the only extended treatment. Although not at all explicit as to what the Incarnation meant to its author, the poem does provide some indirect evidence for a better understanding of his position. The very choice of subject (rather than the Passion) shows his deep interest in the humanity of Christ. But then how was he tempted? as man or as God–man? The question is a difficult one which Miss Pope has answered with a wealth of patristic and later religious material which shows that for Milton Christ was tempted only in his human nature.[26] But there are other pertinent details which appear in christological speculations.

First, the early church found a way around the awkwardness of the temptation of the incarnate God by developing the doctrine of *kenosis*. This

---

that two persons rather than two natures were joined to form one nature. To label Milton a monophysite is to ignore his understanding of essence as well as his definitions of nature and personality.

[26] Elizabeth Marie Pope, *"Paradise Regained": The Tradition and the Poem* (Baltimore, 1947), ch. 2.

represents the emptying ($\kappa\acute{\epsilon}\nu\omega\sigma\iota\varsigma$) of Godhead which the Son is said to have undergone in Philippians 2: 6–8: Jesus, "being in the form of God, thought it not robbery to be equal with God: but made himself of no reputation [or emptied himself] and took upon him the form of a servant, and was made in the likeness of men: And being found in fashion as a man, he humbled himself, and became obedient unto death, even the death of the Cross." He could, therefore, be "in all points tempted like as we are" (Hebrews 4: 15). The concept is a troublesome one, but from his premises about the Incarnation Milton directly profits in understanding it. Because for him two *persons* have been united, he may interpret the "emptying" as a total renunciation of the divine knowledge and power by the Son as he becomes incarnate. The human nature or personality then makes the decisions which the will executes. Milton need not argue kenosis at length, in that his hypothesis of two persons makes such an argument unnecessary; his references to the passage in Philippians are likely to be rather colorless,[27] nor is the conception extensively analyzed in the *Christian Doctrine*. For Milton the exinanition of the Son means that "he emptied himself of that form of God in which he had previously existed" (14: 343) and accordingly "after having 'emptied himself,' he might 'increase in wisdom,' Luke ii: 52 by means of the understanding" (15: 275). That is, the human personality grows and directs the incarnate life since the divine has emptied itself. The temptations in *Paradise Regained* are real and not apparent. Only gradually during their course does Christ come to some understanding of both his divine and human roles.

Why did Milton insist upon the personality of the human element in the Incarnation and run the risk of being labeled a Nestorian? It seems clear that he must have considered himself to be adequately protected from criticism by his insistence upon the true union of the two persons in Christ. Unlike other theorists, he then refused to speculate any further upon the exact mode of this union — an area where if he had tried to clarify his thinking he might have run into trouble, for it is just here that the basic problem lies. Even so, one may speculate about the reason for his taking the risk of emphasizing the union of persons rather than of natures. The basis of his acceptance of the

---

[27] E.g., Nativity Ode, line 12, Circumcision, line 20, *Paradise Lost*, 3. 239, and 10. 214. For some reason Mrs. Lewalski (p. 393, n. 69) has chosen to interpret this statement as denying "that kenosis is an important concept for Milton." Instead, she asserts that "it is of central importance," as, of course, it is and as my argument is attempting to prove. The point, which apparently bears repetition, is that because of his conception of two *persons* in Christ, Milton's problem in utilizing the theory of kenosis was a simple one which he did not need to argue at length, though he employed the idea frequently.

human personality of the incarnate Christ seems in large part to derive from his interpretation of what *person* means. Evidently he was unable to conceive of a complete human nature without personality. As he argued accurately in the *Christian Doctrine* (15: 269), the term is historically a metaphor which originally meant the mask which the actor of antiquity wore and which was called *prosopon* or *persona*.[28] As early as 1630 he had written in "The Passion" of the Incarnation, "O what a Mask was there, what a disguise!," where *Mask* is consciously employed in its etymological sense of *person*. The standard definition traces to Boethius, who used it to attack Eutyches and Nestorius: a person is an "individual substance of a rational nature," [29] a conception which Milton reproduces: for him a person is "any individual thing gifted with intelligence (14: 43) or "an intelligent substance, under any form whatever" (14: 371).

Now for the mature Milton the "intelligent substance" which is man is "the faculties of his mind"; they in turn are composed of "understanding and will" (15: 371). In his *Art of Logic* he affirms that these two faculties are coequal: "as far as art and thought effect anything, the first does not seem to set out from the intellect, the second from the will, but either one seems to set out from the other." [30] More briefly, in *Paradise Lost*, 3. 108, Milton asserts that "Reason also is choice," an observation which also appears in *Areopagitica*. Hooker had stated that "Will, in things tending towards any end, is termed Choice." [31] For Milton, then, the statement that the human nature of Christ was a person meant that it was possessed of an intelligence and will of its own. To put it another way, Christ as a human *person* had a true power of choice which in Milton's judgment his human nature alone would not possess. Accordingly, in the Incarnation the new person, the God–man, seems to have included two wills and two understandings, the divine and human, but Milton does not think it necessary to inquire about this problem (15: 275). It seems probable, therefore, that he approached the Nestorian position, perhaps unconsciously, at least in part because of his emphasis upon man's freedom. In order to emphasize man's freedom he had to emphasize man's personality. Thus he and the Nestorians were moved by similar con-

---

[28] Cf. Clement C. J. Webb, *God and Personality* (London, 1919), pp. 35 f. Milton refers to this etymology again in *Paradise Lost*, 10. 156, and in "the drama of the personalities in the Godhead," *Christian Doctrine*, 14: 197.

[29] *Theological Tractates*, p. 85. Cf. Thomas Aquinas, *Summa Theologica*, i.29.1, and Webb, pp. 47 ff.

[30] *Works*, 11: 41; cf. *Treatise of Civil Power*, 6: 21.

[31] *Ecclesiastical Polity*, 1. 7. 2; cf. Aristotle, *Eth. Nic.*, 3: 2, 3; 6: 2.

siderations; as Harnack says of the latter, "they fully accepted the perfect humanity [that is, the human personality] of Christ. The most important characteristic of perfect humanity is its freedom. The thought that Christ possessed a free will was the lode-star of their Christology." [32] In the same way Milton vindicated Christ's free human will by accepting the theological dangers inherent in the concept of his personality. Its clearest exercise would be found in its free choice when confronted by evil, the subject of *Paradise Regained*. Even before the Incarnation, the Son had possessed the same complete freedom: in *Paradise Lost*, 3, he volunteers for the office of mediator; the *Christian Doctrine* asserts that "He voluntarily submitted himself to the divine justice" (15: 303). It is little short of amazing how Milton's emphasis upon freedom enters his theology as it did his other fields of activity.

---

[32] A. Harnack, *History of Dogma*, 4: 165. Cf. MacArthur, p. 16: "What are the marks of real humanity? Above all, the possession of a will that is capable of moral action." Milton and the Antiochenes were also at one in their literal reading of Scripture, in comparison with the allegorizing of the school at Alexandria. See J. N. D. Kelly, *Early Christian Doctrines* (London, 1965), p. 75, and H. R. MacCallum, "Milton and Figurative Interpretation of the Bible," *UTQ* 31 (1962): 397–413.

Milton's Muse

W. B. HUNTER

A famous crux in *Paradise Lost* is the invocation to light which opens Book 3. In these lines Milton hails "Holy Light" as "offspring of Heav'n first-born," or as "of th'Eternal Coeternal beam," or as "pure Ethereal stream, / Whose Fountain who shall tell." In addition, the poet observes that "God is light" and that God thus dwells in this "Holy Light," which he terms the "Bright effluence of bright essence increate." Commentators have presented analogies from Dante, Ficino, and Spenser; the meaning of the perplexing image has been interpreted as physical light or as representing God as Father, as Son, or as Holy Spirit. I think that the collocation of the two images light–sun and stream–fountain reveals that Milton had in mind the identification of this Holy Light with the Son of God.

Among the earliest patristic writers, the so-called Apologists, there was some difficulty in explaining the relationship of the Christian Father and Son to pagan opponents. In order to make clear the meaning of this mystery they especially employed the same two metaphors that Milton was to use. Justin Martyr first brings forward the image of the sun and its light, developing the idea from biblical suggestions. The Son has power "indivisible and inseparable from the Father, just as they say that the light of the sun on earth is indivisible and inseparable from the sun in the heavens." [1] Hippolytus continues this image and adds to it the stream–fountain simile: "When I say *another* [God, i.e., the Son], I do not mean that there are two Gods, but that it is only as light of light, or as water from a fountain, or as a ray from the Sun." [2]

---

[1] *Dialogue with Trypho*, Chap. 128, in *Ante-Nicene Fathers* (Grand Rapids, 1967), 1.

[2] *Against the Heresy of One Noetus*, chap. 11, in *Ante-Nicene Fathers*, 5.

In the Latin fathers these two similes continue with the same meaning. Lactantius argues that the Father and Son cannot be separated: "the former is as it were an overflowing fountain, the latter as a stream flowing forth from it: the former as the sun, the latter as it were a ray extended from the sun." They cannot be separated: "just as the stream is not separated from the fountain, nor the ray from the sun: for the water of the fountain is in the stream, and the light of the sun is in the ray." [3] Tertullian also employs these two images with the addition of another from a tree and its roots: the unity of God in the Son is declared, "just as the root puts forth the tree, and the fountain the river, and the sun the ray. For these are προβολαί, *or emanations*, of the substances from which they proceed. I should not hesitate, indeed, to call the tree the son or offspring of the root, and the river of the fountain, and the ray of the sun; because every original source is a parent, and everything which issues from the origin is an offspring." Nevertheless, he argues, there is no separation of Son from Father: "But still the tree is not severed from the root, nor the river from the fountain, nor the ray from the sun; nor, indeed, is the Word separated from God. Following, therefore, the form of these analogies, I confess that I call God and His Word — the Father and His Son — *two*. For the root and the tree are distinctly two things, but correlatively joined; the fountain and the river are also two forms, but indivisible; so likewise the sun and the ray are two forms, but coherent ones." These analogies, however, lead to the subordination of the Son to the Father: "Everything which proceeds from something else must needs be second to that from which it proceeds, without being on that account separated." [4]

In the same way, Milton must also mean that the light or stream represents the Logos, and the sun or fountain represents the Father. Since the Father is for him completely transcendent, he cannot be described: as the poem says, "Whose Fountain who shall tell." Later in Book 3 the angels hymn the Father in the same terms: "Fountain of Light, thyself invisible" (1. 375); in *Paradise Regained* all of mankind may receive this "Light from above, from the fountain of light" (4. 289). Milton considers the Logos-light to be either the first of creation ("offspring of Heav'n first-born") or co-

---

[3] *Divine Institutes*, 4: 29, in *Ante-Nicene Fathers*, 7.

[4] *Against Praxeas*, chap. 8, in *Ante-Nicene Fathers*, 3. A similar statement appears in his discussion of the generation of the Son from the Father in his *Apology*, chap. 21. The Nicene Creed describes the Son as "light of light." Further discussion appears in J. H. Adamson, "Milton's 'Arianism'," reprinted elsewhere in this volume; our arguments were proposed in complete independence of each other.

eternal with the Father ("of th'Eternal Coeternal beam"), alternatives which were available to him in the tradition of the Apologists.

It seems altogether probable that in the invocations prefacing Books 1, 7, and 9 Milton is addressing the same divinity as that of Book 3. In these introductory passages, that is, he is invoking the Son of God to mediate for him with the Father. If this thesis is sound, then by the only named divinity, Urania in Book 7, he also understands the Son of God.

Urania has usually been explained as one of the Muses. Her particular subject was astronomy, and Milton prefers her (7. 39) to the Muse of epic poetry, Calliope, even though western culture has never developed any significant myths about her. Indeed, the obvious identification with this Muse has not been at all helpful in expounding Milton's meaning. For many years commentators instead thought that Urania represented the Holy Spirit, to whom Milton thus utters these prayers. But the *Christian Doctrine* argues that the Third Person of the Trinity should never be invoked, and Maurice Kelley's comments seem to have disposed permanently of this interpretation.[5] With some misgivings, Kelley in turn sees the invocation as addressed to "a personification of the various attributes of God the Father."

Besides the Muse of Astronomy, there is a far more important Urania who appears in western traditions: the Uranian Aphrodite or Heavenly Beauty posited in opposition to Popular or Earthly Beauty in Plato's *Symposium*. The former was "of no mother born, but daughter of Heaven [Οὐρανοῦ], whence we name her heavenly; while the other was the child of Zeus and Dione, and her we call Popular [Πάνδημον]" (180D).

Amplification of this distinction took place in the hands of the Neoplatonists. Review of the extensive scholarship upon Spenser's *Fowre Hymnes* in the Variorum, especially that to *Heavenly Beautie* (that is, to Uranian Venus), will reveal the tradition in full. According to Plotinus (*Enneads*, 3. 5. 2), the Heavenly Aphrodite is "no other than Mind [νοῦς] itself"; she is "a divine hypostasis," born of Uranus or Saturn. "Mind" in this system is next to the most highly exalted being: it is the first emanation from the One, which is the source of everything. Marsilio Ficino slightly modifies this judgment, holding rather that Aphrodite Urania is the intelligence (*intelligentia*) of Mind (*Mens*).[6] As I have argued,[7] with the addition of Soul to the One and

---

[5] *Christian Doctrine* in *Works* (New York, 1931–38), 14: 395; *This Great Argument* (Princeton, 1941), pp. 109–18.

[6] In the text and translation of his "Commentary on Plato's *Symposium*" by Sears Jayne, *University of Missouri Studies*, 19 (1944): 142.

[7] "Milton's Arianism Reconsidered," reprinted in this volume.

Mind, these Platonists arrived at a trinity of divinities. The parallel was often drawn between the Neoplatonic trinity of One–Mind–Soul and the Christian Trinity of Father–Son–Spirit. In his interpretation of Plotinus' statement, Ficino explicitly concludes that this chapter of the *Enneads* clearly imitated the conception of the Christian Trinity: the first Venus is not a merely imaginary entity but "naturale aliquid & subsistens (ut arbitror) Christianae trinitatis in hoc mysterium imitatus." [8] Uranian Aphrodite is thus the equivalent of the Neoplatonic Mind, which in turn is partially equivalent to the Christian Son. There were, of course, serious theological difficulties with this identification of pagan and Christian divinities, not the least of which was the fact that the pagan one led to a subordinationist trinity. As Pico comments on Benivieni, "no creature but this first minde proceeds immediately from God: for of all other effects issuing from this minde, and all other second causes, God is onely the mediate efficient. This by Plato, Hermes, and Zoroaster is called the Daughter of God, the Minde, Wisdom, Divine Reason, by some interpreted the Word: not meaning (with our Divines) the Son of God, he not being a creature." [9] The Neoplatonic view of Heavenly Beauty permitted the poetic development of Urania as a goddess of inspiration for poets,[10] though her roots in astronomy were never entirely forgotten. According to the fanciful etymologies of Milton's day, she might also be equated with light, even as he seems to have done in the invocation to Book 3.[11]

The invocation of Book 7 observes that before the creation Urania "with Eternal Wisdom didst converse, / Wisdom thy sister." This figure of Wisdom has long been identified with the personified Wisdom of the apocryphal Wisdom of Solomon and of Proverbs 8, who was present and an active agent of the Father in the creation which is about to be described. Yet it is odd to find the poet confusing cultural traditions by asserting sisterhood between a Greek and a Hebrew. An important source for the Hebrew sister has been recog-

---

[8] *Plotini Divini illius e Platonica familia Philosophi* (Basel, 1559), p. 154v.

[9] As quoted by M. Bhattacherje in the commentary to Spenser's *Heavenly Beautie*; Variorum, pp. 562–63. The equivalence of Daughter of God (Zeus), Mind, Wisdom, and Word are worth attention despite Pico's cautious disclaimer. Another very important study is that by Robert Ellrodt, *Neoplatonism in the Poetry of Spenser* (Geneva, 1960), especially chapter 11. For a particularly interesting development of some of its ideas as they apply to Milton's invocations, see M. Y. Hughes, "Milton and the Symbol of Light," in *Ten Perspectives on Milton* (New Haven, 1965).

[10] See Lily B. Campbell, "The Christian Muse," *Huntington Library Bulletin* 8 (1935): 29–70.

[11] Theophilus Gale, *The Court of the Gentiles* (London, 1672), 2. 2. 3: "As for Οὐρανία *Urania*, it evidently received its *origination* from the Hebrew . . . *Or* or *Ur*; which signifies *Light*, as Gen. 1.5." For Ficino, too, Beauty is synonymous with light ("Commentary," p. 211).

nized in the description of Sapience or Wisdom in Spenser's *Hymne of Heavenly Beautie*, which is addressed to Uranian Venus. Spenser certainly associates Milton's sisters here, but they seem to be identical in his eyes in that only Sapience is personified (ll. 183 ff.) in this poem addressed to Urania.

By Sapience Spenser almost certainly means the Son of God.[12] Beginning with Paul (1 Cor. 1: 24) from earliest Christian times the identification of the quasi-divine Old Testament Wisdom was made with Christ. Among the earliest of the church fathers, Justin Martyr elaborates upon this identification, which is echoed by many of his successors.[13] In addition, there may also be some relationship between this Hebrew figure of Wisdom and her Greek and Latin equivalent, Athena–Minerva, in that they all may represent a secondary divinity. Thus according to Plato (Cratylus 407B), Homer "represents Athena as mind [νοῦς] and intellect [διάνοια]; and the maker of her name seems to have had a similar conception of her, but he gives her the still grander title of 'mind of God.'" But this representation of Athena is, of course, exactly the same as that of the Mind or Intellect which had been the Neoplatonic interpretation of Uranian Aphrodite. As Milton's contemporary, Ralph Cudworth, observed in applying these traditions to Christianity, "God was also called Athena or Minerva, as wisdom diffusing itself through all things: and Aphrodite Urania, the heavenly Venus or Love." [14]

Even if Wisdom should be understood as analogous to Athena, who in turn is the sister of Uranian Aphrodite, how Milton has related the sisters Urania and Wisdom is not clear. On the one hand, as two separate beings like Aphrodite and Athena, he may be indicating that the Son possessed Divine Beauty and Divine Wisdom, and the two beings are thus names for two of his manifestations. Or he may be using "sister" as a metaphor for self-identity: the Greek "Heavenly Beauty" is the same being as the Hebrew "Wisdom" in that they had been used to express a second deity in two different cultures. Milton's statement that Urania conversed with Wisdom "Before the Hills appear'd, or Fountain flow'd" clearly shows that he had in mind Proverbs 8, where these phrases originally appear: Wisdom was "brought forth," that text says, "when there were no fountains abounding with water" and "before the hills." But in this passage Wisdom alone was with the Lord

---

[12] See especially Charles G. Osgood, "Spenser's Sapience," *SP* 14 (1917): 174 f.

[13] *Dialogue with Trypho*, chap. 61. Extensive citations appear in Osgood, p. 174, n. 17.

[14] *The True Intellectual System of the Universe* (London, 1845), 2: 279. Cf. pp. 150 f. and his discussion of Minerva together with the interpretative materials which he quotes from Aristides' oration upon her, pp. 213 ff. It is worth mention that neither Urania nor Athena had a mother, nor did the Son of God (nor his parody Sin).

"and was daily his delight, rejoicing always before him"; there is no Urania. The standard interpretation of Milton's statement that Urania

> with Eternal wisdom didst converse,
> Wisdom thy Sister, and with her didst play
> In presence of th'Almighty Father, pleas'd
> With thy Celestial Song [7. 9–12]

is that their "play" is Milton's interpretation of a word usually translated in Proverbs as "rejoicing"; the argument, first advanced by Newton, is that the poet could adopt this meaning because in the Vulgate the word is *ludens*. The play, that is, is some kind of physical activity in which both Urania and Wisdom participate. Saurat followed this meaning so far as to interpret the play as God's sex life.[15]

But one may question this interpretation. In the first place, there is only one figure who "plays" or "rejoices" in Proverbs 8. Furthermore, in the Latin of the Junius–Tremellius Bible which Milton generally followed, the word is not *ludens* (playing) but *laetificans* (rejoicing). A solution to the difficulty is the possibility that at this point he has conflated with Proverbs 8 yet another famous passage describing creation, Psalm 33, which reads, "By the word of the Lord were the heavens made; and all the host of them by the breath of his mouth." For Milton, in light of the first chapter of John, the "word" is, of course, the creative Logos or Son of God.[16] The "breath" is in Latin *spiritus*. Here indeed are two beings, Word and Spirit, entirely comparable to Urania and Wisdom and directly related to the creative process. One should also consider the context of the biblical statement: because of the greatness of the creation which is being described, one should "Sing unto [the Lord] a new song," as Milton emphasizes that he is doing in these invocations. Indeed, the two beings, the Word and the Spirit, may themselves participate in this new song at the creation and may also "play (*pulsate*) skilfully with a loud noise" to the Lord. In this context one should consider that the "playing" in which Urania and Wisdom jointly participated was not a physical activity but rather the production of music in the singing which accompanied the creative process described in Psalm 33 (as well as when the "stars of the morning sang together" in Job 38) and in *Paradise Lost*, 7. The Father is "pleased" with the "Celestial Song" which results.

---

[15] Denis Saurat, *Milton: Man and Thinker* (London, 1944), p. 240.

[16] As Calvin interprets the verse, "we may truly and certainly infer from this passage, that the world was framed by God's Eternal Word, his only begotten Son." *Commentary on the Book of Psalms*, trans. James Anderson (Grand Rapids, 1963), 1: 543.

But even if Milton has conflated Psalm 33 with Proverbs 8 in the invocation to Book 7, it is still not clear how he understands Urania and Wisdom (or the Word and Spirit of the Psalm). Two major interpretations of the Psalm were available to him. First, the Word and Spirit were considered to be the Second and Third Persons of the Christian Trinity, an interpretation reaching back to the Apologist Theophilus, who identifies the Spirit of the Psalm with Wisdom.[17] Word and Spirit, Urania and Wisdom, in this view represent two different manifestations of the Godhead in two different persons. Almost as ancient, however, is a second tradition originating with Tertullian which insists that both Word and Spirit (Wisdom) represent the same entity, the Son.[18] Inasmuch as Milton's language permits the acceptance of either of these interpretations, it seems probable that the passage is deliberately ambiguous — a basic literary strategy, in fact, which he practiced in all of the invocations. Elsewhere in the poem, however, the Father addresses the Son as "My word, my wisdom, and effectual might" (3. 171), a statement which apparently accepts Tertullian's view.[19]

That Milton understands that the Son embodies the "effectual might" of the Father (who is completely transcendent) helps to explain a difficulty which appears in the brief invocation of *Paradise Regained*:

> Thou Spirit who led'st this glorious Eremite
> Into the Desert, . . .
>   inspire,
> As thou art wont, my prompted Song, else mute [1. 8–12]

If the "Spirit" here is the same being whom Milton had invoked in *Paradise Lost*, that is, the Son as Urania, it seems inconsistent that the Son should lead his incarnate self into the wilderness.[20] A solution to the problem depends upon the agency through which the Father exerts his "effectual might."

The Father, of course, possesses many attributes. Two of particular significance here are his power (*potentia*) and virtue (*virtus*) which according to Milton may be called the Spirit of God (14: 359, 363, 365). He may exercise them directly, without the intervention of any other agent. This is what is happening at the beginning of *Paradise Regained* when the Son is led by the Spirit (that is, for Milton, by the Father's power and virtue) into the wilderness to be tempted. But this Spirit may also be transmitted to man

[17] *To Autolycus*, 1. 7, in *Ante-Nicene Fathers*, 2.
[18] *Against Praxeas*, chaps. 6–7.
[19] Calvin also believes that Word and Spirit in the Psalm refer to the Son alone, p. 543.
[20] Kelley, pp. 113 ff.

through the agency of the Son: "The Spirit," argues Milton, also "signifies a divine impulse, or light, or voice, or word, transmitted from above either through Christ, who is the Word of God, or by some other channel" (14: 367). In the invocations in *Paradise Lost* Milton is invoking this same Spirit of the Father as it is transmitted through Christ, who has become God's "effectual might" in the universe, recipient of the Father's unlimited Virtue (*Paradise Lost*, 6. 703; *Christian Doctrine*, 15: 261).

Let us make an end of the matter. Just as the Father dwells in the Holy Light of the opening of Book 3 which is the "Bright effluence" of his own "bright essence," so his power and virtue are made manifest in the Son.[21] In all of the invocations in *Paradise Lost* Milton is praying for help from the Spirit, that is, from the virtue and power of the Father as they are manifested in the Son, whom he addresses variously as Holy Light, as Spirit, and as Urania. Only by the Son, indeed, may man approach God: "to God is no access / Without Mediator" (*Paradise Lost*, 12. 239 f.), but "there is no other Redeemer or Mediator besides Christ" (*Christian Doctrine*, 15: 257) and hence "it is by the Son that we come to the Father" (14: 395), upon whom "we are taught to call" (14: 379). Since the Incarnation, man calls upon God only through Christ, as Milton does in *Paradise Lost*. Indeed, as he has observed, "when we call upon the Son of God, it is only in his capacity of advocate with the Father" (14: 333). There is nothing in the least revolutionary or surprising here: Protestants of all persuasions have always prayed to the Father "in the name of Thy Son, Jesus Christ. Amen."

---

[21] Minerva also was named "the power and virtue of Jupiter himself": Cudworth, 2: 215, quoting Aristides.

4. Problems of Stylistic Expression

Paradise Lost
and the Theory of Accommodation

C. A. PATRIDES

"Now we know God but imperfectly, enigmatically;
but then we shall know him, with a perfect cleare
Meridian knowledge."

CHARLES ODINGSELLS (1637)[1]

One of the most formidable problems faced by John Milton in *Paradise Lost* was the presentation of the War in Heaven. Critics, as we know only too well, are wont to regard that event as possibly Milton's greatest artistic failure; nor, we must confess, is their judgment wholly wrong. At the same time, however, we must recognize that Milton was constrained: for the conventions of the epic compelled him to introduce a battle of heroic proportions, while the need of an "example" for Adam and Eve necessitated the relation, specifically, of Lucifer's rebellion and fall.

This is not to say that Milton's account of the war is beyond reproach. But at least we must credit him with such wisdom as he manifested in choosing the better of the two unsatisfactory methods of presentation. The other method had been attempted by Thomas Heywood in *The Hierarchie of the Blessed Angells* (1635), where the embattled spirits were allowed "No Lances, Swords, nor Bombards," but only "spirituall Armes." This was the result:

> *Lucifer*, charg'd with insolence and spleene;
> When nothing but Humilitie was seene,
> And Reuerence towards God, in *Michaels* brest,
> By which the mighty Dragon he supprest . . . .[2]

---

[1] *The Pearle of Perfection* (London, 1637), p. 83; being one of the numerous variations of St. Paul's well-known statement in 1 Corinthians 13: 12.

[2] *The Hierarchie of the Blessed Angells* (London, 1635), p. 341. For a similar dilemma faced by a lesser versifier, see John Abbot, *Devout Rhapsodies* (London, 1648), 5.

Milton, in contrast, was sharply aware of his difficulties:

> to recount Almighty works
> What words or tongue of Seraph can suffice,
> Or heart of man suffice to comprehend? [7. 112–14]

Raphael, commissioned to relate the War in Heaven, realizes that the problem is fundamentally one of language:

> for who, though with the tongue
> Of Angels, can relate, or to what things
> Liken on Earth conspicuous, that may lift
> Human imagination to such highth
> Of Godlike Power . . . . [6. 297–301]

But since the "process of speech" cannot be avoided, he resolves to tell of things invisible to mortal sight in such a manner "as earthly notion can receive." His method was to adopt what has been happily described as an "extended metaphor," [3] which begins with the explicit statement that

> What surmounts the reach
> Of human sense, I shall delineate so,
> *By lik'ning spiritual to corporal forms,*
> As may express them best, [5. 571–74]

and ends some twelve hundred lines later with the observation that

> Thus *measuring things in Heav'n by things on Earth*
> At thy request . . . to thee I have reveal'd
> What might have else to human Race been hid . . . . [6. 893–96]

Raphael's method is not distinguished by any remarkable originality; we may safely assume, indeed, that most seventeenth-century readers of *Paradise Lost* would have recognized his procedure as an interesting application of the "theory of accommodation." This theory — one of the great commonplaces of the Renaissance — originated long before in an attempt to explain (perhaps even to explain away) the cruder anthropomorphism of the Bible, and notably that of the Old Testament. The *locus classicus* is St. Augustine's statement in *De Civitate Dei*:

Gods anger is no disturbance of mind in him, but his iudgement assigning sinne the deserued punishment: and his reuoluing of thought is an vnchanged ordering of changeable things: for God repenteth not of any thing he doth, as man doth: but his knowledge of a thing ere it be done, and his thought of it when it is done are both alike firme and

---

[3] Arnold Stein, "Milton's War in Heaven: An Extended Metaphor," *Journal of English Literary History* 18 (1951): 201–20; reprinted in *Answerable Style* (Minneapolis, 1953), pp. 17–37.

fixed. But the Scripture without these phrases cannot instil into our vnderstandings the meaning of Gods workes nor terrifie the proud, nor stirre vp the idle, nor exercise the inquirers, nor delight the vnderstanders. This it cannot do without declining to our low capacities.[4]

This and more explicit formulations are repeatedly echoed throughout the sixteenth and seventeenth centuries. Thus, elaborating on a parallel statement by St. Hilary of Poitiers,[5] a minor apologist had this to say:

Because our dulnes to conceiue the thinges of God is so great as wee cannot perceiue them, but by comparisons drawne from the things of men, for this infirmity of our vnderstanding, the scripture very often speaketh of inuisible thinges by visible, and shadoweth spirituall, by corporall.[6]

Time and again Renaissance England was cautioned against literal misreadings of the Scriptures. As Jean Veron declared in his "litel treatis" written "for the erudition and learnying of the symple & ingnorant peopell":

Whan we do read any where ĩ ỹ scriptures that god is subiecte to passiones, or that he hath humayne lymmis, as a head, heares, eyes, and such lyke, it ought not to be vnderstãdyd carnally, & after ỹ hystorye of the letter . . . . But all thinges thus spoken, must be spiritually vnderstandid, and cõfessyd.[7]

There was, in fact, a veritable chorus of reminders that the faithful should not accept "litterallie" the attribution of human characteristics to God but ought to interpret them in "a spirituall sence"; that God is said to have eyes, for example, only "by an ἀνθρωποπάθεια, after the manner of men"; that passions such as anger "are spoken of him onely by way of resemblance, for teaching sake"; and that this method is employed capitally "for the better appre-

---

[4] 15. 25; trans. John Healey, *Of the Citie of God* (London, 1610), p. 565. For parallel statements, including those by Thomas Aquinas and Calvin, see Roland M. Frye, *God, Man and Satan* (Princeton, 1960), pp. 7–13. Professor Frye's work is an attempt to demonstrate that "the method of accommodation as operative in Scripture is also the basic mode of development in *Paradise Lost.*" A sound thesis, soundly argued; but one fears that, in less competent hands, "the literal sence" may be altogether displaced by what George Gifford called "grosse and foolish allegories" (*Foure Sermons* [London, 1582], sig. A 8 ᵛ). Time and again Renaissance theologians cautioned against such excessive zeal; typically, Calvin attacked all "Allegorimakers," thinking it "an euill thing to dally with the holie scripture by transforming of it intoo allegories" (*Sermons . . . vpon the Booke of Iob*, trans. Arthur Golding [London, 1574], p. 733; for a similar English view, see Richard Montagu, *Immediate Addresse vnto God Alone* [London, 1624], p. 93). Whatever the merit of other interpretations, the literal was given priority — nowhere more clearly evident than in expositions of history's *eschata*, which I have discussed in "Renaissance and Modern Thought on the Last Things: A Study in Changing Conceptions," *Harvard Theological Review* 51 (1958): 169–85.

[5] In *De Trinitate*, 8. 43: "[God] has so far tempered the language of His utterance as to enable the weakness of our nature to grasp and understand it" (trans. E. N. Bennett, *Nicene and Post-Nicene Fathers*, 2d ser. [Oxford, 1899], 9: 150).

[6] Thomas Wilson, *Theologicall Rules* (London, 1615), p. 23.

[7] *Certayne Litel Treatis* (London, 1548), sigs. D 1–D 1 ᵛ. There follows (sigs. D 1 ᵛ–E 7) the usual explanation of what is meant by God's ears, eyes, and so forth.

hension of our dull understanding." [8] One popular writer, persuaded that specific examples are better than mere theory, tabulated his explanatory comments thus:

[God] is said to

Breathe.			That he doth infuse the soule into the body.
Heare.			That he accomplisheth mans request.
See.	by which is meant		That he knoweth all things that are done.
Smell.			His acceptation of mans doings.
Sorrow.			The dislike of the things which causeth it . . . .
Sleepe.			That he is slow in succouring . . . .

And he is said to be by an *Anthropopatheia*.

Angrie.			His threatning of punishment.
Exalted.			That his Majestie is exalted.
Iealous.	by which is meant		His great Indignation against Idolatrie.
Iustified.			That he is justified being just and good . . . .
Silent.			That he heareth not our Prayers . . . .
Patient.			His willing forbearance to punish till sinnes be ripened.[9]

It was not necessary for Milton to have read any of these popular writers of the Renaissance. After all, well versed as he was in the writings of the Fathers and later theologians, he could have gathered as much from earlier sources. And, once aware of the theory of accommodation,[10] he resolved to utilize it as the basis of the "extended metaphor" of the War in Heaven. Thus Raphael's attempt to liken "spiritual to corporal forms" was but an application of the biblical precedent to speak "of inuisible thinges by visible" and of "spirituall, by corporall." In this manner, as another writer maintained, "vnder the vine and the barke of things visible and corporall, we draw neare vnto the flower and the pith of that which is inuisible & spirituall." [11]

---

[8] Seriatim: Roger Hutchinson, *The Image of God* (Cambridge, 1550), fol. 7 ᵛ; John Pelling, *A Sermon of the Providence of God* (London, 1607), p. 8; William Gouge, *Gods Three Arrowes* (London, 1631), p. 67; and John Byshop, *Beavtifvll Blossomes* (London, 1577), fol. 2. Thus also Zacharias Ursinus, *The Svmme of Christian Religion*, trans. Henry Parry (Oxford, 1587), p. 371; John Barlow, *The Trve Gvide to Glory* (London, 1619), p. 8; Richard Stock, *A Stock of Divine Knowledge* (London, 1641), p. 74; et al. But similar comments are to be encountered in nearly every work concerned with the "anger" of God; see in particular Luther's exposition in *Works*, ed. Jaroslav Pelikan (St. Louis, 1958), 1: 14–15. Similarly, John Colet affirmed that the act of creation is described "so as to suit the conceptions of the multitude"; however, he trespassed into heterodoxy when he claimed that the account in Genesis is *merely* "a high and holy fiction." See his four "Letters to Radulphus" in *Ioannis Coleti Opuscula Quaedam Theologica*, ed. and trans. J. H. Lupton (London, 1876), pp. 3–28.

[9] Richard Bernard, *The Bibles Abstract and Epitomie* (London, 1642), p. 3; I have eliminated the author's profuse biblical references.

[10] Discussed at some length in his *De Doctrina Christiana*, 14: 30 ff.

[11] John Wall, *Alae Seraphicae* (London, 1627), p. 1; referring specifically to the Song of Songs.

But the theory of accommodation applies not only to the War in Heaven but also to the Deity of *Paradise Lost*. Comments on Milton's reported anthropomorphism abound, in tones that are often scornful and sometimes even abusive. Surely, however, it is more profitable to consider that Milton's God is conceived not so much anthropomorphically as anthropopathically, "after the manner of men." Not that the anthropomorphic conception of God needs to be frowned upon; indeed, it is a point not widely appreciated, yet one that is of some consequence, that a higher form of anthropomorphism is very much part of the fabric of the Christian faith. There is not only irony but some truth in the observation — usually attributed to Voltaire — that after God made man in his image, man retaliated. As Lewis R. Farnell wrote a number of years ago, it is not possible for us to disregard totally the anthropomorphic conception of God. In Farnell's words,

no one has ever been able to imagine a divine personal power that in its nature, attributes, and activity was wholly non-human; also, we find that the farther the ideal recedes from the human sphere the less is its value for real and practical religion. By its votaries the high-pitched theory of God as pure spirit is probably unattainable.[12]

Specifically, we should regard the Christian faith as "the most extreme and consistent expression" of the anthropomorphic approach. In the fuller statement of the distinguished theologian W. R. Matthews,

The eagerness of some Christian thinkers to disclaim the title for their religion is due to the mistaken notion that such a type of thought about God must be superstitious and childish . . . . [Yet] the religious consciousness of Jesus was fashioned after this mode; and it is surely significant that the two pivotal dogmas of developed Christianity are that man is made in the image of God and that God is manifested fully in the man Christ Jesus. Let us not be afraid of the plain implications of our faith. The Christian doctrine of God depends more than any other on the legitimacy of the anthropomorphic approach.[13]

And so Milton.

---

[12] *The Attributes of God* (Oxford, 1925), p. 61.

[13] *God in Christian Thought and Experience* (London, 1930), p. 39. See also the pertinent comments by Christopher R. North, *The Old Testament Interpretation of History* (London, 1946), pp. 143 ff., and, for a survey of the relevant literature on the subject, Sister M. Hilda Bonham, "The Anthropomorphic God of *Paradise Lost*," *Papers of the Michigan Academy of Science, Arts and Letters* 53 (1968): 329–35.

Paradise Lost
and the Language of Theology

C. A. PATRIDES

βλέπομεν γὰρ ἄρτι δι' ἐσόπτρου ἐν αἰνίγματι

1 Corinthians 13 : 12

At the dawn of this century *Paradise Lost* was described as "a monument to dead ideas," [1] and some three decades later Milton's total dislodgement was hailed as an accomplished fact.[2] Today, however, we are less in haste to make such categorical statements. Milton's consignment to oblivion has not, after all, been accomplished. The dead ideas of *Paradise Lost*, stirring beneath the forgetful snow, have come to life again. Already innumerable commentaries have accumulated about the poem, and though the commentators often seem like clouds of locusts bent on transforming a fertile plain into a wasteland, we can still say that we have gained much more than we have lost. Since none is endowed with the capacity for perfect illumination and since we all see "through a glass darkly," our hope of appraising *Paradise Lost* satisfactorily must depend on the concerted efforts of scholars and critics. As Milton himself declared in *Areopagitica*, the seekers after truth have to imitate Isis' careful search for the mangled body of Osiris, collecting it limb by limb.

I venture here some suggestions on the deployment in *Paradise Lost* of the language of theology. The subject is of some moment since Milton's poem is not only inextricably wedded to theology but also amounts to a "cosmic disclosure." [3] In demonstration I propose not to confine myself to Milton and

---

[1] Sir Walter A. Raleigh, *Milton* (London, 1900), p. 88.

[2] I allude to the celebrated first sentence of F. R. Leavis' essay "Milton's Verse," *Scrutiny* 2 (1933): 123–36; reprinted in *Revaluation* (London, 1936), pp. 42–61.

[3] I borrow the phrase — and much else besides — from I. T. Ramsey's *Models and Mystery* (London, 1964), and especially his *Christian Discourse* (London, 1965), *passim*.

his age but to consider also discussions now in progress concerning the nature of theological language. These discussions, stemming from the recent "revolution" in philosophy precipitated largely by logical positivists, have for some time been posing a challenge to Christianity.[4]

I

The Renaissance view of the Bible may not have comprehended awareness of "parallelism," the main formal characteristic of Hebrew poetry to which Robert Lowth first drew attention in 1753. Yet Renaissance scholars acknowledged that many books of the Bible were poems rather than prose works.[5] Nearly every Renaissance thinker subscribed readily to Donne's thesis that biblical language is often poetic and consistently metaphorical: "the Holy Ghost in penning the Scriptures delights himself, not only with a propriety, but with a delicacy, and harmony, and melody of language; with height of Metaphors, and other figures, which may work greater impressions upon the Readers, and not with barbarous or triviall, or market, or homely language." [6]

Yet enthusiasms of the moment bred many foolish notions, among them one claiming the superiority of Hebrew poets to those of ancient Greece and Rome. Milton himself held the perverse opinion that Hebrew lyric poems are incomparable "in the very critical art of composition," and Donne assured his congregation that while Virgil is "the King of the Poets," David remains "a better *Poet* than *Virgil*." [7] Notwithstanding their convictions, neither

---

[4] See I. T. Ramsey, "The Challenge of Contemporary Philosophy to Christianity," *The Modern Churchman* 42 (1952): 252–69; and "The Challenge of the Philosophy of Language," *The London Quarterly & Holborn Review* (October 1961), pp. 243–49. Cf. H. D. Lewis, "Contemporary Empiricism and the Philosophy of Religion," *Philosophy* 32 (1957): 193–205, as well as his survey of "The Philosophy of Religion 1945–1952," *Philosophical Quarterly* 4 (1954): 166–81, 262–74. The challenge has all too often assumed the proportions of a frontal attack on theology, most notably in A. J. Ayer's *Language, Truth and Logic* (London, 1936), esp. chap. 6, "Critique of Ethics and Theology." See, further, the important collection of essays edited by A. J. Ayer, *Logical Positivism* (Glencoe, Ill., and London, 1959), and his paper "The Vienna Circle," in *The Revolution in Philosophy* (London, 1956), being essays by W. C. Kneale, G. A. Paul, D. F. Pears, et al.

[5] See Israel Baroway, "The Bible as Poetry in the English Renaissance: An Introduction," *Journal of English and Germanic Philology* 32 (1933): 447–80; "The Hebrew Hexameter: A Study in Renaissance Sources and Interpretation," *English Literary History* 2 (1935): 66–91; " 'The Lyre of David': A Further Study in Renaissance Interpretation of Biblical Form," *English Literary History* 8 (1941): 119–42; and "The Accentual Theory of Hebrew Prosody: A Further Study in Renaissance Interpretation of Biblical Form," *English Literary History* 17 (1950): 115–35.

[6] E. M. Simpson and G. R. Potter, eds., *The Sermons of John Donne* (Berkeley and Los Angeles, 1953–60), 6: 55.

[7] John Milton, "The Reason of Church Government," in *Works* (New York, 1931–38), 3: 238, and Donne, ibid., 4: 167. Cf. John Milton, *Paradise Regained*, 4. 356–60. For a similar statement by Luther and another one by Donne, see the present author's *Milton and the Christian Tradition* (Oxford, 1966), p. 149.

Donne in his sermons nor Milton in *De Doctrina Christiana* found himself capable of responding to Hebrew poetry as poetry. Repeatedly they flatten the "height of Metaphors" they claim to have discerned in the Bible to the level terrain of their prosaic theology. Donne and Milton were hardly alone in this. Their unresponsiveness was shared by the host of Christian theologians who contributed so many inglorious chapters to the history of the Church. Interpreters of the Johannine Apocalypse and the hysteria they so often generated by their speculations come to mind. Luther, too, comes to mind, joining hands with his Catholic opponents to denounce the "new philosophy" of Copernicus by invoking Joshua 10: 12–13, which is patently a poem. And last, there is Origen who, dramatizing in his own life a metaphorical statement by Jesus (Matthew 19: 22), castrated himself.

Are we ourselves any more enlightened? Consider, for instance, Professor Maurice Kelley's *This Great Argument* (1941), where the prose of *De Doctrina Christiana* is used to bring a "gloss" to the poetry of *Paradise Lost* and to establish "parallels" between the two. Curious assumptions must yield curious results. Here, chosen at random from a page of Mr. Kelley's study, are three of the numerous passages from the treatise and the poem presented to our scrutiny as "parallels." A statement from *De Doctrina*, "It is clear that the world was framed out of matter of some kind or other," [8] Mr. Kelley claims is a parallel to the Father's address to the Son in *Paradise Lost*:

> ride forth, and bid the Deep
> Within appointed bounds be Heav'n and Earth.
> Boundless the Deep, because I am who fill
> Infinitude, nor vacuous the space. [7. 166–69]

He invites us at the same time to consider part of Uriel's description of the creation of the universe:

> I saw when at his Word the formless Mass,
> This world's material mould, came to a heap . . . . [3. 708–9]

The statement from *De Doctrina* affirms dogmatically the theory of *creatio ex materia praeexistente*. The two excerpts from *Paradise Lost* reiterate the providential creation of order from disorder, good from evil, life from death. Yet disregard of context is the least offense committed here. Far more serious in its implications is Mr. Kelley's calm juxtaposition of two passages from a poem with a passage from a prosaic treatise. Their modes of expression, how-

---

[8] Milton, *Works*, 15: 19; quoted by Maurice Kelley, *This Great Argument* (Princeton, N. J., 1941), p. 124.

ever, are of course utterly different. Does not the poem, "outward-looking" as it is, expand constantly its circumference? Does not the treatise, "inward-looking" as it is, contract always its circumference until circumference and center touch? I have purposely called *De Doctrina* a "prosaic" treatise for I am of the opinion that Milton found its subject to be "above the years he had, when he wrote it, and nothing satisfi'd with what was begun, left it unfinished." I am not arguing that Milton abandoned *De Doctrina* in the same way or for the same reasons that he abandoned *The Passion*, from which I have just quoted. I am arguing, rather, that *De Doctrina* is unfinished in the sense that, Milton's expectations notwithstanding, it is a singularly gross expedition into theology. Not only is it strikingly unoriginal, but it is also utterly lacking in the two qualities which are, as we shall see, the very essence of theological language: an appropriate "oddness" combined with a certain logical behavior. Above all, the treatise is rather seriously marred by its rejection of the co-equality and co-essentiality of the three Persons within the Godhead even while it accepts the participation of the Son and the Holy Ghost in the Father's *substantia*. Unwittingly it tends to uphold, therefore, not one but three gods. Can the prose of this work really be used to bring a "gloss" to the poetry of *Paradise Lost*?

Milton, performing in the cool sphere of theology, largely met with disaster in *De Doctrina*. The same is not, however, true of *Paradise Lost*. Indeed with that epic Milton compensated enormously the failure of his prosaic treatise. In the poem he burst his limitations as a theologian and became the great poet he truly was, answering the call, natural to him, of poetry. Ponder for a second Milton's discussion in *De Doctrina* concerning the inequality of the "essentiae" within the Godhead. Consider not so much his deployment of the biblical evidence as his insensitivity in trampling the metaphors "Father" and "Son" to their death.[9] Milton would have increased by one the number of the literalistic theologians whose corpses litter the highway of church history but for "the inspired gift of God rarely bestowed," his abilities as a poet.

II

"All attempts to explain the nature and relations of the Deity," we have been told, "must largely depend on metaphor, and no one metaphor can exhaust those relations. Each metaphor can only describe one aspect of the

---

[9] It should be noted that at this point I see *De Doctrina* through the eyes of the Christian tradition generally. But as the treatise could, from another standpoint, be seen more precisely as the by-product of literalistic puritanism, one might convincingly argue that it is a far greater achievement than I intimate here.

nature or being of the Deity." [10] In *Paradise Lost* Milton was obviously illumined by such an awareness. Putting away in that poem the childish things of *De Doctrina*, he embarked upon an exploration of the nature and relations of the Deity that took him voyaging through the Christian tradition he had so scrupulously avoided earlier, never failing to expound the very metaphors he had so insensitively ignored in his prosaic treatise. And so the thoughts of *De Doctrina* — thoughts of a dry brain in a dry season — yielded to the throbbing metaphors in Book 3 of *Paradise Lost*:

> Hail holy Light, offspring of Heav'n first-born,
> Or of th' Eternal Coeternal beam
> May I express thee unblam'd? since God is light,
> And never but in unapproached light
> Dwelt from Eternity, dwelt then in thee,
> Bright effluence of bright essence increate. . . .
>
> .   .   .
>
> on his right
> The radiant image of his Glory sat,
> His only Son . . . .
>
> .   .   .
>
> Divine Similitude,
> In whose conspicuous count'nance, without cloud
> Made visible, th' Almighty Father shines . . . .
>
> .   .   .
>
> Thron'd in highest bliss
> Equal to God, and equally enjoying
> God-like fruition . . . .
>
> [3. 1–6, 62–64, 384–86, 305–7]

Milton's *De Doctrina Christiana* is a theological labyrinth. *Paradise Lost* is a window to the sun.

My thesis may be approached, too, from another direction, through the many modern studies of *Paradise Lost* that have so advanced our ability to "see" the poem properly that the giving famishes the craving. We have come to appreciate as never before the multitude of theological ideas underlying the whole of *Paradise Lost* and the significance of its various parts, down to phrases and words themselves. Thus the last two books of the poem, so frequently misunderstood, have emerged of late as indispensable components

---

[10] J. F. Bethune-Baker, *An Introduction to the Early History of Christian Doctrine*, 5th rev. ed. (London, 1933); in I. T. Ramsey, *Religious Language* (London, 1957), p. 164. Students of Milton may also be interested in Kenneth Burke's study of the poet's theology "purely from the standpoint of verbal symbolism"; see "Words anent Logology," in *Perspectives in Literary Symbolism*, Joseph Strelka, ed. (University Park, Pa., 1968), pp. 72–82.

not only of its poetic movement but also of its theological content.[11] Again, we no longer look through a glass darkly at the seemingly ludicrous War in Heaven or the apparently pointless Jacob's Ladder and Paradise of Fools.[12] Phrases and words have also been given their due, yielding studies demonstrating why the Fall occurred at "the hour of Noon" (9. 739), why the prophecy of the woman's "seed" is important (10. 181), as well as implications of Michael's reference to "types and shadows" (12. 232 ff.).[13] But for my purposes here one reading of *Paradise Lost* is particularly relevant. I refer to Professor Roland M. Frye's study of the theory of accommodation in the poem.[14]

The theory of accommodation reached Milton with impressive credentials. Nearly all major theologians, trailed by a host of minor expositors, had already affirmed that God in the Scriptures "accommodated" himself to our low capacities of comprehension, that he has "so far tempered the language of his utterance as to enable the weakness of our nature to grasp and understand it." [15] The theory was obviously framed to justify the cruder instances

---

[11] See F. T. Prince, "On the Last Two Books of *Paradise Lost*," *Essays and Studies* by Members of the English Association, n.s., 11 (1958): 38–52 (reprinted in *Milton's Epic Poetry*, C. A. Patrides, ed. [Penguin Books, 1967], pp. 233–48); L. A. Sasek, "The Drama of *Paradise Lost*, Books XI and XII," in *Studies in English Renaissance Literature*, W. F. McNeir, ed. (Baton Rouge, La., 1962), pp. 181–96; Barbara K. Lewalski, "Structure and Symbolism of Vision in Michael's Prophecy: *Paradise Lost*, Books XI–XII," *Philological Quarterly* 42 (1963): 25–35; and H. R. MacCallum, "Milton and Sacred History: Books XI and XII of *Paradise Lost*," in *Essays in English Literature*, Millar MacLure and F. W. Watt, eds. (Toronto, 1964), pp. 149–68; and Mary Ann Radzinowicz, " 'Man as a Probationer of Immortality': *Paradise Lost* XI–XII," in *Approaches to 'Paradise Lost': The York Tercentenary Lectures*, C. A. Patrides, ed. (London and Toronto, 1968), pp. 31–51.

[12] Cf. seriatim: Arnold Stein, "Milton's War in Heaven: An Extended Metaphor," *English Literary History* 18 (1951): 201–20, reprinted in *Answerable Style* (Minneapolis, Minn., 1953), pp. 17–37; C. A. Patrides, "Renaissance Interpretations of Jacob's Ladder," *Theologische Zeitschrift* 18 (1962): 411–18; and three studies on the Paradise of Fools: by Joseph Horrell in *Review of English Studies* 18 (1942): 413–27; F. L. Huntley in *English Literary History* 21 (1954): 107–13; and E. L. Marilla in *English Studies* 42 (1961): 1–6.

[13] The Fall at high noon is discussed by Albert R. Cirillo, "Noon-Midnight and the Temporal Structure of *Paradise Lost*," *English Literary History* 29 (1962): 372–95; reprinted in *Milton's Epic Poetry*, C. A. Patrides, ed. (Penguin Books, 1967). There are four studies of the woman's "seed": by J. E. Parish in *Rice Institute Pamphlet* 40 (1953), no. 3, pp. 1–24, and in *Journal of English and Germanic Philology* 58 (1959), 241–47; by John M. Steadman in *Studies in Philology* 56 (1959): 214–25; and by C. A. Patrides in *Studies in English Literature* 3 (1963): 19–30. The importance of typology was first discussed in relation to *Samson Agonistes* by F. Michael Krouse, *Milton's Samson and the Christian Tradition* (Princeton, N. J., 1949); it has since been related to the epic by William G. Madsen, "Earth the Shadow of Heaven: Typological Symbolism in *Paradise Lost*," *PMLA* 75 (1960): 519–27, and "From Shadowy Types to Truth," in *The Lyric and Dramatic Milton*, Joseph H. Summers, ed. (New York, 1965), pp. 95–114.

[14] Roland M. Frye, *God, Man and Satan: Patterns of Christian Thought and Life in "Paradise Lost," "Pilgrim's Progress," and the Great Theologians* (Princeton, N. J., 1960).

[15] St. Hilary of Poitiers, *De Trinitate*, 8: 43; in *Nicene and Post-Nicene Fathers*, 2d ser. (Oxford, 1899), 9: 150. To the similar affirmations of the theory by Thomas Aquinas, Calvin, et al., quoted by Frye (ibid., pp. 7–13), I have added the statements by Augustine

of biblical anthropomorphism, though it was also intended as an invitation to consider as metaphors all statements concerning God — "metaphors," wrote St. Gregory of Nyssa, "which contain a deeper meaning than the obvious one." [16] Milton accepted the invitation both in *De Doctrina* and in *Paradise Lost*.[17] In the poem he made it "the basic mode of development," as Mr. Frye argues. In his prosaic treatise he resolutely shielded his eyes from its implications and wholly avoided the invitation when arguing against the equality of the "Father" and the "Son." I cannot believe that such spectacular differences between *De Doctrina* and *Paradise Lost* are attributable to Milton's hesitation publicly to assert his private beliefs. He was never a man who lacked the courage of his convictions. Nor can I believe that these differences spring from his desire to avoid alienating the readers of his poem, since this would involve us in a charge of hypocrisy that might prove rather difficult to substantiate. I am not even prepared to accept the reasonable-sounding theory that such differences are "eventually due to differences in the media and aims of expository prose and epic poetry." [18] A theological treatise not only might, but *ought*, to avail itself of the theory of accommodation and, especially if it aspires to discuss the nature and relations of the Deity, of metaphorical language. We recall the practice of the great theologians who in their attempts to delineate the nature of the Christian "cosmic disclosure" resorted to the kind of metaphorical language that, for example, informs the treatises of St. Athanasius against the Arians.[19]

In the absence in Milton's *De Doctrina* of such language, of any application of the theory of accommodation nominally endorsed in it, and because we can hardly be impressed by its espousal of a form of tritheism, I can only conclude that the treatise represents such an abortive venture into theology that Milton was forced drastically to alter his approach in *Paradise Lost*. It may be that Milton never actually abandoned *De Doctrina*. It may be that he

---

and numerous Renaissance writers in "*Paradise Lost* and the Theory of Accommodation," reprinted in this volume, and in *Milton and the Christian Tradition*, pp. 9 ff. See also the quotations given by Stephen J. Brown, S. J., *The World of Imagery* (London, 1927), part 2, chap. 5, "Metaphor and Theology."

[16] *Contra Eunomium*, 1: 23; in *Nicene and Post-Nicene Fathers*, 2d ser. (Oxford, 1893), 5: 63.

[17] In *De Doctrina* he discusses the theory at some length (*Works*, 14: 30 ff.), and in *Paradise Lost* he uses it as the basis of the "extended metaphor" of the War in Heaven. See esp. *Paradise Lost*, 5: 571–74, and 6: 893–96; cf. Stein, note 12 above.

[18] B. Rajan, "*Paradise Lost*" and the Seventeenth-Century Reader (New York, 1948), p. 35.

[19] No relationship between Arianism and Milton's treatise is here implied. For my belief to the contrary, see the evidence I cited in "Milton and Arianism," reprinted in this volume.

reverted to it often until his death in 1674. No matter. None of us is prepared to acknowledge total defeat, Milton least of all. In any case the treatise never resolved the problems it raised and, probably for that very reason, was never published.

The problems were resolved only in *Paradise Lost*. The achievement was due to several factors. The most decisive was certainly Milton's adoption of a language whose center of gravity is the "model" [20] or — depending on the dictates of our particular critical vocabulary — the image, the metaphor, the symbol or the archetype, the emblem or the icon, perhaps even parabolic language and possibly "myth." [21] Whichever term we finally endorse, it ought to be one that describes adequately the odd behavior of a language that is always more in intention than it is in existence and constantly points to something beyond itself, thereby enabling poet or theologian to be "articulate about an insight." [22] When the "model" is centrally located, it radiates outward in the manner of the passages from Book 3 of *Paradise Lost* I quoted earlier. When the "model" is abandoned, however, articulation about an insight lapses into mere affirmation in the manner of *De Doctrina*. Many readers of Milton would, of course, argue that in *Paradise Lost* he abandons the "model" in certain respects. This seems to be true notably in the last two books, but also in the prolonged attempts of the Father in Book 3 to justify himself. But the interpretation of passages isolated from their context is surely a fruitless pastime. In such fragments all poets are inclined to nod. Consider T. S. Eliot in *East Coker*:

> You say I am repeating
> Something I have said before. I shall say it again.
> Shall I say it again? . . .

— or Yeats at the outset of *Lapis Lazuli*:

> I have heard that hysterical women say
> They are sick of the palette and fiddle-bow,
> Of poets that are always gay,
> For everybody knows or else should know
> That if nothing drastic is done . . .

---

[20] Max Black, *Models and Metaphors* (Ithaca, N. Y., 1962); I. T. Ramsey, *Religious Language* (London, 1957), and *Models and Mystery* (London, 1964).

[21] On parabolic language, see note 30 below. On "myth," two recent readings of *Paradise Lost* may in particular be recommended: Isabel G. MacCaffrey, *"Paradise Lost" as "Myth"* (Cambridge, Mass., 1959), and Wayne Shumaker, *"Paradise Lost*: The Mythological Dimension," *Bucknell Review* 10 (1961): 75–86. As the term "myth" is highly elusive, however, particular care must be taken not to lose sight of the historical claims of the Christian faith.

[22] While quoting from I. T. Ramsey, *Models and Mystery* (London, 1964), p. 53, I have also adapted two phrases from Philip Wheelwright, *The Burning Fountain: A Study in the Language of Symbolism* (Bloomington, Ind., 1954), p. 19, and Paul Tillich, "Theology and Symbolism," in *Religious Symbolism*, F. Ernest Johnson, ed. (New York, 1955), p. 108.

These fragments, set within their proper context in the *Four Quartets* and *Lapis Lazuli,* change utterly. Similarly, the center of gravity of *Paradise Lost* is, as I see it, neither in the Father's address in Book 3 nor in any other single part of the poem. "Other echoes / Inhabit the garden": it is the cumulative effect of these echoes, the total pattern of *Paradise Lost* that fuses leaf, blossom and bole into one chestnut-tree, one great-rooted blossomer.

My point is hardly novel. Professor Frank Kermode has also invited us to see *Paradise Lost* "as a whole." [23] How else, indeed, can we appreciate the poem's marvelous tonal range? Only in the light of Raphael's courteous attitude toward Adam before the Fall, for example, can we best grasp the sense of Michael's manner when coldly he corrects the fallen Adam who misinterprets most aspects of the Vision unfolding before him, including the union between the sons of Seth and the daughters of Cain (11. 556–636). Mr. Kermode rightly concludes that Michael's attitude heralds a change in the divine arrangements: "the evidence of the senses, the testimony of pleasure, is no longer a reliable guide." As Michael pointedly observes,

> Judge not what is best
> By pleasure, though to Nature seeming meet . . . . [11. 603–4]

Here, in poetic affirmation of the fundamental Christian claim that fallen man errs constantly and constantly needs grace to repair mere nature, we have yet another instance of the marriage between poetry and theology in *Paradise Lost.* Michael's reproof of the fallen Adam is quite simply a "model," a "myth," a metaphor that draws a spiritual truth within the compass of our lowly apprehension. The incident by itself, seen out of context, is doubtless "odd"; but seen in context it has its own "distinctive logical behaviour," particularly because it gathers together many of the echoes we have been hearing throughout the poem. The "oddness" and the "logical behaviour" might indeed be said to describe the language of poetry. They certainly *do* describe the language of theology. [24]

Can we regard the prolonged attempts of the Father in Book 3 to justify himself as an aspect of this pattern? It is a possibility. The theory of accommodation certainly offers an adequate precedent for Milton's seemingly

---

[23] Frank Kermode, "Adam Unparadised," in *The Living Milton,* Frank Kermode, ed. (London, 1960), pp. 119 ff.

[24] Cf. I. T. Ramsey, *Religious Language* (London, 1957), chaps. 1–2. On the languages of poetry and theology, see esp. Austin Farrer, *The Glass of Vision* (London, 1948); Ronald W. Hepburn, "Poetry and Religious Belief," in *Metaphysical Beliefs,* Alasdair MacIntyre, ed. (London, 1957), part 2; and H. D. Lewis, *Our Experience of God* (London, 1959), chap. 13, "Art and Religion."

"odd" conception of the Deity. We might with even more profit, however, invoke the context to attest the simple fact that Milton's God appears for the first time not in Books 1 or 2 but in Book 3. This strategy has several important implications. The very first line of Book 3 ("Hail holy Light, offspring of Heav'n first-born") instantly marks the difference between heaven and hell not simply in terms of light and darkness, but — let it be noted — in terms of life and death, fruition and decay, the natural and the perverse.[25] Thereafter the language of Book 3 appears to be less "poetic" than the language of Books 1 and 2, though it has, in fact, become more subtle, more complex, more "outward-looking." The difference is by no means obvious. How could it be? We ascend most reluctantly from hell to heaven, already seduced by the sounds that have charmed our ears, the splendor that has dazzled our eyes, the rhetoric that has gorgonized our total being. We are barely in a position to recognize that Adam's predicament after the Fall has been our predicament and that Michael's reproof of Adam might as readily have been a reproof of ourselves, lately so tempted by the sights, the sounds, the rhetoric of hell:

> Judge not what is best
> By pleasure, though to Nature seeming meet . . . .

To observe Milton's strategy it is better to appreciate the particular way that he is "articulate about an insight," the particular way that his language is always more in intention than it is in existence. Accordingly, the transition from Book 2 to Book 3 is a transition from the spectacular world of hell, where might and grandeur are merely insubstantial reflections in the mirror of poetry, to the relatively still world of heaven, where majesty and glory are the substantial reflections not of any mirror but the still center of the turning world. The basic "model" is now manipulated with deliberate care. Its effect is calculated. No longer is it permitted to lend support to its immediate object as in Books 1 and 2 but is carefully designed to throw light on the whole universe of *Paradise Lost*. Thus it penetrates into hell and undermines the insubstantial nature of its several claims, glances across history and invests it with meaning, reverts to heaven and arrays the angels in enormous circles that connect the still point at the center to the turning world of the periphery. Even the generally decried forensic terms — justice and justification, imputed

---

[25] See esp. the exposition by Joseph H. Summers, *The Muse's Method* (London, 1962), chap. 4. On the light/dark opposition, see the discussion and further references by Merritt Y. Hughes, *Ten Perspectives on Milton* (New Haven, Conn., 1965), chap. 4.

merit and propitiation, ransom and satisfaction[26] — explode far beyond Book 3 to affect the entire structure of *Paradise Lost*. "Merit," for example, links four events: the exaltation of the Son (5. 815; 6. 43; cf. 3. 309); the rebellion of Satan (cf. 1. 98); the nocturnal temptation of Eve (5. 80); and the sacrifice of the God–man (3. 290 ff.; cf. 12. 408 ff.). "Ransom" emerges implicitly during the debate in heaven and explicitly during Michael's revelation of the future (3. 287 ff.; 12. 424; cf. 10. 61), yet in between underlies Eve's offer to die in Adam's place (10. 930 ff.).[27] "Justice," which on the evidence of Book 3 is usually related only to the Father, reappears in direct relation to the Son both during the War in Heaven (6. 824 ff.) and in all visions of the Last Judgment (3. 323 ff.; 12. 458 ff., 545 ff.). Such an exchange of roles confirms afresh a thesis I have argued elsewhere, that Milton's conception of the "Father" and the "Son" in *Paradise Lost* is neither poetry nor dogma; it is both.[28] We persist in distinguishing the dancer from the dance. Milton does not.

The theory of accommodation as it is used in *Paradise Lost* might, from another standpoint, be seen as a valid means of "knowing" God through the finite symbols common enough in religious poetry. Thus Professor Louis A. Reid has authoritatively observed that:

[T]he characteristic of religious poetry as such is that it is forever attempting to express the trans-phenomenal or the transcendent, and forever failing to do so. Perhaps it is fairer to say that it is always partially succeeding and partially failing. It must fail to do so in the sense that the trans-phenomenal, the transcendent, the infinite, can never be more than hinted at by phenomenal, finite symbols. Yet on the other hand it can in its own symbolism suggest or express this very inexpressibility. One gets something of this in the negative language of some mystics, and in the tumbled and contradictory imagery of much prophetic and eschatological writing.[29]

The language of *Paradise Lost* is not negative or even abstract. It is concrete and earth-bound, as is normally the language of the Bible.[30] We must,

---

[26] I have outlined the traditional nature of these terms in "Milton and the Protestant Theory of the Atonement," *PMLA* 74 (1959): 7–13, and *Milton and the Christian Tradition* (Oxford, 1966), pp. 130–42. Cf. Hughes, *Ten Perspectives on Milton*, chap. 5. The same terms are discussed as "models" by I. T. Ramsey, *Christian Discourse* (London, 1965), chap. 2, "Atonement Theology."

[27] The word *ransom* is particularly prominent in *Samson Agonistes* where it is an indispensable element of dramatic irony.

[28] C. A. Patrides, "The Godhead in *Paradise Lost*: Dogma or Drama?" reprinted in this volume.

[29] Louis A. Reid, *Ways of Knowledge and Experience* (London, 1961), pp. 117–18.

[30] For a convenient list of the most common clusters of biblical images — all equally "concrete" — see Stephen J. Brown, S. J., *Image and Truth: Studies in the Imagery of the Bible* (Rome, 1955). The various studies of the parables of Jesus available in English — as by G. C. Morgan (1907), R. M. Lithgow (1914), H. B. Swete (1920), G. A. Buttrick

on the other hand, be alive to the affinities that exist between the language of *Paradise Lost* and the "tumbled and contradictory" imagery of biblical apocalyptic literature, partly because we may then restrain our almost indecent readiness to see the entire poem as "baroque" and partly because we may resolve some of our difficulties over its alleged discrepancies.

The best report on these discrepancies has been ventured by Professor William Empson in *Milton's God* (1961). One of the most significant examples he has cited concerns Milton's repetition of a metaphor with seemingly disastrous implications.[31] The metaphor first appears when God intervenes in the threatened conflict between Gabriel and Satan by hanging forth in heaven the constellation of his golden scales (4. 996 ff.). It reappears when God later "protests his innocence" over the Fall of Man:

> no Decree of mine
> Concurring to necessitate his Fall,
> Or touch with lightest moment of impulse
> His free Will, to her own inclining left
> In even scale. [10. 43–47]

Empson feels that the metaphor is "unfortunate." But might it not be "fortunate" after all? Might not Milton have used it with studied deliberation? Surely we ought to inquire whether this metaphor, this "model," forms part of any larger model such as the "fortunate" Fall? This may seem at best the merest possibility. Yet possibility is transformed into certainty the moment we remind ourselves that *Paradise Lost* is "articulate about an insight" not simply in poetic terms but rather in poetic terms that are bound up inextricably with the whole vocabulary that goes to make up the language of theology. We have already seen this language called "odd." It is indeed *very* "odd"; it is "logically anomalous"; [32] it is, in the last analysis, paradoxical — and "paradoxical and near-paradoxical language," we have been told, "is the *staple* of accounts of God's nature." [33]

(1928), A. T. Cadoux (1931), C. H. Dodd (1935), W. O. E. Oesterley (1936), Hugh Martin (1937), B. T. D. Smith (1937), G. C. Morgan (1943), J. A. Findlay (1950), F. L. Filas (1959), A. M. Hunter (1960), G. V. Jones (1964), et al. — might assist readers of Milton wishing to consider the substantial influence of the parabolic language of the New Testament on *Paradise Lost*.

[31] William Empson, *Milton's God* (London, 1961), pp. 112, 116 ff.

[32] Cf. I. M. Crombie, "The Possibility of Theological Statements," in *Faith and Logic*, Basil Mitchell, ed. (London, 1957), chap. 2.

[33] Ronald W. Hepburn, *Christianity and Paradox* (London, 1958), p. 16. In addition to this entire study, see the symposium on "Paradox in Religion" by I. T. Ramsey and Ninian Smart, *Aristotelian Society Supplementary Volume*, 33 (1959): 195–232. Cf. Wheelwright, *The Burning Fountain*, pp. 70 ff. The reader may care to recall at this point Cleanth Brooks' argument that "the language of poetry is the language of paradox" (in *The Lan-*

The paradox of the "fortunate" Fall in *Paradise Lost* was first noted by Arthur O. Lovejoy in 1937 and has since been the subject of numerous studies.[34] But there are other paradoxes in the poem, among them Adam's sweeping confession that God is

> Merciful over all his works, with good
> Still overcoming evil, and by small
> Accomplishing great things, by things deem'd weak
> Subverting worldly strong, and worldly wise
> By simply meek, [12. 565–69]

which in retrospect lends coherence to the entire epic as the divers activities of God, Man, and Satan fuse into one "logically anomalous" scheme.[35] Part of this scheme is the seemingly vexing problem of God's foreknowledge and man's free will, indeed the whole paradoxical situation that Rosalie L. Colie has lately seen exemplified in the poem's action and demonstrated in its structure.[36] The technique is decidedly Milton's own, but the general method recalls the attempts of many poet–prophets — among them Isaiah, the creator of Job, and Dante — to absorb the merely natural into a far more comprehensive vision until all paradoxes merge into "one simple flame," until "the fire and the rose are one."[37]

---

guage of Poetry*, Allen Tate, ed. [Princeton, N. J., 1942], pp. 37–61; reprinted in *The Well Wrought Urn* [New York, 1947], chap. 1).

[34] Arthur O. Lovejoy, "Milton and the Paradox of the Fortunate Fall," *English Literary History* 4 (1937): 161–79; reprinted in *Essays in the History of Ideas* (Baltimore, Md., 1948), chap. 14; in *Criticism: The Foundations of Modern Literary Judgment*, Mark Schorer et al., eds. (New York, 1948), pp. 137–47; and in *Milton's Epic Poetry*, C. A. Patrides, ed. (Penguin Books, 1967), pp. 55–72. I have noted a number of other uses of the paradox in "Adam's 'Happy Fault' and XVIIth-Century Apologetics," *Franciscan Studies* 23 (1963): 238–43. The studies occasioned by Lovejoy's thesis range from William G. Madsen's brief though suggestive essay in *Modern Language Notes* 74 (1959): 103–5, to Dick Taylor's extremely personal view in *Tulane Studies in English* 9 (1959): 35–51.

[35] I have noted this paradox in *Milton and the Christian Tradition* (Oxford, 1966), pp. 159–61. But see also its exposition by Thomas Greene, *The Descent from Heaven* (New Haven, Conn., 1963), pp. 388–94, and the relevant discussion by MacCaffrey, "*Paradise Lost*" as "*Myth*", pp. 64 ff.

[36] Rosalie L. Colie, "Time and Eternity: Paradox and Structure in *Paradise Lost*," *Journal of the Warburg and Courtauld Institutes* 23 (1960): 127–38. See also her more comprehensive study, *Paradoxia Epidemica: Studies in Renaissance Paradoxy* (Princeton, N. J., 1966). For another approach, cf. Roy Daniells, "*Paradise Lost*: Paradox and Ambiguity," in *Milton, Mannerism and Baroque* (Toronto, 1963), chap. 8. On the medieval predilection for paradox, see Walter J. Ong, S. J., "Wit and Mystery: A Revaluation of Mediaeval Latin Hymnody," *Speculum* 22 (1947): 310–41.

[37] Cf. Dante's "un semplice lume" (*Paradiso* 33. 20), and the last verse of T. S. Eliot's *Little Gidding*. A discussion of Milton as a poet–prophet is very much lacking. I recommend, as a starting point, Austin Farrer's *The Glass of Vision* (London, 1948), chap. 8, and H. D. Lewis' *Our Experience of God* (London, 1959), chap. 13.

Milton in *Paradise Lost* may often have failed to see beyond the dark mirror, to see "face to face." But this was inevitable. As Yeats said of another poet–prophet:

The technique of Blake was imperfect, incomplete, as is the technique of wellnigh all artists who have striven to bring fires from remote summits; but where his imagination is perfect and complete, his technique has a like perfection, a like completeness.[38]

---

[38] William Butler Yeats, "William Blake and His Illustrations to the *Divine Comedy*," in *Essays and Introductions* (London, 1961), p. 127.

A Reading List
on the Language of Theology

C. A. PATRIDES

The studies listed below do not constitute an exhaustive reading list but are recommended as particularly noteworthy contributions to the discussions now in progress. For a simple and lucid introduction, the interested reader might consult John B. Wilson's *Language and Christian Belief* (London, 1958), or *The Truth of Religion* (London, 1958). Thereafter, the following:

BAILLIE, JOHN. *Our Knowledge of God.* London, 1939.

BLACK, MAX. *Models and Metaphors: Studies in Language and Philosophy.* Ithaca, N. Y., 1962.

BRAITHWAITE, R. B. *An Empiricist's View of the Nature of Religious Belief.* Cambridge, 1955. Discussed by J. N. Schofield, D. M. MacKinnon, I. T. Ramsey, and R. B. Braithwaite, in "Religion and Empiricism," *Cambridge Review* 77 (1956): 352–53, 375–78, 404–5, 433–36, and by A. C. Ewing in "Religious Assertions in the Light of Contemporary Philosophy," *Philosophy* 32 (1957): 206–18.

CAMPBELL, A. C. *On Selfhood and Godhood.* London, 1957.

CASSERLEY, J. V. LANGMEAD. *The Christian in Philosophy.* London, 1949. Especially part 2.

CHRISTIAN, WILLIAM A. *Meaning and Truth in Religion.* Princeton, 1964.

CLEOBURY, F. H. *Christian Rationalism and Philosophical Analysis.* London, 1959.

EVANS, DONALD D. *The Logic of Self-Involvement: A Philosophical Study of Everyday Language with Special Reference to the Christian Use of Language about God as Creator.* London, 1963.

FARRER, AUSTIN. *The Glass of Vision.* London, 1948.

FERRÉ, FREDERICK. *Language, Logic and God.* London, 1962.

FLEW, ANTHONY, and ALASDAIR McINTYRE, eds. *New Essays in Philosophical Theology.* London, 1955. Twenty-two essays by various hands; cf. the discussion by Illtyd Trethowan and Leo Williams in "God and Logical Analysis," *Downside Review* 74 (1956): 185–98, as well as by most writers in the present list.

FOSTER, MICHAEL B. *Mystery and Philosophy.* London, 1957.

GLASGOW, W. D. "Knowledge of God," *Philosophy* 32 (1957): 229–40.

HEPBURN, RONALD W. *Christianity and Paradox: Critical Studies in Twentieth-Century Theology.* London, 1958.

HICK, JOHN. *Faith and Knowledge: A Modern Introduction to the Problem of Religious Knowledge* (Ithaca, N. Y., 1957).

HOOK, SIDNEY, ed. *Religious Experience and Truth: A Symposium.* London, 1962. Thirty-six papers by various hands.

KENNICK, WILLIAM E. "The Language of Religion." *Philosophical Review* 65 (1956): 56–71.

KLEMKE, E. D. "Are Religious Statements Meaningful?" *Journal of Religion* 40 (1960): 27–39.

LEWIS, H. D. *Our Experience of God.* London, 1959.

McINTYRE, ALASDAIR, ed. *Metaphysical Beliefs: Three Essays.* London, 1957. Includes Stephen Toulmin's "Contemporary Scientific Mythology," R. W. Hepburn's "Poetry and Religious Belief," and A. MacIntyre's "The Logical Status of Religious Belief."

MACKINNON, D. M. "Metaphysical and Religious Language." *Proceedings of the Aristotelian Society,* n.s., 54 (1953–54): 115–30.

MARTIN, C. B. *Religious Belief.* Ithaca, N. Y., 1959.

MASCALL, E. L. *Words and Images: A Study in Theological Discourse.* London, 1957.

MILES, T. R. *Religion and the Scientific Outlook.* London, 1959. Especially part 3.

MITCHELL, BASIL, ed. *Faith and Logic: Oxford Essays in Philosophical Theology.* (London, 1957). Eight essays by various hands.

MUNZ, PETER. *Problems of Religious Knowledge.* London, 1959.

RAMSEY, IAN T. *Religious Language: An Empirical Placing of Theological Phrases.* London, 1957.

———. *Freedom and Immortality.* London, 1960.

———. *Models and Mystery.* London, 1964.

————. *Christian Discourse: Some Logical Explorations.* London, 1965.

RAMSEY, IAN T., ed. *Prospect for Metaphysics: Essays of Metaphysical Exploration.* London, 1961. Twelve essays by various hands.

RAMSEY, IAN T., and NINIAN SMART. "Paradox in Religion," *Aristotelian Society Supplementary Volume,* 33 (1959) : 195–232.

REID, LOUIS A. *Ways of Knowledge and Experience.* London, 1961. Especially part 2, "Knowledge and Religion."

THOMAS, IVO, O. P. "Logic and Theology." *Dominican Studies* 1 (1948) : 291–312.

WISDOM, JOHN. "Metaphysics and Verification." *Philosophy and Psychoanalysis.* Oxford, 1953.

WOODS, G. F. *Theological Explanation.* London, 1958.

ZUURDEEG, WILLEM F. *An Analytical Philosophy of Religion.* Nashville, Tenn., 1958, and London, 1959.

————. "The Nature of Theological Language," with a "Reply" by Samuel Thompson. *Journal of Religion* 40 (1960) : 1–17.

See also a number of essays by various hands in "Contemporary Philosophy and Christian Faith," *The Socratic*, no. 5 (1952), and especially in "Faith and Verification," *The Christian Scholar* 43 (1960) : 163–230. For further references consult H. D. Lewis' survey of "The Philosophy of Religion 1945–1952," *Philosophical Quarterly* 4 (1954) : 166–81, 262–74, and A. J. Ayer's full bibliography in *Logical Positivism* (Glencoe, Ill., and London, 1959).

BRIGHT ESSENCE was set in Intertype Baskerville with foundry Baskerville and Visual Graphics Inserat Grotesque display types. Typography and hand composition by Donald M. Henriksen. Design by Keith E. Montague of Bailey-Montague & Associates.